D1497033

Image Transmission
Techniques

Advances in Electronics and Electron Physics

Edited by

L. MARTON   CLAIRE MARTON

Smithsonian Institution
Washington, D.C.

SUPPLEMENTS

Image Transmission Techniques

Edited by
WILLIAM K. PRATT

IMAGE PROCESSING INSTITUTE
UNIVERSITY OF SOUTHERN CALIFORNIA
LOS ANGELES, CALIFORNIA

1979

ACADEMIC PRESS   New York   San Francisco   London
A Subsidiary of Harcourt Brace Jovanovich, Publishers

ACADEMIC PRESS, INC.
111 Fifth Avenue, New York, New York 10003

United Kingdom Edition published by
ACADEMIC PRESS, INC. (LONDON) LTD.
24/28 Oval Road, London NW1 7DX

LIBRARY OF CONGRESS CATALOG CARD NUMBER: 63–12814

ISBN 0–12–014572–3

PRINTED IN THE UNITED STATES OF AMERICA

79 80 81 82   9 8 7 6 5 4 3 2 1

Dedicated to the references
This book is merely a summary of
their cumulative contributions.

Contents

Image Transmission Techniques

WILLIAM K. PRATT

Image Coding Applications of Vision Models

DAVID J. SAKRISON

Predictive Image Coding

HANS GEORG MUSMANN

Transform Image Coding

ANDREW G. TESCHER

Hybrid Transform/Predictive Image Coding

JOHN A. ROESE

Frame Replenishment Coding of Television

BARRY G. HASKELL

Binary Image Compression

RONALD B. ARPS

List of Contributors

RONALD B. ARPS* (219), *Department of Electrical Engineering, Linkö-ping University, Linköping, Sweden S-581 83*

BARRY G. HASKELL (189), *Radio Communications Research Department, Bell Laboratories, Holmdel, New Jersey 07724*

HANS GEORG MUSMANN (73), *Lehrstuhl für Theoretische Nachrichten-technik und Informationsverarbeitung, Technische Universität, Han-nover, Germany*

WILLIAM K. PRATT (1), *Image Processing Institute, University of South-ern California, Los Angeles, California 90007*

JOHN A. ROESE (157), *Naval Ocean Systems Center, San Diego, Cali-fornia 95152*

DAVID J. SAKRISON (21), *Department of Electrical Engineering and Com-puter Sciences, Electronics Research Laboratory, University of Cali-fornia, Berkeley, California 94720*

ANDREW G. TESCHER (113), *Engineering Sciences Operations, The Aero-space Corporation, Los Angeles, California 90045*

* Present address: IBM Department F08/G26, 555 Bailey Avenue, San Jose, Cali-fornia 95150.

Foreword

The subject of image transmission techniques is one of wide interest and has application in many areas. Professor William K. Pratt has drawn together a group of eminent collaborators and achieved very comprehensive coverage in this volume.

The subject matter fits well with the past articles *Advances in Electronics and Electron Physics* has presented dealing with image transmission, and we welcome having this Supplement complement our earlier presentations.

We extend our thanks to the Editor and authors of this volume for the splendid job they have done.

L. MARTON
C. MARTON

Preface

Designers of image transmission systems have available an abundance of information in the form of scientific and engineering papers, articles, and reports to assist in their systems design. The problem in this field is that there has been too much information published to comprehend fully. Furthermore, the literature is widely dispersed among many international journals, and some key literature has been published in relatively obscure journals or inaccessible reports. Finally, there has been the difficulty of evaluation of this wealth of information. What information is truly fundamental and essential? These factors have supplied the motivation for this volume.

An attempt has been made to produce a volume that will serve as a practical guide to the designer of image transmission systems, one that will provide answers to the following pertinent questions:

What are the major competitive image transmission techniques?
How do they work?
What is their expected performance?
What are their advantages and limitations?
What are the major considerations in their implementation?
What is the state of the art of these techniques?
Where can further detailed information be obtained?

The volume is made up of seven articles. The first is a general introductory discourse on the field of image transmission techniques and is written by the Editor. This article also provides an elementary description of the major image transmission techniques. The remaining articles present sophisticated reviews of these techniques, each written by an eminent expert on that particular method.

In any publication that is a compilation of articles from different authors, there is a danger of unevenness of presentation, divergence of style, repetition of material, and voids in important topics. Every effort has been made by the Editor to avoid these pitfalls by a recursive writing and editing process. The contributors have had to suffer the unaccustomed wrath of a liberal red pencil wielded by the Editor in the preparation of their manuscripts. Their indulgence has been greatly appreciated.

WILLIAM K. PRATT

Image Transmission Techniques

WILLIAM K. PRATT

Image Processing Institute
University of Southern California
Los Angeles, California

Since the first laboratory demonstrations of television transmission in the 1920s, there has been considerable investigation into efficient transmission techniques. Applications include broadcast and relay television, facsimile, remote image sensing, biomedical imaging, surveillance, and other specialized applications. The usual goal in the design of an efficient image transmission system is to maximize the transmission rate for a specified acceptable limit to image quality. Transmission rate can be expressed as the analog transmission bandwidth of an analog communication link, as a bit rate for digital transmission, or as picture or document transmission speed for a facsimile system.

During the past decade there has been much progress toward the design of more efficient image transmission systems. This progress is at-

1

tributable to two major factors: the discovery and refinement of new image-coding methods, and the advent of relatively inexpensive, compact, high-speed, solid state signal-processing circuitry. Modern image transmission equipment is now beginning to incorporate rather sophisticated image-coding processes to improve transmission efficiency. This trend is likely to increase dramatically with the rapid growth of digital transmission links.

This chapter provides a general introduction to the subject of image transmission techniques in preparation for the subsequent chapters that present more detailed descriptions of specific methods. The following sections introduce a characterization of image transmission systems, discuss image quality measures, and summarize the operating principles of major image-coding systems.

1.1 IMAGE TRANSMISSION SYSTEM CHARACTERIZATION

An image transmission system is a particular type of communication system—particular in the sense that physical characteristics of the image source and image destination are vital in its system design. Efficient image transmission systems cannot be realized by a "black box" design approach based on communication theory alone.

Figure 1-1 contains a general block diagram of an image transmission system. The model contains a source of images obtained from a television camera or facsimile scanner, for example, followed by a source coder that transforms the source data into a form with minimal transmission requirements. Next, the coded image source is converted to a format suitable for transmission. This step involves modulation of the transmission carrier and, often, error correction coding for channel errors caused by noise. The channel decoder and source decoders invert the coding processes to produce a reconstructed source of images presented to the image destination. The image destination consists of an image display or photographic recorder *plus,* in most cases, a human observer. Attention is now directed to characterization of the image source and destination.

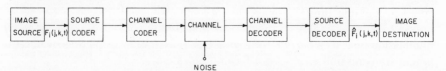

FIG. 1-1.   Image transmission system.

1.1.1 Image Source Characterization—Deterministic Models

The image source of Fig. 1-1 contains photoelectric sensors that are sensitive over different spectral bands. Each produces an electronic image $F_i(x, y, t)$ whose amplitude is proportional to the optical radiation incident on the sensor at space coordinates (x, y), time (t), and spectral band (i). For monochrome image sources, there is only a single sensor whose image function $F(x, y, t)$ is proportional to the luminance of the incident light, and for natural color imagery, the set $F_i(x, y, t)$ for $i = 1, 2, 3$ usually denotes the red, green, and blue content of the incident radiation. Multispectral image sources typically operate over 4 to 12 spectral bands, some of which may extend into the infrared or ultraviolet wavelengths. The designer should be aware that image sensors often respond in a non-linear manner to the amplitude of optical radiation, typically with a square-law response. This nonlinearity can significantly affect the image signal characteristics. The image source model of Fig. 1-1 accommodates single-frame sources of independent images, such as produced by a facsimile scanner, and also multiple-frame sources of correlated images in a real-time television system.

Each electronic image field $F_i(x, y, t)$ is spatially sampled by the image sensor. Solid state array sensors, such as a charge-coupled-device (CCD) sensor array, perform an inherent spatial sampling by averaging the continuous field image over the surface of each array element to produce a discrete array. Let $F(j, k, t)$ denote the discrete array where $1 \le j \le J$ and $1 \le k \le K$ with an implied sample spacing of Δx and Δy units. In a conventional television camera, such as an image orthicon or vidicon camera, an electron beam scans the continuous image field along one spatial coordinate in a line-by-line raster scanning process. For analog transmission, the line-scanned image signal is transmitted directly, while for discrete or digital communication links, the line-scanned signal is time sampled to produce an equivalent discrete array $F_i(j, k, t)$. Facsimile and other line scanners operate in a similar manner. Spatial sampling is normally subject to two sources of degradation: resolution loss and aliasing error. Resolution loss occurs as a result of sampling with sample pulses of finite extent, which effectively blur the ideal image. Aliasing error, which results from sampling too coarsely, appears as a spurious low-spatial-frequency pattern. Both effects should be considered in developing a model for the sampled image source.

Color and multispectral image planes are often combined by linear or nonlinear processing before coding. For example, in the United States color television standard (Fink, 1957), the red, $R(j, k, t)$, green, $G(j, k, t)$, and blue, $B(j, k, t)$ tristimulus signals are linearly combined to produce a monochrome luminance signal Y(j, k, t) and two chrominance signals, I(j, k, t) and Q(j, k, t), as shown in Fig. 1-2. This process is invertible. For transmission, the I and Q signals are low-pass filtered and modulated onto a subcarrier wave that is frequency interleaved with the luminance signal. The resultant "composite" video signal is then transmitted over a communications carrier. At the receiver, inverse processes reproduce the Y, I, Q and R, G, B tristimulus values. As a result of the low-pass-filtering step, the receiver tristimulus values are not exact replicas of the transmitter tristimulus values, but the degradation is relatively small. Image coding can be performed on the R, G, B or Y, I, Q component tristimulus values either separately or jointly, or on the composite video signal. The choice is strongly dependent on the type of coding employed.

1.1.2   Image Source Characterization–Stochastic Models

In the design of image coders, it is often useful to regard an image source from a stochastic viewpoint. Under this characterization, each image is assumed to be a time sample of a two-dimensional stochastic process. The image source can then be represented by the joint probability density between all pixels of all image functions $F_i(j, k, t)$. Some simple models will now be considered.

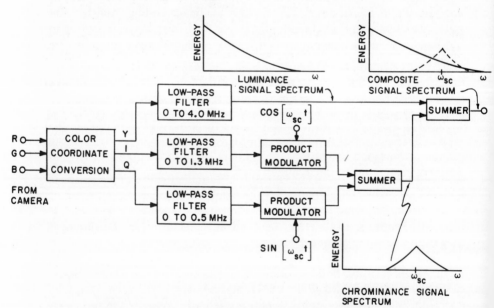

FIG. 1-2.   Formation of color composite signal.

For analytic compactness, it is convenient to regard a discrete image array at frame time (t) as a $Q = J \cdot K$ vector $\mathbf{f}$ of pixels obtained by column scanning the array and linking its columns (Pratt, 1975). The vector density

$$p(\mathbf{f}) = p\{f(1), f(2), \ldots, f(Q)\} \tag{1}$$

denotes the joint probability density relationship among all Q pixels in the image frame. It is common to describe $\mathbf{f}$ in terms of its ensemble averages or moments. The mean vector

$$\boldsymbol{\eta}_f = E\{\mathbf{f}\} \tag{2}$$

where $E\{\cdot\}$ denotes the expectation operator, represents the average image amplitude at each pixel. The mean can be estimated, in principle, by averaging corresponding pixels of a large number of representative images. The $Q \times Q$ image covariance matrix

$$\mathbf{K}_f = E\{(\mathbf{f} - \boldsymbol{\eta}_f)(\mathbf{f} - \boldsymbol{\eta}_f)^T\} \tag{3}$$

provides an indication of the spatial relationship between all pixel pairs within an image. If the image is wide-sense stationary, then its mean vector $\boldsymbol{\eta}_f$ will be constant valued, and the covariance relationship between pairs of pixels will be dependent only on their geometrical separation and not on their coordinate values. This is the common assumption made, for analytic simplicity, in developing models for image coding. Another simplifying assumption is to consider the covariance function to be orthogonally separable along image rows and columns. Under this assumption, the covariance matrix can be written as the direct product

$$\mathbf{K}_f = \mathbf{K}_C \otimes \mathbf{K}_R \tag{4}$$

of the $J \times J$ column covariance matrix $\mathbf{K}_C$ and the $K \times K$ row covariance matrix $\mathbf{K}_R$. Jain (1976) has investigated the accuracy of this model. A final step in simplication is to utilize a Markov process model for the row and column covariance matrices. For example, the Markov process row covariance matrix takes the symmetric form

$$\mathbf{K}_R = \sigma_R^2 \begin{bmatrix} 1 & \rho_R & \rho_R^2 & \cdots \\ \rho_R & 1 & \rho_R & \cdots \\ \cdot & \cdot & \cdot & \\ \cdot & \cdot & \cdot & \\ \cdot & \cdot & \cdot & \cdots \end{bmatrix}$$

where σ_R^2 represents the pixel variance along each row and ρ_R is the adjacent pixel correlation. Most designs of image-coding systems are based only on second-order statistics, the mean and covariance matrices.

There has been some recent work on the development of simple probability density models that may be useful for design purposes. Hunt and Cannon (1976) have proposed a joint Gaussian density model

$$p(\mathbf{f}) = (2\pi)^{-Q/2}|\mathbf{K}_f|^{-1/2} \exp\{-\frac{1}{2}(\mathbf{f} - \boldsymbol{\eta}_f)\mathbf{K}_f^{-1}(\mathbf{f} - \boldsymbol{\eta}_f)\} \qquad (6)$$

where $|\mathbf{K}_f|$ denotes the determinant of the covariance matrix and $\mathbf{K}_f^{-1}$ is its matrix inverse. In this model, the covariance function is assumed stationary, but the mean vector is considered to be spatially varying. Hunt suggests that $\boldsymbol{\eta}_f$ can be estimated by spatially blurring representative images. It should be observed that the Gaussian density is bipolar, and therefore the model will only be effective for low-contrast images for which the negative tail of the Gaussian density is small. Huhns (1975) has developed a joint density model in which the marginal (single-pixel) densities assume some desired form, for example, unipolar Rayleigh or lognormal densities, and pairs of pixels possess specified covariance. The model has been successfully employed in the design of postprocessors to reduce the effect of quantization error for PCM, DPCM, and transform coding.

A discrete image may be regarded as an array of $Q = J \cdot K$ numbers representing pixel amplitudes each of which assumes B amplitude levels. A total of $T = B^Q$ different images can be represented in this manner. With conventional binary coding, called pulse-code modulation (PCM), each of the pixels is treated as being independent and is coded with $b = \log_2(B)$ bits. For simplicity, b is assumed to be an integer. Thus, $b \cdot Q$ bits are required to code the image with standard binary coding. This baseline value is quite large: approximately 5×10^7 bits/sec for monochrome television; as many as 1.5×10^8 bits/sec for color television; and about 10^6 bits/document for binary facsimile. These transmission requirements for PCM are large because the statistical redundancy of the source is ignored by a PCM coder.

The statistical redundancy of an image source can be expressed in terms of the source entropy (Shannon, 1949) in bits per image as

$$H = -\sum_{i=1}^{T} p_i \log_2 p_i \qquad (7)$$

where p_i denotes the *a priori* probability of the ith image of a total of T images that can be produced by the source. In principle, a source code that will require an average code rate quite close to the entropy can be found. The coding concept is quite simple; short code words are assigned to image patterns with high relative probability, and long words are assigned to rarely occurring patterns. Since the total number of images T that could be generated by the source is so enormous, it is not practical to attempt to measure the probability set $\{p_i\}$ and then estimate the source entropy. The only potential solutions to this problem are to establish an analytic model for the probability distribution of the source and compute the entropy by Eq. (7), or to break the image up into small blocks so that T is small and it becomes practical to measure the source probability set $\{p_i\}$. The second approach, that of block division, has proved feasible only for relatively small blocks, 2 or 3 neighbors for monochrome images, and perhaps 10 or so neighbors for binary facsimile. Table 1-1 lists measurements by Schreiber (1956) for a 64 gray-level image and by Preuss (1975) for binary facsimile. Also included for reference are entropy measurements of the GIRL image, which is widely used as a test image in image-coding computer simulation studies.

1.1.3 Image Destination Characterization

Proper modeling of the destination or receiver of images is vital to the effective design of image transmission systems that produce images for visual display. There are two major considerations: image reconstruction and human observer performance.

At the image destination, the array of decoded pixel samples $\hat{F}(j, k, t)$ must be interpolated to produce a continuous image field $\hat{F}(x, y, t)$ for dis-

TABLE 1-1

IMAGE ENTROPY MEASUREMENTS

Conditioning	Entropy (bits/pixel)
Schreiber's measurements of 6-bit image	
None	4.4
1 left neighbor	1.9
2 left neighbors	1.5
Pratt's measurements of 8-bit GIRL image	
None	6.41
1 left neighbor	4.04
Preuss's measurements of 1-bit business letter image	
	0.240
	0.226
	0.204

play or recording. For cathode-ray-tube displays, interpolation is inherently performed by the bell-shaped writing spot. Flying spot scanner recorders also employ bell-shaped writing spots, while electromechanical recorders usually utilize nonoverlapping square writing apertures. This type of interpolation is not optimal, but if the sample spacing is sufficiently close (500–600 lines at normal viewing distances), the interpolation error is not significant. However, for lower-spatial-resolution image transmission systems, more sophisticated interpolation is necessary. The simplest approach is to employ pixel replication to "fill out" the display. Much better visual results can be obtained by bilinear interpolation (Andrews, 1976) in which intermediate pixels are approximated by sequential linear interpolation along image rows and columns.

Most image displays and recording systems possess a nonlinear point response. The emitted light from a cathode-ray tube or the reflected light from a photographic print is seldom linearly proportional to the driving pixel $\hat{F}(j, k, t)$ unless there is electronic or digital compensation. Such compensation improves display fidelity but often results in better visibility of coding distortion.

Cognizance of the human observer is vital in image-coder design. Ideally, image distortion should be controlled such that "it cannot be seen" even though it is numerically present. In practice, the coding system design is optimized to present minimal visible distortion by exploiting limitations of human vision. To accomplish this, it is necessary to understand the mechanics of human vision, at least to the point of developing models that adequately predict visual phenomena. The most important visual phenomena in regard to image coding are point contrast and chrominance sensitivity, spatial response, and the masking effect.

It has been long established that the sensitivity of a human observer to contrast changes in monochrome imagery is about 2%. Furthermore, the sensitivity to chrominance changes is well documented; an observer is most sensitive to changes in green light, moderately sensitive to red changes, and least sensitive to blue changes (Wyszecki and Stiles, 1967). It is known that the receptors of the retina, the rods and cones, respond nonlinearly to excitation. Several empirical models have been suggested (Cornsweet, 1970). The most widely adopted are a scaled logarithmic response and a cube-root response. Knowledge of these point characteristics of human vision is useful in designing quantizers in image-coding systems.

There have been many studies of the spatial frequency response of human vision. The general conclusions are that the human eye acts as a nonlinear bandpass filter, as qualitatively indicated in Fig. 1-3. High-spatial-frequency attenuation is attributable to spatial response limita-

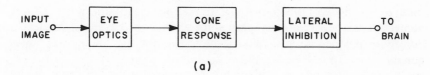

(a)

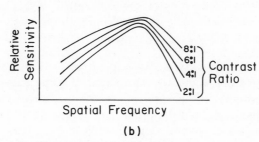

(b)

FIG. 1-3.   Human vision modeling. (a) Model; (b) transfer function.

tions of the "optics" of the eye. Spatial interaction of the rods and cones, called lateral inhibition, produces a spatial differentiating effect and results in an attenuation of low spatial frequencies. The nonlinear photoreceptor response accounts for the contrast-dependent response. Information of this nature has been used to develop "front end" models of the human visual system that have proved quite effective in predicting visual phenomena such as contrast sensitivity and the Mach band effect.

The masking effect of human vision refers to the reduction of contrast sensitivity in the vicinity of luminance and color edge gradients. In such regions there is a reduced perception of coding distortion.

1.2 IMAGE QUALITY MEASURES

A reliable quantitative measure of image quality is of prime importance in the design and performance assessment of image transmission techniques. With such a measure, it would be possible to definitively rate the fidelity of an image transmission system in comparison to some standard. Furthermore, if the measure were an analytic function, it would be possible to employ the measure as a goal or objective function for optimization of the image transmission system parameters. It would be pleasant to be able to state that analytic, subjectively qualified measures exist for various image transmission applications. But this is not the case. Rather, there are available numerous subjective scales, test pattern procedures, numerical ad hoc relations, plus some indicators based on models of human visual perception, all of which attempt to characterize image quality.

In this section no attempt is made to review the field of image quality or to assess various measures. This brief discussion merely presents some of the more common methods of image quality measurements and attempts to summarize their advantages and disadvantages.

1.2.1 Subjective Scales

Any "good" image quality measure must correlate well with subjective assessments of image quality formulated as some subjective annotated scale. For image-coding applications there are two relevant subjective scales: absolute quality and perceived impairment. An absolute quality scale consists of several steps, usually 5 to 7, labeled from unsatisfactory to excellent, for example. Each labeling is intended to indicate judged image quality in terms of some reference set of pictures A perceived impairment scale is simply a labeled scale indicating the degree of degradation present in a coded image relative to some perfect rendition. Table 1-2 provides some examples of subjective rating scales common in the field of image transmission (Pearson, 1972).

The normal procedure in image quality measurement by subjective testing is to establish some set of standard images of varying degrees of

TABLE 1-2

IMAGE QUALITY SCALES

Overall goodness scale
  5. Excellent
  4. Good
  3. Fair
  2. Poor
  1. Unsatisfactory

Impairment scale
  1. Not perceptible
  2. Just perceptible
  3. Definitely perceptible, but only
     slight impairment to picture
  4. Impairment to picture, but not
     objectionable
  5. Somewhat objectionable
  6. Definitely objectionable
  7. Extremely objectionable

quality. These images are then employed as a test calibration. Viewers may be shown the standard images before a test, during a test as a "refresher," or even in a side-by-side format. During the course of a test, each viewer rates a set of unknown images, and a mean rating is formed for each test image. It is obviously important that the test be conducted with a sufficient number of subjects to reduce statistical irregularity to tolerable limits. Also, care must be taken to properly "randomize" the presentation format to avoid viewer bias and to compensate for learning and fatigue factors. Proper testing is not a trivial matter.

1.2.2 Test Pattern Performance

A common approach to quality measurement of image scanners and displays is to record their response to test signals or test patterns. For example, if a television camera views a gray-scale test chart, the departure of its signal voltage from a perfect step waveform could be utilized as a measure of camera quality. The "raised cosine pulse," an impulselike function, is often used for testing television transmission systems (Lewis, 1954). System distortion is measured by fitting a scaled template to the output version of the test pulse. The utility of these types of testing procedures is highly dubious when applied to digital image transmission. It is entirely conceivable that one could design a digital image coder to transmit raised cosine pulses with great fidelity, but yet distort images horribly!

1.2.3 Numerical Measures

Numerical image quality measures fall into two classes: univariate and bivariate. Univariate measures are formed for a single picture only, and the measurement scale is calibrated by evaluation of the departure of a test image from a standard image. Bivariate measures are "before and after" differential indicators of image quality.

Univariate measures are usually based on the spatial frequency spectrum of an image. In the continuous domain, the spatial frequency spectrum of an image with a spatial luminance distribution $F(x, y)$ is specified in terms of its two-dimensional Fourier transform defined by

$$\mathcal{F}(\omega_x, \omega_y) = \int_{-L}^{L} \int_{-L}^{L} F(x, y) \exp[-(\omega_x x + \omega_y y)\} \, dxdy \qquad (8)$$

where L represents the spatial limits of the image, and ω_x and ω_y denote spatial frequencies. The discrete Fourier transform

$$\mathcal{F}(u, v) = \frac{1}{(JK)^{1/2}} \sum_{j=0}^{J-1} \sum_{k=0}^{K-1} F(j, k) \exp\left\{-2\pi i \left(\frac{uj}{J} + \frac{vk}{K}\right)\right\} \qquad (9)$$

may be utilized for discrete image arrays $F(j, k)$ where the image is assumed uniformly sampled over a $J \times K$ grid and (u, v) represent discrete spatial frequency components. Typical quality measures include the integrated energy over all frequencies or the mean energy value. Such measures have proved useful when assessing image transmission system performance for systems that are linear in response. In the case of nonlinear coding systems, however, these measures are often erratic and contradictory.

Another class of univariate measures is based on statistical characteristics of an image. Examples include the experimental mean and variance of the samples of a discrete image array. Gray-scale histograms provide much useful information about an image field. The first-order histogram is simply a listing of the number of pixels in an image of a specified luminance level. It can be considered to be an approximation to the image first-order probability distribution. Similarly, a second-order histogram provides an approximation to the joint probability distribution relating pairs of pixels. Image contrast can be inferred from the shape of the first-order histogram. A narrow spread about the mode of a unimodal histogram implies a low-contrast image, and vice versa. A spread about the diagonal of the two-dimensional histogram array is an indicator of the spatial correlation of the corresponding image. A number of one- and two-dimensional histogram measures have been developed for image feature extraction (Haralick *et al.*, 1973; Pratt, 1978), but there has been little quantitative application to image quality.

Bivariate image quality measures are extremely useful for image transmission applications, since they can provide an indication of the relative coding degradation between the input and output images of a coding system. The most common bivariate measure is the least-squared difference or error between the pair, often referred to as the mean-square error (MSE). Usually, the measure is normalized by the energy or peak magnitude of the input image. In the discrete domain, the image-normalized mean-square error between an image $F(j, k)$ and its coded reconstruction $\hat{F}(j, k)$ is defined as

$$\mathscr{E}_N = \sum_{j=0}^{J-1} \sum_{k=0}^{K-1} [F(j, k) - \hat{F}(k, k)]^2 / \sum_{j=0}^{J-1} \sum_{k=0}^{K-1} [F(j, k)]^2 \tag{10}$$

The amplitude-normalized error is specified as

$$\mathscr{E}_A = \sum_{j=0}^{J-1} \sum_{k=0}^{K-1} [F(j, k) - \hat{F}(j, k)]^2 / JKA^2 \tag{11}$$

where A denotes the maximum amplitude of $F(j, k)$.

The major advantages of the mean-square error are its intuitive appeal (large errors are given more importance than small errors), its ease of computation, and its mathematical tractability. On the debit side, the MSE is often found to correlate poorly with subjective ratings. To overcome this defect, many researchers have attempted preprocessing the pair of images under examination prior to formation of the mean-square difference. Logarithmic, square-root, and cube-root weightings have been considered. A Laplacian operation forming spatial second partial derivatives of the images to emphasize their edge content has also been explored. Another approach investigated is to pass each image through an operator designed to model the processing steps of the human visual system. Although these processing steps possess a rational basis and do indeed seem to improve the correlation of the MSE with subjective rating, they have not been sufficiently tested to warrant adoption as a standard.

1.2.4 Recommendation

In the introductory paragraph of this section on image quality, it was stated that many measures exist, but none are completely acceptable. Research is continuing in the search for qualified measures. In the interim, the designer of image transmission systems obviously must make do with existing measures. The recommendation from these quarters is to utilize the amplitude-normalized mean-square error between the input and output images of a transmission system.

1.3 IMAGE-CODING TECHNIQUES

The principal goal in the design of an image-coding system is to reduce the transmission rate requirements of the image source subject to some image quality constraint. There are basically only two ways to accomplish this goal, reduction of the statistical and psychophysical redundancy of the image source.

An image source is normally very highly correlated both spatially and temporally; there is a strong dependence among the values of individual pixels. This dependence can be regarded as statistical redundancy of the image source. Knowledge of the statistical redundancy of the source in terms of the amplitudes of previously coded pixels can be utilized to reduce its transmission requirements. The advantage of this type of coding is that it is information preserving, that is, error free.

If the images to be coded in an image transmission system are to be viewed by a human observer, then the perceptual limitations of human vision can be exploited to reduce transmission requirements. Human observers are subject to perceptual limitations in amplitude, spatial resolution, and temporal acuity. By proper design of the coder, it is possible to discard statistical information of the source without affecting perception at all, or at least, with only minimal degradation.

Some image coders, most notably those used for binary facsimile transmission applications, are based entirely on statistical coding concepts. Most coders allow some degradation in order to achieve a reduction in transmission requirements. This leads to a trade-off between transmission rate and coding distortion.

The following sections present a summary description of the major image-coding techniques developed. Since these techniques are covered in much greater depth in subsequent chapters, referral to references has been limited here to reduce "redundancy." Instead, readers are guided to the special issues of journals on the subject plus books and review journal articles listed in the general references at the end of the chapter.

1.3.1   PCM Coding

Pulse-code-modulation (PCM) coding is the simplest, most basic, form of image coding. In this system the image signal is sampled, and each sample is quantized and binary coded for transmission. For binary facsimile transmission, the image signal is quantized to only two levels, black or white, and coded with 1 bit per sample, zero or one. Monochrome imagery is usually quantized with from 64 to 256 levels per sample, corresponding to a 6- or 8-bits-per-sample, fixed-length, binary-coded word. Digital color television systems usually use 6 to 8 bits each for the red, green, and blue tristimulus values. PCM coding may be considered as a baseline coding system. Transmission-rate reductions are usually calculated with respect to PCM coding.

Reduction in the number of quantization levels for monochrome or color image PCM coding leads to an effect called contouring, in which discrete jumps between quantization levels are observed in image regions that are slowly changing in luminance or tristimulus value. This contouring effect can be reduced substantially by adding a small amount of pseudorandom noise (Roberts, 1962) or deterministic dither (Bisignani *et al.*, 1966) to the image signal before quantization. With such coders, at least 3 bits per sample are required, and there is noticeable residual error in the form of a snowlike appearance or a structured quantization error pattern.

1.3.2 Statistical Coding

PCM coding is inefficient because it ignores the spatial dependency among pixels, and because it treats all quantized amplitude levels as equally likely. Substantial transmission-rate reductions are possible, theoretically, by coding groups of pixels and allocating code words whose length is inversely proportional to the probability of occurrence of the group amplitude pattern. The Huffman (1952) coding procedure can be used to develop a minimal average-length code for a given set of pattern probabilities.

Statistical coding forms the basis for most binary facsimile coding techniques. For such sources, the number of possible binary patterns is of reasonable size. But, for multiple gray-level and color images, the number of patterns can be enormous. For example, a 4×4 group of pixels, each quantized to 256 levels, corresponds to about 10^{40} possible patterns. Consequently, application of statistical coding to multiple-level images has been limited to very small neighborhoods of about two or three pixels. A considerable saving in coder complexity can be obtained by simply coding the running difference of pixels by a variable-length statistical code. This type of coder can achieve about a $2:1$ bit-rate reduction (Davisson and Kutz, 1971).

The effectiveness of statistical coding is limited by knowledge of the source probabilities. For most image sources, the source probabilities can vary drastically from image to image and even within an image. Good coding results can only be obtained by adaptively estimating the source probabilities and revising the source code appropriately.

Because of the relatively poor "return of investment" in terms of a small coding compression for high coder complexity, statistical coding has not found much application in the coding of monochrome and color images. But the concepts have proved useful in combination with other coding methods, such as predictive and transform coding.

1.3.3 Predictive Coding

Figure 1-4 contains a general block diagram of a predictive image-coding system. In such a system, the amplitude of each scanned pixel is predicted on the basis of the history of previously scanned pixels. Then, the predicted estimate $\bar{F}(j, k, t)$ is subtracted from the actual pixel amplitude $F(j, k, t)$, and the difference signal $D(j, k, t)$ is quantized, coded, and transmitted. At the receiver, the quantized difference signal $\hat{D}(j, k, t)$ is used to form a reconstruction $\hat{F}(j, k, t)$ of the ideal image by summing the receiver prediction $\bar{F}(j, k, t)$ with the quantized difference signal. A

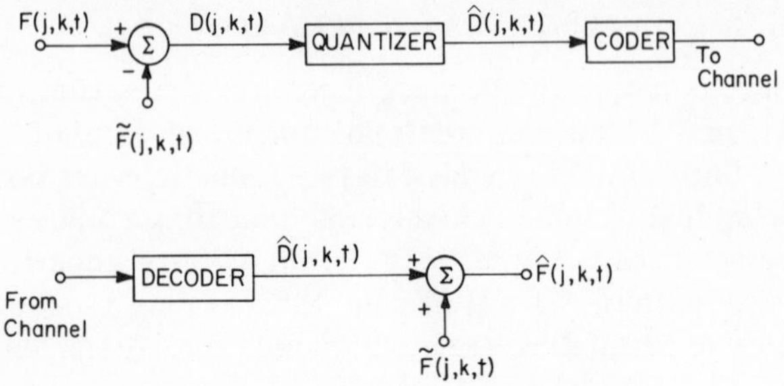

FIG. 1-4.   Predictive image-coding system.

transmission-rate reduction is achieved by coarsely quantizing the difference signal.

The simplest form of a predictive image coder is the delta modulation system in which the prediction is formed from the previous prediction value quantized to only two levels. Differential pulse-code-modulation (DPCM) systems utilize previous pixel prediction with from 4 to 16 quantization levels allocated to each prediction difference signal. Tapering of the quantization scale to provide a narrow spacing of quantization levels for small prediction differences and a wider spacing for large differences results in minimum-mean-square coding error and nearly best subjective performance. The coding error can further be reduced by utilizing previous prediction differences in an image frame or from previously scanned frames. Additional improvement can be obtained by adapting the quantizer to the instantaneous image activity and statistically coding the quantization levels.

1.3.4   Transform Coding

In a transform coding system, as illustrated in Fig. 1-5, a two-dimensional unitary transform is taken over an entire image, or repeatedly over subsections called blocks. Fourier, sine, cosine, Hadamard, Haar, Slant, and Karhunen–Loeve transforms have been extensively utilized for image coding. The transformation produces an array of relatively decorrelated, energy-compacted transform coefficients that can be efficiently quantized and coded for transmission.

After transformation, the transform samples are selected for transmission in accordance with a zonal or threshold sampling strategy. For zonal sampling, only those coefficients lying in a prespecified zone, usually the low-spatial-frequency samples, are selected for transmission. With threshold sampling, a coefficient is transmitted if its magnitude is greater

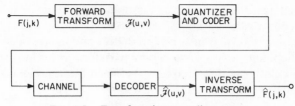

Fig. 1-5.   Transform image-coding system.

than a threshold value. The quantizer and coder then individually quantize and code each coefficient zone in each transform block. Transform samples in each zone are then quantized with the same number of quantization levels set proportional to the expected variance of the transform coefficients. For a constant-word-length code, the number of bits assigned to each coefficient is set proportional to the logarithm of the variance of a coefficient. The transform coefficient variance can be determined for a given spatial domain correlation model. Probability density models of the transform coefficients are utilized to select quantization levels to minimize the mean-square coding system. At the receiver the incoming code bits are decoded, and the quantized transform coefficient array is reconstructed. An inverse transformation produces the reconstructed image array.

Monochrome images can be coded at rates of 1.0 to 1.5 bits/pixel with mean-square-error distortion less than 0.5%. Color images require an additional 0.5 to 1.0 bit/pixel.

1.3.5   Hybrid Transform/Predictive Coding

Transform and predictive image-coding systems perform a decorrelation of an image source to produce a sequence of variables that are individually quantized and coded. Two-dimensional transform coding produces a lower mean-square-error image reconstruction than predictive coding at low transmission rates, but a transform coder is more complicated to implement than a predictive coder. The hybrid transform/predictive image-coding concept provides an effective compromise of the advantages and disadvantages of the two coding methods.

In the operation of the intraframe hybrid coder, a one-dimensional transform is taken along each image line of an image block to produce a sequence of transform coefficients. Predictive coding is then applied along columns of the transform coefficients. Thus, the coder only requires memory for the transform coefficients of a single image line. Subjectively, the performance of the intraframe hybrid coder is quite good for coding rates approaching 1.0 bit/pixel, and in some applications results may be adequate at coding rates as low as 0.5 bit/pixel.

The concept of hybrid transform/predictive coding has been extended to interframe coding. A two-dimensional transform is performed within a frame, and predictive coding is applied between frames. Good quality results have been obtained at rates as low as 0.25 bit/pixel.

1.3.6   Frame Replenishment Coding

In real-time television systems a majority of picture elements remain virtually unchanged from frame to frame. This fact forms the basis of an interframe coding system called frame replenishment coding. In a frame replenishment coder, each frame is digitized at 8 bits. The first frame of a sequence is stored at the coder as a reference frame and is also transmitted to act as a reference at the receiver. Each subsequent frame is digitized and then compared to the reference. If the difference is significant, the old pixel value in the frame memory is replaced by the new value, and the new value is transmitted along with its frame address to replace the old value at the receiver. There are several extensions to the basic coding concept. Frame differences can be coded in clusters to improve the address coding efficiency. Also, a further transmission-rate reduction can be obtained by subsampling the frame diffrences in moving image areas.

Simulations of frame replenishment coding systems have been reported at rates of about 1.0 bit/pixel with quality rated as excellent except for periods of violent motion. Coding at rates of 0.25 bit/pixel is feasible for classroom television applications.

1.4   Summary

This chapter has provided a brief introduction, to the important topics and considerations associated with the design of image-coding systems. The following chapters present more detailed, state-of-art analyses of the major coding techniques.

Bibliography

Andrews, H. C., Tescher, A. G., and Kruger, R. P. (1972). Image processing by digital computer. *IEEE Spectrum* **9**, No. 7, 20–32.

Habibi, A., and Robinson, G. S. (1974). A survey of digital picture coding. *IEEE Comput.* **7**, No. 5, 22–34.

Huang, T. S. (1965). PCM picture transmission. *IEEE Spectrum* **2**, No. 12, 57–60.
Huang, T. S., and Tretiak, O. J., eds. (1972). "Picture Bandwidth Compression." Gordon & Breach, New York.
Huang, T. S., Schreiber, W. F., and Tretiak, O. J. (1971). Image processing. *Proc. IEEE* **59**, No. 11, 1586–1609.
Pratt, W. K. (1978). "Digital Image Processing." Wiley (Interscience), New York.
Special Issue on Digital Picture Processing (1972). *Proc. IEEE* **60**, No. 7.
Special Issue on Redundancy Reduction (1967). *Proc. IEEE* **55**, No. 3.
Special Issue on Signal Processing for Digital Communications (1971). *IEEE Trans. Commun. Technol.* **19**, No. 6, Part I.

References

Andrews, H. C. (1976). *IEEE Trans. Comput.* **c-25**, 196–202.
Bisignani, W. T., Richards, G. P., and Whelan, J. W. (1966). *Proc. IEEE* **54**, 376–390.
Cornsweet, T. N. (1970). "Visual Perception." Academic Press, New York.
Davisson, L. D., and Kutz, R. L. (1971). *Natl. Telemeter. Conf. Rec.*, 1971 34A-1 to 34A-4.
Fink, D. G., ed. (1957). "Television Engineering Handbook." McGraw-Hill, New York.
Haralick, R. M., Shanmugam, K., and Dinstein, I. (1973). *IEEE Trans. Syst., Man Cybernet.* **3**, 610–621.
Huffman, D. A. (1952). *Proc. IRE* **40**, 1098–1101.
Huhns, M. (1975). "Optimum Restoration of Quantized Correlated Signals," USCIPI Rep. No. 600. University of Southern California, Image Processing Institute, Los Angeles (summarized in Pratt, 1978, 132–134).
Hunt, B. R., and Cannon, T. M. (1976). *IEEE Trans. Syst. Man Cybernet.* 876–882.
Jain, A. K. (1976). *In* "Image Science Mathematics" (C. O. Wilde and E. Barrett, eds.), 201–223. Western Periodicals, North Hollywood, California.
Lewis, N. W. (1954). *Proc. IEEEE* **101**, Part III, 258–270.
Pearson, D. E. (1972). *In* "Picture Bandwidth Compression" (T. S. Huang and O. J. Tretiak, eds.), 47–95. Gordon & Breach, New York.
Pratt, W. K. (1975). *J. Comput. Graph. Image Process.* **4**, 1–24.
Pratt, W. K. (1978). "Digital Image Processing." Wiley (Interscience), New York.
Preuss, D. (1975). *Int. Commun. Conf.* **1**, 7.12–7.16.
Roberts, L. G. (1962). *IRE Trans. Inf. Theory* **8**, 145–154.
Schreiber, W. F. (1956). *IRE Trans. Inf. Theory* 94–105.
Shannon, C. E. (1949). "The Mathematical Teory of Communications." Univ. of Illinois Press, Urbana.
Wyszecki, G., and Stiles, W. S. (1967). "Color Science." Wiley, New York.

Image Coding Applications of Vision Models*

DAVID J. SAKRISON

Department of Electrical Engineering and Computer Sciences
and the Electronics Research Laboratory
University of California
Berkeley, California

If one considers image encoding carefully, it is clear that there are two factors that make data compression possible. These are the statistical structure of the source and the fidelity requirements of the end user. Heuristically, the contributions of these are as follows. The source image must be regarded as probabilistic in nature, since the encoder does not know beforehand exactly what it will be called on to transmit. However, the ensemble of images that might be generated by a realistic source model will not be completely random, i.e., all pixels being independent and having maximum entropy. There is considerable statistical structure in the image in that a pixel intensity value may be quite accurately predicted

* Research sponsored by the National Science Foundation Grant ENG75-10063.

from values of adjacent pixels. By exploiting this statistical regularity, one may reduce the average number of bits per raster required to describe the image. The requirements of the user enter in a different way. Since the accuracy of perception for a human user or the measurement accuracy for an instrument make certain perturbations unnoticeable or negligible in importance, the encoder can introduce certain errors into the encoded– decoded representation of the image presented to the user (indeed any finite-rate encoder *must* do so). This also allows a reduction in rate. Different methods of encoding at a fixed rate introduce errors with different characteristics; by picking the method that introduces errors of the most unobtrusive nature, the encoding efficiency can be optimized.

This chapter is concerned with the increase in efficiency that can be obtained by appropriately tailoring the characteristics of the distortion introduced by the encoding–decoding procedure. The chapter proceeds in the following sequence. The above description relates in an intuitive way how redundancy and distortion can be used to reduce source rate. Section 2.1 gives a brief analytic discussion of the optimum performance that can be achieved in encoding a source characterized by its probability distribution and user-fidelity requirements. The structure of an optimum code depends in an involved way on both of these considerations. Thus a special situation is considered in which, via the Shannon lower bound, the effect on encoding performance of the source distribution and fidelity requirements can be separated. Having developed an analytic base for how the distortion requirements affect the optimum encoding rate, the chapter then turns to the distortion requirements germane to image encoding. Since the end user in an image transmission system is usually a human viewer, this entails a brief examination of the properties of the human visual system. Section 2.2 gives a brief description of the properties of the human visual system as determined by physiological and psychophysical measurements, followed by a discussion of how these facts can be reduced to mathematical models.

Sections 2.1 and 2.2 provide the background information for the subject. The real question is then to what extent the use of a visual model and distortion criterion can actually result in improved encoding methods. The number of image-encoding studies that have incorporated the use of a fidelity measure are a small fraction of the total simulation and experimental work done in image encoding, and here only the more representative of these efforts are described. These naturally divide into two categories, discussed in Sections 2.3 and 2.4. Section 2.3 considers simulations involving encoding methods whose physical implementations are sufficiently simple that they are of current or potential interest, and the primary emphasis is on exploring how to improve this class of encoding methods. Section 2.4 considers simulations whose objective was simply to better model the visual system in the coding context, and which were carried out without any consideration for the ease of coding implementation. In either case a class of visual models or distortion criteria is chosen, encoding is simulated (usually at a fixed rate), and the quality of images is compared for different members of the class. This gives a limited (because of the restricted class considered) but direct way of judging the appropriateness of a distortion criterion and the extent to which inclusion of visual criteria can improve encoding performance. The discussion is limited to still images with primary emphasis on achromatic (gray-scale) images.

2.1 RATE DISTORTION THEORY; OPTIMUM POSSIBLE PERFORMANCE

2.1.1 Summary of Results

The purpose of this section is to lay a theoretical understanding for how the statistical characteristics of the source and the distortion measure determine the character of an optimum encoding method. The mathematical basis for this is Shannon's rate distortion theory. This section gives a brief statement of the principal results. The reader who wishes a fuller treatment should read the classical work by Shannon (1948) or consult the texts by Gallager (1968), Berger (1971), or Sakrison (1970).

An achromatic still image source produces a sequence of images that can be defined as intensity functions $i(x, y)$ defined on a raster $0 \leq x \leq X$, $0 \leq y \leq Y$. To simplify the mathematics, we introduce a number of mathematical idealizations. First, for reasons to be stated in Section 2.2.1, the image will not be characterized by its intensity but by some memoryless function, such as the logarithm, of the intensity

$$u(x, y) = \log[i(x, y)] \tag{1}$$

Second, in order that the discussion may proceed using only multidimensional calculus, the log-intensity pattern on the continuous raster will be approximately described by the pattern defined on a number of discrete picture elements (pixels). The source output is thus thought of as

$$u_{ij} = u(i\Delta x, j\Delta y) \tag{2}$$

where $i = 1, 2, \ldots, N_x$ and $j = 1, 2, \ldots, N_y$ for $N_x = X/\Delta x$ and $N_y = Y/\Delta y$. The array of $N_x N_y$ log-intensity values will be denoted by the vector $\mathbf{u}$. By making the increments Δx and Δy sufficiently small, this finite dimensional representation can be made to represent the original function $u(x, y)$ arbitrarily closely. At this point the use of the discrete representation is just for mathematical simplification; the reader should keep this in mind and make appropriate associations with the original image defined on the continuous raster. The last assumption to be made is that the source produces a sequence of images that are statistically independent. The output of the random-source model will be denoted by $\mathbf{U}$ ($\mathbf{u}$ denotes a particular image or *sample image*). The assumption then is that the sequence of source outputs $\mathbf{U}_n$, $n = 1, 2, \ldots$, are statistically independent, i.e., that the distribution of $\mathbf{U}_n$ is independent of any observations of $\mathbf{U}_i$ for values of i unequal to n. This assumption would be a reasonable one for a sequence of still images to be transmitted from a satellite or over a wirephoto service; it would be utterly inappropriate for a succession of frames from a TV camera.

The output of the image source is to somehow be encoded, the encoded data transmitted over a channel of *capacity C* bits per image raster or frame, and the channel output decoded to yield an approximation $\bar{u}(x, y)$ or $\bar{\mathbf{u}}$ to the image generated by the source. The reader unfamiliar with the information-theoretic notion of channel capacity should simply associate the channel with a digital channel of very low probability of error and transmission rate C bits/raster.

The source is characterized by an $N_x N_y$ dimensional probability distribution; certain entities will depend on this distribution and the variable α will be used to index this distribution; the source is thus characterized by a probability density $f_\alpha(\mathbf{u})$. For transmission purposes the source is characterized not only by the probability distribution α describing the source distribution, but also by a distortion criterion imposed *by the user* of the system. One might ask to minimize the channel capacity required to transmit the source, subject to certain fidelity constraints. In order to minimize the transmission rate, the fidelity constraints must be stated quantitatively. For this purpose a numerical measure of distortion is introduced; this assigns a nonnegative number to the distortion introduced when the source produces an image $u(x, y)$ and the decoder produces a decoded approximation $\bar{u}(x, y)$. An example of such a distortion measure is

$$d(u, \bar{u}) = \int_0^X \int_0^Y dx dy [u(x, y) - \bar{u}(c, y)]^2 \tag{3}$$

or for the vector representation of pixel samples, the integral is replaced by a sum yielding

$$d(u, \bar{u}) = \sum_{i,j} [u_{ij} - \bar{u}_{ij}]^2 = \|\mathbf{u} - \bar{\mathbf{u}}\|^2 \tag{4}$$

With the above entities defined, it is possible to define the rate distortion function. The physical source imposes a distribution on $\mathbf{u}$, $f_\alpha(\mathbf{u})$. Let

$f_\gamma(\bar{\mathbf{u}}|\mathbf{u})$ denote an arbitrary (dummy or test channel) transition distribution for $\bar{\mathbf{u}}$ given $\mathbf{u}$. The variable γ is used to index such a transition distribution; the subscripts α and γ are used to indicate dependencies on the source and transition densities, respectively. The density $f_\alpha(\mathbf{u})$, together with such a transition density $f_\gamma(\bar{\mathbf{u}}|\mathbf{u})$, define a joint density $f_{\alpha\gamma}(\mathbf{u}, \bar{\mathbf{u}})$. This joint density has associated with it an average distortion

$$E_{\alpha\gamma}\{d(\mathbf{U}, \bar{\mathbf{U}})\} = \int\int d\mathbf{u}\,d\bar{\mathbf{u}}\ d(\mathbf{u}, \bar{\mathbf{u}})f_\alpha(\mathbf{u})f\gamma(\bar{\mathbf{u}}|\mathbf{u}) \qquad (5)$$

and an average mutual information

$$I_{\alpha\gamma}(\mathbf{U}; \bar{\mathbf{U}}) = \int\int d\mathbf{u}\,d\bar{\mathbf{u}}\ \log\left[\frac{f_\gamma(\mathbf{u}|\bar{\mathbf{u}})}{f_{\alpha\gamma}(\bar{\mathbf{u}})}\right]f_\alpha(\mathbf{u})f_\gamma(\bar{\mathbf{u}}|\mathbf{u}) \qquad (6)$$

in which $f_{\alpha\gamma}(\bar{\mathbf{u}})$ denotes the marginal density induced on $\bar{\mathbf{u}}$ by the joint density $\alpha\gamma$. Let

$$\Gamma_\alpha(d^*) = \{\gamma\colon E_{\alpha\gamma}\{d(\mathbf{U}, \bar{\mathbf{U}})\} \leq d^*\} \qquad (7)$$

denote the set of all transition densities that yield average distortion less than or equal to d^*. The rate distortion function of the source is then defined to be

$$R_\alpha(d^*) = \min_{\gamma\,:\,\in\Gamma_\alpha(d^*)} \{I_{\alpha\gamma}(\mathbf{U}; \bar{\mathbf{U}})\} \qquad (8)$$

Note that this function is determined by the probability density α of the source and the distortion measure $d(\mathbf{u}, \bar{\mathbf{u}})$ imposed by the user. It can be shown that $R_\alpha(\cdot)$ is a convex $\cup$ monotone-decreasing function of d^*.

The rate distortion function may have some intuitive meaning; however its real meaning stems from Shannon's source-coding theorem and its converse, which together determine $R_\alpha(d^*)$ to be exactly the minimum transmission rate required to achieve average distortion level d^*.

CONVERSE TO THE CODING THEOREM.   *Given a source with rate distortion function $R_\alpha(d^*)$ and any channel of capacity C bits/raster, there does not exist any coding–decoding method of transmitting the source output U over the channel with average distortion less than d^*, where d^* is the solution of the equation*

$$R_\alpha(d^*) = C \qquad (9)$$

The reader should note the generality of this statement. It states that the source need only be characterized by its *rate distortion function* and the channel *independently* characterized by its *capacity*. This statement of what cannot be done contains *no qualification* as to the complexity or nature of the encoding method (PCM, transform code, video FM, etc.).

This converse is proved by juggling a number of information-theoretic inequalities. Although these inequalities have some intuitive interpretation and lend some insight into the problem of source encoding, they are not reproduced here; the interested reader should consult Gallager (1968, p. 449), Sakrison (1970, p. 143), or Berger (1971, Section 3.2).

The converse theorem by itself is not tremendously exciting; what makes it of interest is the positive side of the coding theorem which states that it is possible to approach the performance limit of the rate distortion level set by Eq. (9) arbitrarily closely. While the converse to the coding theorem states what cannot be done by *any* method of encoding, the coding theorem by contrast considers a fairly specific method of encoding. A number of source outputs $\mathbf{u}_1, \mathbf{u}_2, \ldots, \mathbf{u}_L$ are blocked together to form an $L' = N_x N_y L$-dimensional vector $\mathbf{u}^L$. This L'-dimensional vector is quantized into one of M possible L'-dimensional vectors, $\mathbf{u}_m{}^L, m = 1, \ldots, M$. The index of this vector is then converted to a digit stream, which is transmitted over the channel, and the decoder constructs $\mathbf{u}_m{}^L$ as the approximation to the source output $\mathbf{u}^L$. The distortion between these blocks of L source images is measured as the average over the block

$$d(\mathbf{u}^L, \bar{\mathbf{u}}^L) = (1/L) \sum_{l=1}^{L} d(\mathbf{u}_l, \bar{\mathbf{u}}_l) \tag{10}$$

(Note that the same notation $d(,)$ is used for a function of a single output pair and blocks of output pairs.) The encoder functions by picking as the code vector or vector to represent the source outputs $\mathbf{u}^L$, that vector $\mathbf{u}_m{}^L$ for which $d(\mathbf{u}^L, \mathbf{u}_m{}^L)$ is a minimum for $m = 1, 2, \ldots, M$. Shannon's source coding theorem then makes the following statement about this method of encoding:

SOURCE-CODING THEOREM. *Given a source with rate distortion function $R_\alpha(\cdot)$, an average distortion level d^*, and any small positive numbers ϵ and δ, there exists a block length L and a set of M code words $\mathbf{u}_1{}^L, \mathbf{u}_2{}^L, \ldots, \mathbf{u}_M{}^L$, with M the largest integer satisfying*

$$M \leq 2^{L[R_\alpha(d^*)+\delta]} \tag{11}$$

and the average encoding–decoding quantization distortion satisfying

$$E_\alpha\{d(\mathbf{U}^L, \bar{\mathbf{u}}^L)\} \leq d^* + \epsilon \tag{12}$$

Since the M code vectors can be described by $L[R_\alpha(d^*) + \delta]$ bits, the rate per raster is $R_\alpha(d^*) + \delta$, and this code approaches arbitrarily closely the performance given by Eq. (9).

The primary utility of the rate distortion function is that the coding theorem and its converse show that $R_\alpha(d^*)$ specifies the minimum achievable rate required to achieve average distortion d^*. It thus is very valuable as an absolute yardstick of performance. *However interesting this is to the image-coding problem, this is not really the motivation for describing this theory in this chapter;* rather it is to dig into *how the choice of a distortion measure affects the characteristics of optimum encoding.*

First note that the coding method described in the coding theorem blocked together L (and L may have to be large) $N_x N_y$ pixel images for *simultaneous* quantization. Lest the impact of this fact be lost on the reader, let it be stated explicitly: A number of images (L) are stored, represented to a high degree of accuracy, and then quantized by picking one L-tuple of images to represent them; the values of the pixels are *not* quantized *individually*. The complexity of such a scheme is such as to stagger the mind of any sane person. It is thus worthwhile to examine why the coding theorem expects the encoder designer to cope with a problem of such large dimensionality. This will be accomplished by considering several examples. Rather than coping with the complex problem of image transmission, these examples will assume that the source output is a sequence of independent identically distributed random variables U_1, U_2, . . . , rather than a sequence of random images.

Before considering an example, it is to be remarked that an optimum code, i.e., a set of $M = 2^{LR_\alpha(d^*)}$ L-tuples (M an integer) or M L-dimensional vectors, could be generaged by picking M vectors independently at random with a distribution that chose the L components of the vector independently according to a density

$$f_{\alpha\gamma^*}(\tilde{u}) = \int_{-\infty}^{\infty} du \, f_\alpha(u) f_{\gamma^*}(\tilde{u}|u)$$

in which γ^* is the transition density that achieves the minimization in Eq. (8). Note that the probability density for generating or drawing code vectors thus depends *both* on the source distriution α and this minimizing transition density γ^*. The examples now consider how α and the distortion measure determine the distribution of the code vectors and the dimensionality required for effective encoding.

First consider a source random variable which is uniformly distributed between -1 and 1 and a distortion measure

$$d(u, \tilde{u}) = \begin{cases} 0, & |u - \tilde{u}| \le \epsilon \\ 1, & |u - \tilde{u}| > \epsilon \end{cases} \tag{13}$$

In this case $d^* = E\{d(U, \tilde{U})\}$ is the probability that the error is greater than $\dot{\epsilon}$. Let ϵ^{-1} be an integer. It can be shown (Berger, 1971, Theorem 4.3.1) that for this case the optimum distribution for selecting code vectors is just to draw components of the code vectors according to a distribution that assigns probability ϵ to the points $-1 + \epsilon, -1 + 3\epsilon, \ldots,$ $1 - \epsilon$. *In fact an optimum code in this case simply consists of quantizing each source output* $U_1, U_2, \ldots$ *separately with a uniform A–D converter of dynamic range* $[-1, 1]$ *and quantization interval* $[-\epsilon, \epsilon]$. In this case it is unnecessary to block a number of source outputs together. An optimum encoder of block length 1 functions as shown in Fig. 2-1a, while an optimum encoder of block length 2 functions as the repetition of such an encoder used twice, as shown in Fig. 2-1b.

Does this mean that near-optimum encoding does not generally require simultaneous quantization of a block of L random variables? Not hardly; the simplification that resulted here for a uniform source density and uniform error criterion has caused the problem to "factor," but this is hardly typical. Suppose next that the error criterion remains the same but that the source random variable has a Gaussian distribution of variance $\sigma^2 = 1$. Consider encoding an L-dimensional block of source variables. Under the condition $\epsilon \ll 1$, a near-optimum code still has all the code vectors occurring on a rectangular lattice with spacing 2ϵ in each direc-

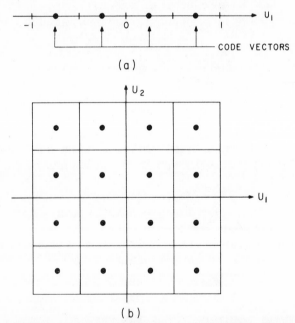

Fig. 2-1.   Optimum quantizing (coding) for a random variable uniformly distributed on $[-1, 1]$ with the distortion measure of Eq. (13) and $\epsilon = 1/2$. (a) Block length $L = 1$; (b) block length $L = 2$.

tion, $u_l = \epsilon + 2i\epsilon$; $l = 1, \ldots, L$; $i = 0, \pm1, \pm2, \ldots$. Now, however, there is a big difference. First the entire L-dimensional space cannot be covered with a finite number of points; the average distortion (probability of an error $> \epsilon$) will therefore be nonzero. For some fixed value of this distortion, $d^* < 1$, one wants to pick the minimum possible number of code points. The source density for an L-dimensional block of independent Gaussian variables is

$$f_\alpha(\mathbf{u}^L) = \prod_{l=1}^{L} 1/(2\pi)^{1/2} \exp[-u_l^2/2] = (1/2\pi)^{L/2} \exp[-\|\mathbf{u}^L\|^2/2] \quad (14)$$

The density thus drops off exponentially with radial distance from the origin, and the set of code vectors should thus be picked on the lattice points but within a sphere of radius just sufficient to yield average distortion D^*, as depicted in Fig. 2-2. The code is thus multidimensional in that the value of the lth coordinate of the code vector (the receiver output) depends on coordinates of the source vector other than the lth. However, the quantization can still be performed coordinate by coordinate. If one used an A–D converter on the source variables, this is equivalent to having code

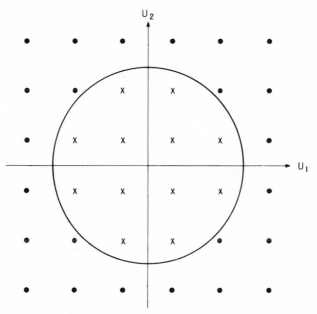

FIG. 2-2.   A near-optimum set of code points and quantization points for a Gaussian source with block length $L = 2$ and distortion criterion of Eq. (13). The circle contains probability mass $1 - d^*$. X: code points. ●: quantization (lattice) points that are not code points.

points at all the vertices of spacing 2ϵ. One would introduce only a small amount of error (for $\epsilon \ll 1$, $d^* \ll 1$) by simply mapping the quantized points (lattice vertices) outside the circle into the closest point inside the circle. A more optimum solution would be to use optimum digital source-encoding methods [such as Huffman coding (Gallager, 1968, Section 3.4)] to encode the quantized variables. As will be shown in the next section, this encoding is in fact optimum. *The above statements seem innocuous, but the reader should carefully note the following implications, which generalize under conditions to be discussed in the next section. First, for $\epsilon \ll 1$, the structure of the code was determined independently* by two considerations: the *distortion measure* dictated that the code vectors fall on a *rectangular lattice,* while the *source distribution* dictated that the subset of lattice points to be used fall inside an L-dimensional sphere. *Second,* this separation occurred because of the condition $\epsilon \ll 1$; the reader should draw the diagram for $\epsilon \approx {}^1/_2$, noting that for large L nearly all the probability mass falls within a sphere of radius $L(1 + \delta)$. *Third,* the curse of having to *simultaneously encode a long block* of variables, here *imposed by the source distribution,* could be pushed off onto *simultaneously digitally coding* a number of quantized variables, the *quantization* being performed simply by A–D *conversion of each variable, variable by variable.* The practical implications of this are very, very significant, for simultaneous digital encoding of a number of discrete variables is not beyond practical digital implementation, while the task of multidimensional quantization staggers the imagination.

Given the third point above, one asks whether optimum encoding ever requires (for small distortion) simultaneous quantization? The answer is yes, and this is the reason for this section delving as deeply into the coding problem as it has, for the factor that determines the nature of optimum *quantization* is the *distortion measure.* This will be shown by modifying the above example further; instead of the distortion criterion of Eq. (13), the distortion measure is now taken to be the squared-error criterion

$$d(u, \bar{u}) = [u - \bar{u}]^2 \qquad (15)$$

so that the distortion measured over a block of L source outputs is

$$d(\mathbf{u}^L, \bar{\mathbf{u}}^L) = 1/L \sum_{l=1}^{L} [u_l - \bar{u}_l]^2 = (1/L)\|\mathbf{u}^L - \bar{\mathbf{u}}^L\|^2 \qquad (16)$$

For this distortion criterion the independent quantization method depicted in Figs. 2-1b and 2-2 for two dimensions is not optimum; the large errors in the corners contribute significantly because distortion is measured as the square of the error. As discussed in the next section, the optimum distribution for the quantization errors is a Gaussian distribution of variance d^*. A much better (and in fact optimal) quantization pattern for block length $L = 2$ is the hexagonal pattern shown in Fig. 2-3; for a given mean-square quantization error, the density of hexagons required is less than that of squares. However, note that this requires a complicated two-dimensional A–D converter.

The reason for the discussion above in a chapter on vision modeling should at last be apparent: What can be gained by *appropriately choosing a distortion measure can only be gained by tailoring the shape or distribution of the quantization errors*. These remarks are made quantitative in the next section. They should serve as a sober warning to those looking for an easy or large payoff by making use of a distortion measure, for *multidimensional quantization is very unattractive from the standpoint of implementation*. A quick benchmark as to the gain to be had is found in the work of Goblick and Holzinger (1967). They considered encoding a Gaussian random variable and showed (among many other useful things) that uniform quantization (A–D conversion) followed by digital encoding yielded a data rate only 0.25 bit per source output (random variable) higher than the minimum rate given by $R_{gauss}(d^*)$ that could be achieved by multidimensional quantization. The cost of multidimensional quantization is clearly not worth this modest improvement in most applications. Lest the reader be dissuaded from reading further, it will be shown in Section 2.2 that there are some properties of the visual system that can be exploited with only modest implementation penalties.

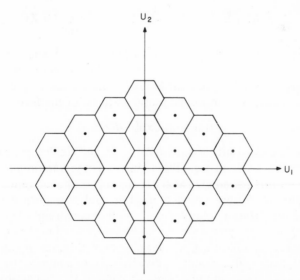

FIG. 2-3. An optimum quantizer for $L = 2$ and a square-error criterion. •: code points.

2.1.2   The Shannon Lower Bound

Although the sensitivity of the visual system depends in nontrivial ways on properties of the image **u** itself, this subsection considers *difference distortion measures* in order to give quantitative substance to the insights built up in the preceding examples. A difference distortion measure is one that depends only on the error

$$d(\mathbf{u}, \tilde{\mathbf{u}}) = d(\mathbf{u} - \tilde{\mathbf{u}}) \tag{17}$$

(again we use the same notation d for two different functions). For such a distortion measure the expression (8) can be manipulated as follows (Shannon, 1948, Part V):

$$
\begin{aligned}
R_\alpha(d^*) &= \min_{\gamma \in \Gamma_\alpha(d^*)} [I_{\alpha\gamma}(\mathbf{U}; \tilde{\mathbf{U}})] \\
&= \min_{\gamma \in \Gamma_\alpha(d^*)} [H_\alpha(\mathbf{U}) - H_{\alpha\gamma}(\mathbf{U}|\tilde{\mathbf{U}})] \\
&= H_\alpha(\mathbf{U}) - \max_{\gamma:\, E_{\alpha\gamma}\{d(\mathbf{U}-\tilde{\mathbf{U}})\}\le d^*} [H_{\alpha\gamma}(\mathbf{U} - \tilde{\mathbf{U}}|\tilde{\mathbf{U}})] \\
&\ge H_\alpha(\mathbf{U}) - \max_{\gamma:\, E_{\alpha\gamma}\{d(\mathbf{U}-\tilde{\mathbf{U}})\}\le d^*} [H_{\alpha\gamma}(\mathbf{U} - \tilde{\mathbf{U}})] \tag{18}
\end{aligned}
$$

in which the H's denote the differential (integral) entropy for the variables indicated. Now the maximization on the right-hand side of Eq. (18) does not depend on α or **U**; specifically letting $\mathbf{Z} = \mathbf{U} - \tilde{\mathbf{U}}$,

$$R_\alpha(d^*) \ge R_{\alpha L}(d^*) \triangleq H_\alpha(\mathbf{U}) - \max_{E\{d(\mathbf{Z})\}\le d^*} [H(\mathbf{Z})] \tag{19}$$

The maximization to be carried out in Eq. (19) is much simpler than that in the original expression for $R_\alpha(d^*)$; it depends *only* on the distortion *criterion* and not on the source distribution. This maximizing distribution is easily determined by variational methods to be of the form

$$f(\mathbf{z}) = c_1 \exp[-d(\mathbf{z})/c_2] \tag{20}$$

with c_1 and c_2 picked such that $E\{d(\mathbf{Z})\} = d^*$ and $f(\mathbf{z})$ has probability mass 1. The right-hand side of Eq. (19) is known as the *Shannon lower bound*.

How does this bound give analytic support to the inference made from the examples of the preceding subsection and how does it bear on the problem of quantization relative to a distortion constraint? The bound consists of two *separate* terms which can be interpreted in the context of the coding theorem as follows. Consider blocks of L-tuples of source vectors $\mathbf{u}^L$; let the space of such blocks be divided up into a number (not necessarily finite) of quantization regions $\mathcal{U}_m$ of volume V_m. All source blocks $\mathbf{u}^L$

falling in $\mathcal{U}_m$ are to be represented at the receiver by a representation or code block $\mathbf{u}_m{}^L$. The probability of $\mathbf{U}^L$ falling in the mth region $\mathcal{U}_m$ is denoted by

$$p_m = \int_{\mathcal{U}_m} \cdots \int_{\mathcal{U}_m} d\mathbf{u}^L p(\mathbf{u}^L) \tag{21}$$

The entropy or rate per output of the encoded or quantized block of source outputs is then

$$(1/L)H = -(1/L) \sum_m p_m \log p_m$$

$$= -(1/L) \sum_m \int_{\mathcal{U}_m} \cdots \int_{\mathcal{U}_m} d\mathbf{u}^L p(\mathbf{u}^L) \log p_m \tag{22}$$

Now suppose that the source density varies only a small amount over $\mathcal{U}_m$ as would be the case if the density $p(\mathbf{u}^L)$ was smooth and $d^* \ll E\{d(\mathbf{U})\}$; then

$$p_m \approx V_m p(\mathbf{u}^L) \tag{23}$$

for $\mathbf{u}^L \in \mathcal{U}_m$, and Eq. (22) can be written

$$(1/L)H \approx -(1/L) \sum_m \int_{\mathcal{U}_m} \cdots \int_{\mathcal{U}_m} d\mathbf{u}^L \, p(\mathbf{u}^L) \log[p(\mathbf{u}^L)V_m]$$

$$= (1/L)H_\alpha(\mathbf{U}^L) - (1/L) \sum_m p_m \log V_m \tag{24}$$

The first term in Eq. (24) is the entropy term appearing in the Shannon lower bound [if the different source outputs are independent, then $H(\mathbf{U}^L) = LH(\mathbf{U})$; the rate for the block is L times the rate for a single output]. How can the second term in Eq. (24) be made to look like the second term in Eq. (19)? Suppose all the quantization regions are translates of each other so that the V_m are equal, $V_m \equiv V$. Then

$$(1/L)H \approx H_\alpha(\mathbf{U}) + (1/L) \log V^{-1} \tag{25}$$

Suppose further that the $\mathcal{U}_m$ are translates of the set

$$\mathcal{U} = \{\mathbf{u}^L: d(\mathbf{u}^L) \le d^*\} \tag{26}$$

For L sufficiently large, nearly all the volume of this region lies in a thin shell near the boundary, and if the code vector $\mathbf{u}_m{}^L$ is located at the center, the distortion is d^*. The distribution formed for $\mathbf{Z}^L$ by taking each component in the block independently with the optimizing distribution of Eq. (19) also has nearly all of its probability mass near the boundary; this implies that

$$H(\mathbf{Z}) = 1/L \, H(\mathbf{Z}^L) = -1/L \, \log V^{-1} \tag{27}$$

making the entropy or rate of Eq. (25) equal to the Shannon lower bound. The last equality in Eq. (27) is not immediately obvious, but the concerned reader should be able to convince himself of it; the process will force an understanding of the statements made above.

The above analysis has been somewhat involved, but it is very much germane to the question of the use of a distortion measure. The analysis gives a more general justification for the statement made in the preceding subsection: In optimum encoding *the distortion measure determines the shape of an optimum quantizing region; the source statistics determine the digital encoding of the quantized output.* Further, Eq. (26) tells us what the shape of an optimum L-dimensional quantization region should be and gives a standard of comparison for practical quantization schemes. For quantization methods in which the quantization regions are translates of a basic region $\mathcal{U}$, one can calculate the scale or size of the region required to have the quantization distortion equal d^*; from Eq. (23) errors are approximately uniformly distributed throughout $\mathcal{U}$. The quantity $\log(V^{-1})$ can then be compared to the quantity

$$\max_{E\{d(Z)\}\leq d^*} [H(Z)]$$

to study the effectiveness of a quantizer. For example, for a scalar-valued random variable with square-error distortion measure, $f(\mathbf{z})$ as given by Eq. (20) is Gaussian. The *ideal* quantization region is an L-dimensional sphere of radius $(LD^*)^{1/2}$, and

$$\max_{E\{d(Z)\}\leq d^*} [H(Z)] = \tfrac{1}{2}\log_2(2\pi e d^*) = 2.047 + \tfrac{1}{2}\log_2 d^* \quad \text{bits} \tag{28}$$

For a simple uniform one-dimensional quantizer (A–D converter), the quantization interval is $[-(3d^*)^{1/2}, (3d^*)^{1/2}]$ and

$$\log(V^{-1}) = \tfrac{1}{2}\log_2[12d^*] = 1.792 + \tfrac{1}{2}\log_2 d^* \quad \text{bits} \tag{29}$$

For a two-dimensional hexagonal quantization region, the "radius" is $[128 \, d^*/13(3)^{1/2}]^{1/2}$. Since the quantization region is two dimensional, $L = 2$ and the relevant quantity is

$$\tfrac{1}{2}\log(V^{-1}) = \tfrac{1}{2}\log_2(192 \, d^*/13) = 1.942 + \tfrac{1}{2}\log_2 d^* \quad \text{bits} \tag{30}$$

This provides a derivation of the statement made in the preceding section that an optimum multidimensional quantitizer gains only 0.25 bit per scalar variable over simple uniform A–D conversion, and further shows that this loss can be cut to only 0.1 bit per variable for two-dimensional conversion. This two-dimensional hexagonal quantization could be simply achieved by two pairs of A–D converters and a comparator, but the savings of 0.15 bit per variable hardly seems worth the modest added complexity.

The results above permit a significant simplification of the design problem by breaking it into two parts and isolating that portion of the problem relevant to the choice of the distortion measure. However, they are really significant only when equality holds in Eq. (19). This point thus needs clarification. Berger (1971, Section 4.3.1) has a derivation of Eq. (19) which yields the following useful result:

$$R_\alpha(d^*) = R_{\alpha L}(d^*) \tag{31}$$

if and only if the source variable U can be expressed as the sum of two independent variables $U = W + Z$, with Z having the probability density of Eq. (20). Note that as $d^* \to 0$, this condition becomes weaker and weaker; thus even when there is not equality in Eq. (19), $R_{\alpha L}(d^*)$ approaches $R_\alpha(d^*)$ as d^* approaches 0 for a broad class of source distributions and distortion measures. The reader should check that the first and third examples of Section 2.2.1 satisfy this criterion exactly, and that the second example does nearly so for small ϵ.

The following section considers properties of the visual system. After discussing these properties, the remarks of this section are used as a guideline in abstracting the more relevant of those properties into a quantitative distortion criterion.

2.2 PROPERTIES OF THE HUMAN VISUAL SYSTEM

This section is divided into three subsections. The first describes briefly what is known about achromatic properties of the visual system, and the second gives a description of color vision. These descriptions are general in nature and not specific to the coding problem. The third subsection abstracts the more relevant of these properties into a quantitative measure of distortion appropriate for the context of image encoding.

2.2.1 Spatial Properties of the Visual System

The visual system has been studied by several methods. The first is by anatomical study, in which structure is observed and its function deduced from the structure. The second is physiological, in which recordings of nervous activity in anesthetized animals are made in response to various visual stimuli. The last is through psychophysical studies, in which alert human subjects are asked to respond in some manner ("I detected a change," "the stimulus was in the left half field," etc.) to a sequence of stimuli. A recent review article (Sakrison, 1977) written for communication engineers describes briefly the physiology of the visual system and some of the more pertinent psychophysical experiments and cites fairly extensive references to the subject. The reader interested in such a description is referred to that article and the references given therein; here only a brief summary of the results of the experiments that pertain to still images is given. This subsection deals specifically with achromatic images.

Some of the most useful information comes from psychophysical measurements that have determined the sensitivity of an observer to sinusoidal gratings presented at the threshold of visibility (detectability) using stimuli of the form

$$i(x, y) = I_0 + k \cos[2\pi f_0(x \cos \theta - y \sin \theta)] \tag{32}$$

These experiments have been performed by a large number of investigators and for different choices of spatial frequency f_0, background illumination I_0, and grating angle θ. The principal conclusions are these: At photopic levels of illumination (from a moderately well-lighted room on up to bright sunlight) detectability, for any fixed values of f_0 and θ, depends only on the contrast of the grating, k/I_0, and not separately on k and I_0. The sensitivity depends both on f_0 and θ. This is usually stated in terms of the *contrast sensitivity,* the value of I_0/k at the threshold of detectability (the sensitivity is inversely proportional to the contrast required for detection). As a function of spatial frequency f_0, this sensitivity increases nearly linearly from low spatial frequencies up to a maximum in the midfrequency range and then falls off rapidly with increasing frequency. Spatial frequencies are usually referred to as the number of cycles occurring in 1.0 degree of arc subtended in a viewer's field of vision. The frequency of maximum sensitivity varies somewhat from viewer to viewer, but is typically between 3.0 and 4.5 cycles/degree. Typical contrast sensitivity curves for both sinusoidal gratings and narrow-band random patterns are shown in Fig. 2-4. The sensitivity also depends on θ, being a maximum for horizontal and vertical gratings and decreasing with the angle from either axis, being down about 3 dB at an angle of 45°.

Measurements using sinusoidal gratings have been broadened to measurements using periodic gratings of various waveshapes and complex gratings consisting of two sinusoids of different frequencies. A number of such experiments suggest that frequency components separated by about an octave are detected by the observer *independently;* i.e., if one frequency component is close to its level of detectability, the level at which

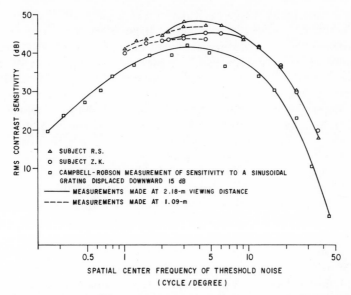

FIG. 2-4. Contrast sensitivity of the human visual system to sinusoidal gratings (lower curve) and narrow-band isotropic noise (upper curve) (from Mostafavi and Sakrison, 1976; and Campbell and Robson, 1968).

it is detected is unaffected by the presence and level of a second sub-threshold component. This has led workers in the field to the hypothesis that the visual perceptive system is composed of a number of independent parallel detection mechanisms, which they term spatial channels, each tuned to a different spatial frequency and orientation angle. A considerable number of relevant experiments have been performed to test this hypothesis, and all are consistent with this model. Such a model is shown in block diagram form in Fig. 2-5.

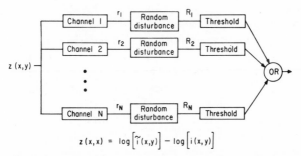

$$z(x,x) = \log\left[\tilde{i}(x,y)\right] - \log\left[i(x,y)\right]$$

FIG. 2-5. General structure of a visual system model with parallel channels followed by OR detection.

Some experiments have been performed to determine the properties of an individual channel. A number of these have dealt with the bandwidth of the channel. These results have varied, but those which are least ambiguous of interpretation yield a bandwidth of about $\pm \, ^1/_2$ the center frequency in the radial direction and about $\pm 10°$ angle subtended in the frequency plane in the angular direction. This broad-band frequency tuning corresponds in the inverse Fourier transform domain to a narrow-point-spread function (impulse response) consisting of one main lobe flanked by two opposing lobes whose amplitude is about one-fourth the amplitude as that of the center lobe. A single channel responds to a stimulus broader than the extent of this point-spread function. Unfortunately there do not exist reliable measurements of the spatial extent (visual field subtended) of this summation of a spatial channel, but it is perhaps several times broader than the extent of one of these point-spread functions and perhaps something like $1°$ (foveal or detailed vision is confined to about $1°$ around the observer's point of fixation). This would indicate the presence of incoherent spatial summation in addition to the spatial summation performed by the point-spread function; certain experiments with mixtures of gratings of different phases also indicate this.

The remarks so far might be summarized analytically as follows. There exist a number of parallel processors that produce real-valued outputs r_k, $k = 0, 1, 2, \ldots$. Whenever any one or more of these response variables r_k exceeds threshold, the observer detects a stimulus as being present. The behavior of the response variables is consistent with the following model. Let $c(x, y) = [i(x, y) - I_0]/I_0$ denote the contrast of the intensity pattern $i(x, y)$ of an image with average illumination I_0. The response variables will be functionals of $c(x, y)$, since it is observed that detectability depends only on contrast. If an error pattern $\bar{i}(x, y) - i(x, y)$ is to be detected on a background (or useful) image $i(x, y)$, then the appropriate contrast variable would be

$$
\begin{aligned}
z(x, y) &= \frac{\bar{i}(x, y) - i(x, y)}{i(x, y)} \\
&\approx \log[i(x, y) + \bar{i}(x, y) - i(x, y)] - \log[i(x, y)] \\
&= \bar{u}(x, y) - u(x, y)
\end{aligned}
\tag{33}
$$

in which

$$
u(x, y) = \log[i(x, y)]
\tag{34a}
$$

and

$$
\bar{u}(x, y) = \log[\bar{i}(x, y)]
\tag{34b}
$$

In point of fact, the logarithmic sort of nonlinearity occurs within the photoreceptors and the first two levels of neural transduction in the retina. Thus there is a linear operation that precedes the logarithmic operation, and $i(x, y)$ in Eq. (34) should be replaced by a version of $i(x, y)$ subjected to low-pass filtering. However, in an emmetropic (optically normal) or optically well-corrected eye, this low-pass filtering has a notably slower drop-off with increasing frequency than that of the neural processing that follows the logarithmic nonlinearity (Campbell and Green, 1965). Thus to keep the model as simple as is consistent with including first-order effects, the optical filtering is neglected. The functions or response variables r_k are then generated from $z(x, y)$ in the following manner. Let $v_k(x, y)$ denote the result of filtering $z(x, y)$ with a bandpass filter of center frequency f_k, radial bandwidth $\pm 0.5 f_k$, and angular bandwidth $\pm 10°$. Let $g(\cdot)$ denote a pointwise nonlinearity. Then the behavior of the r_k is consistent with

$$r_k = \iint\limits_{\text{raster}} dxdy \; g[v_k(x, y)] \qquad (35)$$

This sequence of operations is depicted in the block diagram of Fig. 2-6. The nonlinearity $g(\cdot)$ has not been determined by a number of consistent experiments, but the most recent indicate something like a sixth-power law out to a value v_0 followed by a linear characteristic. The value v_0 is about at the peak value at which a sinusoidal grating of spatial extent $1^1/_2$ cycles wide and several cycles high is at threshold; i.e., grating patches of this small size or larger have amplitudes below the linear portion of the characteristic at threshold.

The above model is not the only one that is consistent with the observed facts, but it is functionally straightforward and consistent with the observed data. However, it pertains only to situations in which the observer is attempting to detect the presence of a stimulus $i(x, y)$ on a uniform background. If, instead, the observer is attempting to detect the presence of the error $i(x, y) - \bar{\imath}(x, y)$ on the image $i(x, y)$, the image $i(x, y)$ has an effect that must be taken into account. If an observer is asked to detect the difference between

$$i(x, y) = I_0 + i_m(x, y) \qquad (36)$$

and

$$i(x, y) = I_0 + i_m(x, y) + i_n(x, y) \qquad (37)$$

then the sensitivity of the observer to detecting $i_n(x, y)$ is reduced, approximately inversely proportional to the quantity [Constant + rms value of $i_m(x, y)$]. This reduction in sensitivity depends on the relative

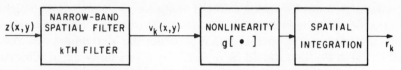

FIG. 2-6.   Block diagram of a simple model for a single-channel detector.

spatial frequency content of $i_m(x, y)$ and $i_n(x, y)$, the reduction being maximum when both i_m and i_n are bandpass functions with the same center frequency. However, this frequency tuning is broad, and the reduction of sensitivity extends for one to two octaves about the center frequency of i_m. If $i_m(x, y)$ is also localized in position, then the reduction of sensitivity to $i_n(x, y)$ is localized to that same spatial area. Unfortunately no direct measurements have been made on the spatial extent of this reduced sensitivity. The above remarks are often expressed in a direct ad hoc fashion by the comment that a viewer's sensitivity to errors is reduced in regions of the image where the image itself has sharp edges or large gradients. Analytically, these remarks might be expressed by modifying the response variables r_k to be

$$r_k = \iint\limits_{\text{raster}} dxdy \; g \left[\frac{v_k(x, y)}{1 + s(x, y)} \right] \tag{38}$$

in which $s(x, y)$ is defined as follows. Let $u(x, y) = \log i(x, y)$ be filtered with a filter having a linear increase with radial spatial frequency from about 2.0 to 20 cycles/degree and falling off thereafter. The output of this filter, $q(x, y)$, thus approximates the magnitude of the gradient of $u(x, y)$. The function $s(x, y)$ is then a spatially smoothed rms measure of $q(x, y)$.

This brief discussion of the visual system and its behavior is thus summarized by the model predicting that the observer will detect the difference between $i(x, y)$ and $\tilde{i}(x, y)$ for any pair of stimuli for which any one of the r_k given by Eq. (38) is above a certain threshold. The remarks here to this effect have been only of a summary nature; for a fuller description of the rationale for these remarks, the reader is again referred to Sakrison (1977) and the considerable number of articles referenced therein.

2.2.2   Color Properties of the Visual System

Achromatic properties of the visual system have been studied extensively both by psychophysical experiments on humans and physiological studies based on cell recordings from other species, usually other primates. Further, the key experiments have been performed sufficiently often that most of the first-order properties are fairly well resolved. In the case of color vision, the picture is not nearly so complete. There exist a few psychophysical studies, but the bulk of knowledge comes from physiological studies of monkeys, chiefly the macaque. For an introductory discussion of color vision, the reader is referred to Weale (1968, Chapter 4). An up-to-date summary of current knowledge in the field is to be found in the very readable chapter by DeValois and DeValois (1975).

The first important fact about human perception of color dates back to the time of Thomas Young and earlier. This is the principle of trichromacy that states that a stimulus of any apparent color may be matched by an appropriate combination of three appropriately chosen light sources, X, Y, and Z. The sources X, Y, and Z need not be monochromatic, but they must be linearly independent in that no one of them can be matched by a combination of the other two. By match it is meant that a human observer is unable to distinguish between the two stimuli. If the three sources X, Y, and Z are appropriately chosen from distinct regions of the spectrum, this trichromacy principle is correct as stated. If the sources are simply linearly independent, a match might require a combination $\alpha X + \beta Y + \gamma Z$ in which one of the α, β, or γ (say α) is negative. This is not possible. In this case the statement may be altered to Grassman's law of color mixtures, which says that a combination $\beta Y + \gamma Z$ can be found to match the combination (stimulus $+ \alpha X$).

The trichromacy principle dictates that there are at least three types of receptors with different spectral absorption characteristics and that in the central nervous system, signals from these receptors appear in exactly three linearly independent combinations. The simplest situation would be for there to exist three types of receptors, each consisting of only a single photopigment (light-absorbing and -converting chemical). However, that need not be the only possibility. Another would be for there to exist three types of photoreceptors, each containing more than one photopigment but with all receptors of a given type consisting of the same proportions of photopigments. A still more complicated possibility would be for there to exist more than three types of photoreceptors, but for signals from these to be transmitted to the central nervous system in only three linearly independent combinations. Although nature usually observes an efficiency of complexity, physiologists did not rule out the more complex possibilities until just recently. However, within the past 10 years it seems to have been reasonably established (DeValois and DeValois, 1975) that there exist only three types of photoreceptors (in addition to the rods which are used in dim lighting), each consisting of a single photopigment. The maximum absorbencies of these are at wavelengths 445, 535, and 570 nm, and they are termed, respectively, the S (short), M (medium), and L (long) receptors. Note that color names are not appropriate since all three photoreceptors have broad spectral absorbency characteristics and since two (M and L) have their peak absorbency bunched together in the green–greenish yellow portion of the spectrum.

The next question is how information from these three sets of photoreceptors is encoded for transmission to the central nervous system. A communications engineer whose interest is in efficient transmission would feel that the information should be encoded into a format that makes for efficient transmision. The nervous system sometimes opts for this approach and other times sticks with an inefficient scheme that is easy to implement (as the pulse-rate modulation used to transmit along all ganglia). Recent measurements in the lateral geniculate nucleus, a midway station between the retina and the visual cortex, have in fact revealed the existence of six, and apparently only six, types of cells. These are termed by DeValois (1971) WH $-$ B (white minus black, $L + M$), B $-$ Wh; R $-$ G (red minus green, more accurately $L - M$), G $-$ R; Y $-$ B (yellow minus blue, more accurately $L - S$), and $B - $ Y. For each of these, the receptive field consists of a center excitatory spot surrounded by a torroidal inhibitory region. The firing rate is increased when the first-named stimulus is shown on the excitatory region and decreased when the second-named stimulus is shown on that region. For the inhibitory region the response pattern is reversed; i.e., the second-named stimulus increases the firing rate. Note that the six types of cells are grouped into three complementary pairs. Each member of the pair is necessary since a firing rate cannot go negative. A white spot with dark surround is thus signaled by a Wh $-$ B cell (no appreciable information being transmitted by a B $-$ Wh cell), and a black dot with a white surround is signaled by a B $-$ Wh cell. The Wh $-$ B and B $-$ Wh cells convey no chromatic information and, together with subsequent processing in the visual cortex, are the basis for the properties of achromatic vision discussed in the previous subsection. The R $-$ G and Y $-$ B cells signal chromatic information by transmitting color differences.

As mentioned in the preceding subsection, the achromatic portion of the visual system responds to contrast, or for simplicity of modeling, to the log of intensity. This remark generalizes to the R $-$ G and Y $-$ B cells; the response of an R $-$ G cell being approximately equal to the log of the intensity absorbed by the L receptors minus the log of the intensity absorbed by the M receptors.

The above remarks perhaps indicate that the Wh $-$ B, R $-$ G, and Y $-$ B systems form a canonical system for describing an image and hence perhaps an orthogonal basis for describing errors. If this is to be made quantitative, these systems need to be better defined than Wh $-$ B, R $-$ G, Y $-$ B; specifically numerical relations giving the spectral characteristics of these three systems need to be specified. Suppose $l(\lambda)$, $m(\lambda)$, and $s(\lambda)$ represent the absorption curves estimated for the three types of photoreceptors. Then let

$$L(x, y) = \int I(x, y, \lambda)l(\lambda) \, d\lambda \tag{39}$$

in which $I(x, y, \lambda)$ denotes the incident intensity as a function of position (x, y) and wavelength λ; $M(x, y)$ and $S(x, y)$ are defined by similar equations. Then a triple of response fields is formed as

$$\begin{bmatrix} z(x, y) \\ c_1(x, y) \\ c_2(x, y) \end{bmatrix} = B \begin{bmatrix} \log(L(x, y)) \\ \log(M(x, y)) \\ \log(S(x, y)) \end{bmatrix} \tag{40}$$

in which B is a three-by-three matrix. The functions $z(x, y)$, $c_1(x, y)$, and $c_2(x, y)$ are intended to represent, respectively, the Wh $-$ B, R $-$ G, and Y $-$ B systems. The functional form of this model is shown in Fig. 2-7.

What is a rational method for picking the matrix B? If the z, c_1, c_2 are to represent canonical representations of the color system, then it would be logical to pick B such that errors in the three systems are uncorrelated, i.e., so that surfaces of confusion or threshold errors are circles in this system of coordinates. Brown and MacAdam (1959) in fact measured errors in an an observer's ability to match colors for 39 different choices of color and luminance and calculated ellipses of matching errors for each (a truly gargantuan experimental undertaking). Under the mapping from their set of coordinates (the C.I.E. standard observer absorption set) to the z, c_1, c_2 coordinates, their ellipses should be mapped into circles. Faugeras (1976) and Frei (1974) both considered this approach and made calculations of B to minimize the eccentricity of the resulting ellipses. Both unfortunately assumed $b_{22} = -b_{21}$, $b_{23} = 0$, and $b_{33} = -b_{31}$, $b_{32} = 0$ and checked only the eccentricity and not the orientation of the

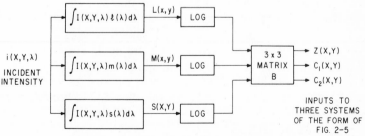

FIG. 2-7. Color model of Faugeras and Frei.

resulting ellipses. Faugeras obtained the following values for determining this triple of canonical response fields:

$$b_{11} = 22.6(0.612) \qquad b_{12} = 22.6(0.369) \qquad b_{13} = 22.6(0.019)$$
$$b_{21} = 64$$
$$b_{31} = 10$$

The spatial properties of the achromatic response system $z(x, y)$ have been described in some detail in the preceding subsection. Some attention will now be given to the spatial characteristics of the c_1 and c_2 ($R - G$, $Y - B$) systems. It is useful to first make some qualitative remarks. The bandwidth of the spatial channels of the achromatic system discussed in the preceding subsection would be expected to correspond (inversely) to the width of a receptive field. The frequency range spanned by the response variables r_k would also be expected to correspond to the various sizes of receptive fields occurring for the Wh $-$ B system. Psychophysical and physiological evidence seems consistent in this respect: The spatial frequency range spanned by the achromatic visual system is quite broad, and a wide range of sizes of receptive fields is observed. For the $R - G$ and $Y - B$ systems, this is not true. The receptive fields all seem rather broad in spatial extent and correspondingly they are much less sensitive to high frequencies than the achromatic system. Subjectively, observers looking at a grating of uniform luminance but alternating color report a uniform field of color for frequencies that would be perceptible if there were alternations of luminance as well as chrominance. Unfortunately beyond these qualitative remarks there is not a wealth of data available. The only quantitative work in this area to date is that of Faugeras (1976). He makes estimates only of the low-frequency portions of the contrast sensitivity curves for the Wh $-$ B, $R - G$, and $Y - B$ systems. These measurements indicate a power law behavior for all three systems at low frequencies with the maximum for the $R - G$ system occurring at about one-half the frequency of the maximum for the achromatic system and that of the $Y - B$ occurring at about one-half that of the $R - G$ system. This one set of measurements is not comparable to the numerous detailed measurements performed for achromatic images by a very large number of investigators, and further measurements need to be made of the contrast sensitivity of the two chrominance systems.

The above somewhat qualitative remarks summarize much of what is known about the properties of color vision; they do not provide nearly as complete a picture as the quantitative model of achromatic vision built up in the preceding subsection.

2.2.3   Summary of Visual System Properties and Formulation of an Analytic Distortion Measure for Image Encoding

This subsection reflects on the model for detecting errors in an image that has been discussed in the preceding subsections. The goal is to arrive at a numerical measure of distortion for use in image encoding. It will be necessary to make some compromises with accuracy for the sake of analytic tractability. The discussion in Section 2.1 of coding errors and their effects on encoding efficiency is used as a guide to the compromises adopted.

Consider first the case of achromatic images. The conclusion of Section 2.2.1 was that an error was detected whenever any one of the r_k defined by Eq. (35) [or (38) to include the effects of masking] and Fig. 2-6 was above threshold. The problem is now to formulate a quantitative measure of perceived error that is consistent with that model of detection. Compared to the number of detection experiments, the results concerning perceived contrast at suprathreshold levels are modest. Some of the more recent and useful results are found in the work of Hammerly et al. (1977). They asked subjects to compare the contrast of various test gratings with that of a comparison sinusoidal grating and give a subjective rating of the contrast of the test pattern relative to that of the test grating. The test patterns consisted of sinusoidal gratings, narrow-band random gratings, compound sinusoidal gratings, and compound random gratings (bimodal power spectra).

For the single-component (sinusoidal or random) patterns, perceived contrast was a piecewise linear function of physical contrast for contrast levels above threshold; near threshold the functional dependence between perceived and actual contrast was the same form as the function $g(\cdot)$. This implied that for narrow-band stimuli, a single response variable r_k is itself an appropriate measure of perceived contrast. For the compound gratings, they reported that a peaks-adding and peaks-subtracting phasing of two sinusoids had equal measures of perceived contrast. Also, for varying magnitudes of the component stimuli, the quantity $r_i + r_j$ (i and j corresponding to the two frequency components) gave an accurate fit to perceived contrast.

The conclusion of these remarks and of the preceding subsections is that a useful measure of perceived distortion might be given by

$$d(u - \tilde{u}) = \sum_k r_k = \sum_k \iint dxdy \, g[v_k(x, y)] \qquad (41)$$

with the $v_k(x, y)$ the responses to the channel bandpass filters described in Section 2.2.1, the common input to these filters being

$$z(x, y) = u(x, y) - \tilde{u}(x, y) = \log i(x, y) - \log \tilde{i}(x, y) \qquad (33)$$

While Eq. (41) may succinctly sum up the dominant first-order properties of the visual system in a measure of perceived contrast, it is too complex analytically to use in incorporating visual properties into the design of an image-encoding system. The goal is thus to simplify Eq. (41), but to do so in such a manner that the system optimization done according to the simpler distortion measure would not be too suboptimal to an optimization carried out for the measure of Eq. (41). The guide for such a choice is the discussion of Section 2.1 on the role of the distortion measure in determining an optimum encoding system: specifically, the observation that, for a difference distortion measure, the error field should have maximum entropy subject to the distortion constraint. With this in mind, it is expedient to simply consider several analytically convenient measures and compare them with Eq. (41) on the basis of their relative entropies.

The sum of a number of nonlinear functionals appearing in Eq. (41) is particularly cumbersome. Let $v(x, y)$ denote the sum of the $v_k(x, y)$. The field $v(x, y)$ could be obtained as the response to $z(x, y)$ of a single filter whose impulse response was the sum of the filters in the various channels, i.e., a filter whose transfer function is equal to that of the contrast sensitivity function shown in Fig. 2-4. One might then be tempted to replace the sum in Eq. (41) by the single integral

$$d(u - \tilde{u}) = \int\int dxdy \, g[v(x, y)] \qquad (42)$$

If one wanted to incoporate the masking effect, the argument of $g(\cdot)$, $v(x, y)$, could be replaced by $v(x, y)/[1 + s(x, y)]$ to yield

$$d(u, \tilde{u}) = \int\int dxdy \, g\left[\frac{v(x, y)}{1 + s(x, y)}\right] \qquad (42a)$$

A further sacrifice to analytic tractability would be to replace the function $g(e)$, which resembles $|e|^6$ for subthreshold e and $|e| - c$ for suprathreshold e, by simply $|e|^p$, yielding

$$d(u - \tilde{u}) = \int\int dxdy|v(x, y)|^p \qquad (43)$$

What have the simplifications of Eqs. (42) and (43) cost in effectiveness versus the measure of Eq. (41)? It depends on how they are used. It would not be difficult to find error fields for which these different distortion measures give noticeably different values. The most outstanding example would be a compound grating consisting of two somewhat disjoint frequency components. The measure of Eq. (41) would be sensitive to the phase between the two components, while that of Eq. (42) would vary considerably as a function of the phase; the measure of Eq. (43) would be independent of phase for $p = 2$ because of the (near) orthogonality of the two disjoint frequency components. For values of $p > 1$, the criterion of Eq. (43) weights large suprathreshold errors more severely than that of Eq. (41) or (42). Error fields that have nonuniform behavior in that they concentrate errors in certain frequencies or in certain amplitude levels will be measured differently by the three criteria of Eqs. (41)–(43). *Thus if the intent is to use the distortion criterion to measure grossly suboptimum coding methods, the simplified distortion measures can be of dubious value.*

However, as discussed in Section 2.1, an error field generated by an optimum encoder does not isolate errors in frequency or amplitude nor consist of isolated frequency components with crucial relative phasing; thus such error patterns are not subject to these differences in behavior among Eqs. (41)–(43). *Thus if the intent of the distortion measure is to act as a guide in designing quantizers or in judging near-optimum encoding methods, the above criteria are roughly equivalent.* The basis for this statement is that if one asks to maximize the entropy of the distribution of the quantization error subject to a distortion constraint (as in the Shannon lower bound), all of the above criteria produce roughly comparable distributions, and the optimum under one distortion constraint will not be grossly suboptimum under another. All of them produce optimum distributions that contain errors spread throughout the spatial frequency band with a spectrum determined by the contrast sensitivity function. Further, although the distribution of error size depends on p for any $p \geq 2$, the distribution discriminates against large infrequent errors and does not waste space with a large fraction of errors that are well below threshold. To make this quantitative, a Gaussian distribution (which is optimum for $p = 2$) of a given entropy produces root-mean-sixth-moment errors only 12.3% larger than a distribution of the same entropy optimized for $p = 6$.

To conclude the above, all of the above measures incorporate the important fact that the visual system depends on contrast and not absolute luminance and the considerable variation in sensitivity with spatial frequency (all of them however do not incorporate effectively the independence of errors of different frequencies). These facts are important to include not only because they are primary properties of the visual system, *but also because an encoding system can effectively exploit them* by the simple means of companding and prefiltering. The designer should keep in mind that these criteria do not place as stringent a penalty on frequency bunching of errors as does the visual system. The fact that the different measures weight errors of different sizes differently is not too crucial, both in view of the fact that the optimal distribution for one measure is only slightly suboptimal for another, *and,* as seen in Section 2.1, trying to exploit this particular aspect requires multidimensional quantization, which is very difficult to implement. Finally, whether one includes the term $[1 + s(x, y)]$ to include the effects of edges on sensitivity depends both on whether the encoding method can make effective use of this and whether the fraction of raster-containing edges makes this savings significant.

For a color image, a reasonable distortion measure would seem to consist of a sum of three terms, each of the terms being functionally the same as the distortion measures of Eqs. (42) and (43) but operating, respectively, on functions $v(x, y)$, $v_1(x, y)$, and $v_2(x, y)$, which are filtered versions of $z(x, y)$, $c_1(x, y)$, and $c_2(x, y)$. The filters would be the contrast sensitivity functions for the achromatic and two chrominance (R − G and Y − B) channels, respectively. Such a model has been proposed and studied by Frei (1974) and further investigated by Faugeras (1976); it will be discussed in Section 2.4.2.

2.3 SIMULATION OF IMPLEMENTABLE CODING METHODS

This section and Section 2.4 discuss the simulation of several methods of encoding that make use of a measure of distortion: this section discusses encoding methods that are in use or can be reasonably implemented and Section 2.4 discusses simulation of nearly optimum encoding methods. The separation is essentially between those investigations that have attempted to exploit properties of the visual system with the main goal of optimizing a workable encoding method and those that have performed simulation primarily for confirming or obtaining a better model of the visual system directly within the encoding context. In neither section is the selection of work discussed comprehensive, nor is any effort made to attribute proper credit to past work in the field. Only a few methods are discussed. The choice has been of those methods that most directly and effectively use distortion criteria, and the work discussed is that which is most recent and tends to subsume previous work. The work described necessarily builds on the effort of others, and the reader should consult this work and the references cited therein in order to form a more composite picture of the contributions made by various workers in the field.

Section 2.3.1 discusses the methods of subjectively rating picture quality and Section 2.3.2 then discusses the visibility function that has been used to optimize the performance of DPCM and interpolative encoding systems. The work relating to optimizing these two systems is described in Sections 2.3.3 and 2.3.4, respectively.

2.3.1 Rating Methods

This subsection is intended to describe rating methods only to the extent necessary for understanding the experiments described subsequently. For a comprehensive discussion of the use of rating methods and the techniques employed, the reader is referred to Pearson (1972).

In the kind of experiments to be described, some encoding parameter, say β, that directly relates to an assumption concerning the visual system is usually varied. Some other threshold parameter that directly controls the transmission rate R is also varied. A two-dimensional array of images is thus produced for various values of R and β. One might then ask observers to subjectively rate the pictures and assign some measure of quality or, inversely, some measure of impairment or distortion to each picture. One could then select some fixed value of R and ask which value of β yielded the image with least distortion. Hopefully, that value of β will be the same for different values of R. If so, the resulting functional relationship not only specifies the optimum encoder and the encoder's sensitivity to the parameter β, but also helps determine a model that more accurately describes the behavior of the viewer in the coding context. An equally valid approach to looking at different fixed values of R would be to sort through the array and for the different values of β compare the rates of images that have constant impairment ratings. As a practical matter, it might be easier to use the first method of sorting (comparing pictures of constant rate), since it is usually desirable to minimize the number of images that need to be generated and judged. During the process of simulation the rate can be observed and controlled, while the impairment ratings will not be known until the subjects have viewed the images.

One might ask to what extent the above procedure depends on a visual model and how it is different from just random knob twiddling. The answer is that one does not twiddle knobs at random; one uses the distortion criterion to provide guidance as to how to structure parameters of the encoding system to provide some improvement. For example, first-order properties of the visual system dictate that error visibility depends on: (1) luminance of the area surrounding the error, (2) rate of change or masking properties of the image in the immediate area around the error, and (3) frequency content of the error pattern. Thus an effective encoder will provide some form of companding and, if possible, some control of errors dependent on the masking level and some control of the frequency content of the errors. Thus one might profitably study variations in companding characteristic, masking threshold, or preemphasis filtering.

Let us now consider how subjects might rate encoded images. The depth of discussion will be limited to the immediate purposes of the remainder of this chapter.

If the encoded images are generated by simulation on a computer, they are often reproduced photographically. In this case the whole array of images is available to the subject at one time, and they are all available simultaneously for comparison. They might typically be arranged in columns, each column corresponding to a common transmission rate and different values of the parameter β. The subject can then make as many pairwise comparisons as necessary (using a bubble sort or any convenient sequence of pairwise comparisons) to rank the images in one column. The subject can then assign a rating to the different images, comparing them against the original image. A five-scale rating used at Bell Telephone Laboratories is listed below:

(1) Impairment is not noticeable.
(2) Impairment is just noticeable.
(3) Impairment is definitely noticeable, not objectionable.
(4) Impairment is objectionable.
(5) Impairment is extremely objectionable.

In order to stabilize ratings from one session to the next, an "anchor" set of images previously rated by the subject can be available for comparison. However, this may mean trying to equate impairment for different types of errors (edge busyness versus granular noise in flat areas), which is not easy for untrained observers.

The above rating task is the easiest one for a subject to perform because the multitude of pairwise comparisons available allow for consistency checks. However, in many cases the images are generated on a prototype encoder (as a DPCM encoder) and are not stored but are simply available one at a time for comparison against the original image. In this situation good results demand the use of experienced subjects, a long training period to allow the subjects' criteria and judgment to stabilize, and observation of the same image a number of times (but interleaved randomly with other images) to average out observation errors. Further, the ratings are usually correlated with a quantitative measure of distortion as a consistency check.

2.3.2   The Visibility Function

The work described in this section is concerned primarily with exploiting the loss of sensitivity to errors that occurs in regions where the image itself is varying rapidly. To do this, it is necessary to have some quantitative measure of this loss of sensitivity due to the activity of the image. One such measure is the cumulative visibility function originated by Candy and Bosworth (1972). Another measure is the differential visibility function of Netravali (1977a) and Netravali and Prasada (1977). This visibility function $f(T)$ is based on a masking function $m(x, y)$, which depends on the image $i(x, y)$. Let $i_x(x, y)$ and $i_y(x, y)$ denote, respectively, the first x and y differences of successive pixels from the image $i(x, y)$ [or, in the case of a continuous video signal $i_x(x, y) = \partial/\partial x\, i(x, y)$]. The masking function

$$m(x, y) = |i_x(x, y)| \tag{44}$$

is commonly used because it is easily obtained from the video signal. More complicated masking functions might be obtained by taking a weighted spatial average of both $|i_x(x, y)|$ and $|i_y(x, y)|$ in a neighborhood of points about (x, y). The visibility function $f(T)$ expresses the visibility of noise added in an interval of width ΔT about a masking level T, i.e., noise added in those regions of the image in which $|m(x, y) - T| \le \Delta T/2$. Specifically, it is hypothesized that quantization noise of power P_{quant} added to this portion of the image is equivalent to an amount of white noise added to the whole image, where the power of this equivalent white noise is given by

$$P_{\text{equiv}} = P_{\text{quant}}\, f(T)\, \Delta T \tag{45}$$

Thus $f(T)$ expresses the relative strength of noise power added at places where the masking function has value T. One might question whether P_{equiv} and P_{quant} are related linearly for various values of P_{quant}; both Candy and Bosworth (1972) and Netravali (1977a) report measurements for a number of values of P_{quant} and find that the relationship is closely fit by a linear one.

The method of measurement used by these workers is as follows. The image is stored on a drum to provide a video signal with the same frame repeated, yielding a still image on a TV monitor. In the simplest case in which $m(x, y)$ is given by Eq. (44), $m(x, y)$ can be obtained from the video signal by a differentiator. For a more complicated masking function, $m(x, y)$ is generated by a computer linked to the disk. At whatever times the masking signal so generated falls in the interval $|m - T| \le \Delta T/2$, a sample from a noise process of power P_{quant} is added to the video signal by a switch controlled by m. This noise process is to simulate encoding (quantization) error. This is done a number of times in random order for various values of T and P_{quant}. On any such trial, the observer alternately switches back and forth between this image and an image to which white noise is added. The power of the additive white noise P_{equiv} is controlled by an attenuator, and the subject, while switching, adjusts this attenuator until he feels the two images are subjectively equivalent (this procedure is a version of the so-called "method of adjustment"). In this way the function $f(T)$ is determined as the constant of proportionality for various values of T.

The function $f(T)$ has been determined both by Candy and Bosworth (1972) and Netravali (1977a) for several scenes. It decreases steeply with T and is scene dependent, but does not vary drastically for head-and-shoulders scenes. It should be noted that $f(T)$ includes *both* the effect of the probability density of the masking function and the decreased sensitivity of the human observer. The function decreases faster with T than does the density function for the masking function. This combined dependence is directly useful in optimizing encoding systems and hence was the appropriate quantity for the experimenters to measure. However, from the standpoint of developing a model of vision, it would have been desirable to measure *just the change in sensitivity* due to $m(x, y)$. This could have been done by controlling the area into which the white noise was introduced.

The following two subsections describe the use of $f(T)$ in optimizing two different encoding methods.

2.3.3   Use of Masking to Optimize DPCM

Differential pulse-code modulation (DPCM) encodes the video signal generated along a scan line. From this signal, $i_x(x, y)$ is directly available. This method of encoding thus allows direct measurement of masking and direct control over errors. Hence optimizing DPCM by making use of masking is a natural match.

DPCM is a form of predictive encoding, which is covered in full in Chapter 3. The description here is thus intended only to be adequate to allow understanding of the remainder of the section. DPCM takes advantage of the fact that the intensity $i(x, y)$ varies continuously in a rather predictable way as a function of x. This redundancy can be exploited by encoding and transmitting only the information required to correct the prediction. If this correction information or prediction error is quantized, it can be transmitted digitally, i.e., by pulse-code modulation (PCM). However, this means the predictor at the receiver has only the quantized version of the prediction error to work with. Since this predictor is to emulate the predictor used in the encoder, the predictors at both the encoder and decoder must work from this quantized information. Figure 2-8 shows the block diagram of a DPCM system that operates in this fashion. As seen from this block diagram, the error in this transmission system, *assuming no channel errors,* is simply the quantization error $q(t)$. The quantizer characteristic is thus crucial to system performance, and this is the logical place to try to exploit the effect of the masking function on sensitivity.

The visibility function measures the effective noise power of quantization errors located in regions of various masking levels. Suppose the masking function is chosen to be simply $|i_x(x, y)|$ or, in the notation of Fig. 2-8, $s(t) - s(t - 1)$. Suppose further that the predictor is taken to be simply the previous video sample, $\hat{s}(t) = s(t - 1)$. Then the signal being quantized is $e(t) = s(t) - s(t - 1)$, and the masking function is $|e(t)|$. The equivalent visible noise or, as Netravali terms it, the mean-square subjective distortion (MSSD) is thus given by

$$\text{MSSD} = \int q^2(e)f(e) \, de \qquad (46)$$

in which $f(e)$ is the visibility function and $q(e)$ denotes the quantization error in quantizing the error value e. Note that this error criterion incor-

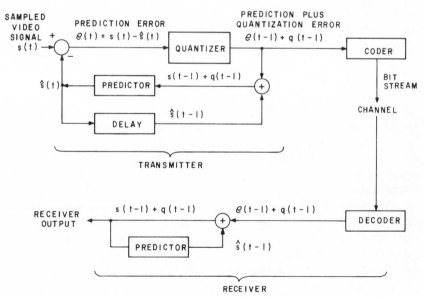

FIG. 2-8. Block diagram of a basic DPCM system.

porates *only* the masking effects and does not take into account the logarithmic compansion or frequency response characteristics of the visual system. Comment on this will be made at the end of this subsection; for the present discussion, let the validity of the MSSD distortion criterion be accepted. Given this measure of distortion based on measurements of the visibility function, the optimum quantizer is the one that minimizes the MSSD, as given by Eq. (46), subject to a constraint on the entropy of the quantizer output (this entropy being equal to the digital transmission rate required by the system).

The visibility function measurements thus determine the optimum quantizer characteristic. To confirm that these measurements do in fact apply directly to the encoding situation, it is useful to compare this quantizer characteristic with a number of others to see if it does in fact optimize the performance. Netravali considers four quantizers chosen as optimum under the following criteria:

(1) minimum-mean-square error (weighted according to frequency of occurrence, not visibility function) with a constraint on the number of quantization levels,

(2) minimum-mean-square error with a constraint on the entropy of the quantizer output,

(3) minimum-mean-square subjective distortion [weighted as in Eq. (46)] with a constraint on the number of quantization levels, and

(4) minimum-mean-square subjective distortion with a constraint on the entropy of the quantizer output.

The behavior of these four quantizers, as judged both by the MSSD of Eq. (46) and the average rating determined by a number of experienced subjects, is shown as a function of quantizer output entropy in Fig. 2-9 (Netravali, 1977a, Fig. 10). The scene used is a head and shoulders of a girl wearing a checkered shirt. Quantizer number (2) is in fact very nearly uniform, particularly for small error, and curve (2) in the figure is actually for a uniform quantizer. The results are consistent with the distortion measure of Eq. (46) being the subjectively appropriate one; at all rates, quantizer 4, which is optimized for this criterion, is noticeably (albeit not dramatically) superior to the other three quantizers.

As a practical matter, the value of this optimization would be lost if the quantizer and visibility functions depended critically on the scene, for although transmitting the quantizer characteristic for each image would entail negligible overhead rate, measuring the visibility function is out of the question. However, Netravali used two quantizers optimized for two different head-and-shoulders scenes on several images. For these images the output entropy of each quantizer varied only -0.3 to $+0.2$ bit/pixel

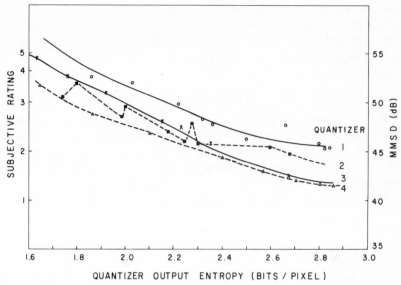

FIG. 2-9.   Mean-square-subjective distortion and average subjective rating shown as functions of quantizer entropy for the four quantizers described in the text.

from the value obtained when it was used on its "own" image (the one for which it was optimized).

Netravali and Prasada (1977) extended the results described above in several ways. First, rather than taking the masking function to be simply the magnitude of the first horizontal intensity difference, they considered a number of masking functions using local spatial averages of both x and y differences. Going to a two-dimensional, single-point masking function yielded an improvement of only 0.15 bit/pixel, and incorporating a locally weighted average of two-dimensional differences yielded negligible further improvement. This indicates that the exact modeling of the masking phenomenon is not crucial.

The final comment to be made regarding this work is the fact that it studied only the effect of the masking function and ignored the other two major properties of the visual system: the near-logarithmic effect of luminance on sensitivity and the variation in sensitivity with spatial frequency. The first property is easily incorporated into an encoding system by preceding the encoding with a compander. To a certain extent this compansion may be achieved by the γ characteristic of the TV camera. However, it is unfortunate that this characteristic was not controlled and studied because it might have a nonnegligible interaction with the masking phenomenon. The spatial frequency variation in sensitivity could be included by using a preemphasis filter. However, for a DPCM system only one-dimensional filtering is practical. It is not clear whether this would have a substantial effect on system optimality or any strong coupling with the investigation of the masking effect.

2.3.4   Optimization of Interpolative Encoding Methods

The incorporation of both masking effects and spatial frequency dependence was used by Limb (1973) in a visual model for optimizing interpolative encoding. A recent paper by Netravali (1977b) builds on this general approach but considers more effective interpolation methods; hence it is this later work that is described in detail here.

The encoding scheme considered by Netravali is described first. In order to avoid double subscripts, let z_i, $i = 1, 2, \ldots$, denote the pixel intensity values on the last line to have been encoded and let x_i denote the pixel intensity values on the line currently being encoded. In a single-field raster the line x_i would be immediately below the line z_i; in a TV raster with two fields, there would be an interlaced line between z_i and x_i. Suppose that the x line has been encoded up to the ith element. A number of elements from x_i on are then encoded using the following algorithm:

(1) Start with $N = 2$.

(2) Extrapolate the values x_i and x_{i+N} by DPCM (operating *vertically*) from z_i and z_{i+N}, respectively.

(3) Interpolate the values of $x_{i+1}, \ldots, x_{i+N-1}$ using x_i, x_{i+N}, z_i, z_{i+1}, $\ldots$, z_{i+N}.

(4) Calculate the interpolation distortion d, using a visual model.

(5) If d is less than a threshold (determining the image quality and rate), increase N by one and return to (2); otherwise exit and use the interpolation found for the preceding value of N.

This approach provides the opportunity to study different possibilities for both the interpolation algorithm and the visual distortion criterion. Although Netravali considered four interpolation methods, only the most effective is described here. Starting at x_i, the value of x_{i+1} is taken to be x_i if $|x_i - z_i| \geq |z_{i+1} - z_i|$ or z_{i+1} otherwise (i.e., the adjacent horizontal or vertical pixel is taken, whichever is in the direction of lesser change). This process is continued until $x_{i+N/2}$ is reached, and a similar process is then started at x_{i+N} and used to work back to $x_{i+1+N/2}$.

Since the interpolation algorithm must be carried out by computer, it is possible to have the measure of distortion incorporate visual properties in a more involved way than is possible in a real-time DPCM system. Netravali incorporates several properties of the visual system as follows.

First, the spatial frequency sensitivity dependence is used by filtering the values of the error between the actual and interpolated values. The filtering is one dimensional along the span of the interpolation interval i to $i + N$, and the filtered error sequence is denoted by $\bar{\epsilon}_k$, $k = i, \ldots ,$ $i + N$. Second, the weighting of filtered errors is considered by taking

$$d_1 = 1/(N + 1) \sum_{k=1}^{i+N} |\bar{\epsilon}_k|^\gamma \qquad (47)$$

and using the exponent γ to determine the relative importance of errors of various sizes, or by using

$$d_2 = \text{number of values of } k: |\bar{\epsilon}_k| > T, \qquad k = i, \ldots , i + N \quad (48)$$

Finally the masking effect is incorporated. A two-dimensional masking function averaging both x and y first differences on a 3×3 set of pixels is used, and the visibility function defined previously is used to incorporate the masking sensitivity into the above distortion measures:

$$d_1' = 1/(N + 1) \sum_{k=i}^{i+N} |\bar{\epsilon}_k|^\gamma f(M_k) \qquad (49)$$

$$d_2' = \text{number of values of k: } |\epsilon_k| f(M_k) > T, \qquad k = i, \ldots , i + N$$
$$(50)$$

The interpolative encoding method thus gives a richer study of the effect of the distortion measure than is the case with DPCM.

In evaluating the simulation, a DPCM system using previous element prediction and a 13-level quantizer with an entropy (bit rate) of 2.60 bits/pixel was used as a reference standard. Experienced observers were used as subjects, and their task was to set the threshold level for the interpolation method to a level that gave the same image quality as this 2.60-bit/pixel DPCM image.

The results of Netravali's experiments are summarized as follows. The first variable studied was the choice of distortion criterion from among those given by Eqs. (47)–(50). For all these distortion criteria, the filter used was five equal weights, averaging the errors at k, $k \pm 1$, and $k \pm 2$ equally. For the distortion criterion, d_1 different values of γ were tried from 1.0 to 4.0 in increments of 0.5. Netravali reports that at reference-level quality (equal to that of the DPCM system), the lowest transmission rate was obtained for $\gamma = 2.0$ on one head-and-shoulders image and for $\gamma = 2.5$ on a second such image; he unfortunately does not state how sensitive the rate at reference quality is to changes in γ. The rate at reference quality was also measured for distortion measure d_2; since this rate was lower than that for d_1, only the rate for d_2' was measured among the distortion measures employing the visibility function. The rates for these three distortion measures are shown in Table 2-1 for two head-and-shoulders images. The visibility function $f(m)$ was approximated by a stepwise function of m on four segments of the range of m. As can be seen from the table, use of d_2 yields a noticeable but rather small decrease in rate over the use of d_1. This is of interest on two counts. Netravali terminated the interpolation for d_2 whenever the number of points with $|\bar{\epsilon}_k| > T$ was greater than 1. This corresponds to a distortion measure of

$$d(\epsilon) = \begin{cases} 0, & \sum_{k=1}^{i+N} g(\bar{\epsilon}_k) \le 1 \\ 1, & \text{otherwise} \end{cases} \tag{51}$$

with

$$g(\epsilon) = \begin{cases} 1, & |\epsilon| > T \\ 0, & |\epsilon| \le T \end{cases} \tag{52}$$

Recall from Section 2.2.1 that an error-weighting function

$$g(\bar{\epsilon}) = \begin{cases} |\bar{\epsilon}|^6 & |\bar{\epsilon}| \le T \\ T^5[6]|\bar{\epsilon}| - 5T], & |\bar{\epsilon}| > T \end{cases} \tag{53}$$

was considered to give the best match to a number of psychophysical experiments. This function behaves more nearly like $g(\bar{\epsilon})$ of Eq. (52) than does $|\bar{\epsilon}|^\gamma$ for any γ, and for values of $|\bar{\epsilon}|$ close to T it is a good match to this function. The second point to note is that the savings in rate that accrues from fine tuning this choice of error-weighting function is just barely noticeable. This corroborates the remarks made in Section 2.2.3 and further

TABLE 2-1

DEPENDENCE OF INTERPOLATIVE CODING ON DISTORTION MEASURE

Distortion measure	Rate at reference quality (bits/pixel)	
	Girl with checkered shirt	Teri
d_1	$(\gamma = 2.5)$	$(\gamma = 2.0)$
	2.17	2.03
d_2	2.11	1.98
d_2'	1.85	1.81
d_2' With adaptive error filtering	1.57	1.64

justifies the use of the analytically attractive square-error criterion. However, the caveat must again be raised that this indifference to the choice of error-weighting function only applies in a situation in which the error distribution is near optimum for either criterion.

It should also be noted from Table 2-1 that use of the masking function to set the error threshold decreased the rate at reference quality by several times the decrease that resulted from tuning the error-weighting function. Not only does the error level that can be tolerated depend on the masking value, but the resolution required does as well. Netravali incorporated this into his encoding method by making the support of the filter averaging the errors depend on the value of m. Rather than taking $\bar{\epsilon}_k$ as the average of 5 spatial adjacent error samples, the average of 3, 5, 7, or 11 samples was used, increasing as the value of the masking function increased. The results are shown as the last row in Table 2-1. Incorporation of this aspect of masking results in another moderate but substantive decrease in rate. Incorporation of both these aspects of the masking yields a 20–25% decrease in rate.

Netravali did not investigate the shape of the spatial averaging of the errors, using always a uniform weighting. The rationale for this was the earlier work of Limb (1973), who also found a nonnegligible dependence on the spread of the error averaging but no noticeable dependence on the shape of the averaging.

The work described in this section does much to round out our knowledge of the effects of the visual system on the efficiency of encoding, particularly in regard to the effects of masking. It makes a valuable contribution in this respect. It would be even more useful if the effects of the visual system and distribution of different masking levels were separated out, so that other workers could incorporate the use of a masking function to images of different content without having to measure a visibility function for that class of images.

2.4   Simulation of Optimum
Encoding Methods

The real distinctions between the simulations described in the preceding section and this one are the motivation and objectives of the experiment. The work described in the preceding section was carried out with the primary goal of using knowledge of the visual system and the results of the experiment to determine how much a given coding system could be improved. The encoding methods were either of real practical interest because of their ease of implementation (DPCM) or gave considerable opportunity to manipulate the error distribution while still being realizable by a feasible implementation (interpolative encoding). The objective of justifying a model or, more accurately, of determining a model of the visual system was only a secondary one. This section describes simulations that were carried out solely for more accurately determining a visual model for use in the encoding context. No consideration was given to problems of implementation; in fact, the simulation did not actually perform encoding but introduced errors with the same distribution as that of an optimum encoder.

One of the earlier simulations performed with the goal of verifying a visual model was that of Stockham (1972). Stockham used the distortion measure of Eq. (43) with $p = 2$. He was led to this choice primarily because the homomorphic filtering used in obtaining $v(x, y)$ corresponded to separating out a high-frequency reflectance pattern from a slowly varying luminance pattern while greatly reducing the dynamic range of the reflectance component (Oppenheim et al., 1968). However, Stockham also noted the correspondence of the logarithmic operation to the relation between excitation and response in photoreceptors (Weber's law) and the possible connection between the bandpass filtering operation and neural inhibition. He thus did some experiments to see if this model could explain certain contrast illusions known as Mach bands (Ratliff, 1965) and used this method to obtain estimates of the shape of the contrast sensitivity function. Stockham reported that shaping the stimulus so that the pattern $v(x, y)$ corresponded to the perceived pattern was successful in eliminating the illusion.

This led him to consider using the model in the coding context. The approach was direct and used a simple coding scheme due to Roberts (1962) that adds a known pseudorandom dither pattern at the transmitter, quantizes each pixel of the image for transmission, and subtracts the dither pattern at the receiver. Stockham (1972) used only 1-bit quantization and tried encoding the intensity image $i(x, y)$, the log-intensity $u(x, y)$, and the filtered image $v(x, y)$. He found that encoding $u(x, y)$ (and then regenerating $i(x, y)$ at the receiver) produced subjectively less distortion than encoding $i(x, y)$, and that encoding $v(x, y)$ produced distortion that was subjectively still less objectionable.

This provided some verification for the model in the encoding context, but it remained to do a thorough study to accurately determine the characteristics of the model. Such a study was done by Mannos and Sakrison (1974) for achromatic still images; the results are described in Section 2.4.1. The following and final Section, 2.4.2, describes work that extends this approach to color images.

2.4.1 Simulation of Optimum Encoding
of Achromatic Images

The first problem to face in such a simulation study is what sort of encoding should be used in the simulation. As pointed out in Section 2.2.3, this is a real concern: An analytical distortion criterion that accurately models the visual system would be too complex to be of analytical use. One must therefore settle for a model that sacrifices accuracy for tractability; such a model will typically be reasonably accurate for some error distributions and less accurate for others. Thus one must consider for which error distributions the model should most accurately portray a viewer's evaluation: A worker who was interested in some particular encoding method would carry out a simulation that generated error distributions of the sort generated by different variations of that encoding method. However, someone interested in the long-range problem of designing the best possible encoders would want to find a model that accurately represented the viewer for error distributions that would be generated by the optimum encoder.

This was the approach followed by Mannos and Sakrison (1974). They considered distortion criteria of the form of Eq. (43) with $p = 2$. This class was considered because it is the only class for which it is possible to explicitly determine the rate distortion function and the attendant optimum distribution of errors. The choice of $p = 2$, although accepted solely for analytical tractability, was not a serious compromise to reality for the reason pointed out in Sections 2.2.3 and 2.3.4, namely, the relative insensitivity to p for near-optimal distributions. The omission of the masking effect is more serious, for as was seen in the preceding section, it can be used to achieve a modest but nonnegligible reduction in rate. The significance of the masking effect was not appreciated by Mannos and Sakrison; however, there is no obvious tractable way to incorporate it into their type of simulation of optimum errors. Within the class of distortion criteria defined by Eq. (43) ($p = 2$) they explored the best choice for the nonlinearity relating the intensity $i(x, y)$ and $u(x, y)$ and the best choice of the linear filter relating $u(x, y)$ and $v(x, y)$. This was accomplished by considering some family of transformations, for example, a family of functions f_j, $j = 1, \ldots, N$ relating u and i, $u(x, y) = f_j[i(x, y)]$. For each member of a family, an image was generated by simulating the effect of optimum [under that choice of $f_j(\cdot)$] encoding at several different fixed rates, $R = 0.5$, 1.0, and 2.0 bits/pixel. The resulting images were than evaluated by a rating experiment; in almost all cases the parameter value or choice of function that yielded the image with the best subjective rating at one rate did so at all rates. The choice was also consistent from subject to subject. Three subjects were used: a lay person, a student interested in image processing but unfamiliar with the simulation procedures, and the student doing the research. The parameter or function chosen as yielding the best subjective rating was determined to be the model characteristic most accurately modeling the subject's criterion.

In carrying out the procedure described above, it is necessary to make some assumptions concerning the source in order to calculate the transmission rate R. Mannos and Sakrison calculated the rate given by the rate distortion function of a Gaussian source with the power spectral density estimated for the image $U(x, y) = f[I(x, y)]$ [this depends on $f(\cdot)$; the dependency was taken into account]. This calculation was not made under the presumption that the source was Gaussian, for it obviously is not, but rather because the Gaussian source was the only one for which the rate could be calculated *and* because a code for a Gaussian source is robust, i.e., it will yield the same rate distortion performance when used with any other source with the same power spectrum (Sakrison, 1975). However, the Shannon lower bound will apply for sufficiently small d^*, and when it does

$$R(d^*) = H(\mathbf{U}) - \max_{E\{d(\mathbf{U}-\tilde{\mathbf{U}})\} \leq d^*} [H(\mathbf{U} - \tilde{\mathbf{U}})] \qquad (54)$$

Thus if $H(\mathbf{U})$ were fixed [did not depend on $d(\cdot)$], the effect of various choices of $d(\cdot)$ affects only the second term. Knowledge of the source distribution affects $R(d^*)$ only through the *additive* term $H(\mathbf{U})$; studying the effect of $d(\cdot)$ by subjective comparison of image quality at a fixed transmission rate thus does not depend on what the value of that fixed rate is. Unfortunately

$$H(\mathbf{U}) = H[f(\mathbf{I})] \qquad (55)$$

depends on $f(\cdot)$, and this dependency could be exploited by a digital encoder following the quantizer. Those experiments of Mannos and Sakrison that consider changes in $f(\cdot)$ and compare images based on a constant rate are thus making a comparison on a less than optimum encoding strategy, for they fail to take advantage of this change in $H(\mathbf{U})$. This is somewhat unfortunate, but would have greatly increased the complexity of their rate calculations and probably would have had only a second-order effect.

Let us now consider the rate distortion calculations and the error distributions that were used under the Gaussian source assumption. These are well known (Berger, 1971, Section 4.5; Gallager, 1968, Section 9.7; Sakrison, 1970, Section 6.4).[1] Let $U(x, y)$ be a homogeneous (stationary or translation invariant) random field with power spectral density $S_u(f_x, f_y)$. Let $A(f_x, f_y)$ denote a frequency-error-weighting function and $S_v(f_x, f_y) = S_u(f_x, f_y) |A(f_x, f_y)|^2$. Then the rate distortion function under a weighted-square-error criterion [Eq. (43) with $p = 2$] is given parametrically in terms of a parameter μ by

$$R(\mu) = \frac{1}{2} \int\!\!\int_{\overline{f_x, f_y: \; S_v(f_x, f_y) > \mu}} df_x df_y \log_2[S_v(f_x, f_y)/\mu] \tag{56}$$

$$d^*(\mu) = \int_{-\infty}^{\infty} \int_{-\infty}^{\infty} df_x df_y \min[\mu, \; S_v(f_x, f_y)] \tag{57}$$

This function is obtained with an error distribution that deletes all frequency components from $V(x, y)$ for those frequencies for which $S_v(f_x, f_y) \leq \mu$, scales the remaining components by a factor of $1 - [\mu/S_v(f_x, f_y)]$, and adds Gaussian noise of spectral density $\mu[S_v(f_x, f_y) - \mu]/S_v(f_x, f_y)$.[2]

The statements above are strictly true only in the limit as the raster becomes infinitely large in both the x and y directions; however they are approximately true if the raster size is large compared to the correlation distance of $V(x, y)$. Although considerable computation is involved, simulation of optimal transmission at a given rate [with R and d^* related by Eqs. (56) and (57)] is conceptually straightforward and is not described here; the reader is referred to Mannos and Sakrison (1974) for further details.

The results of their simulation are now summarized. In order to minimize the number of images that needed to be made, only one parameter of the distortion criterion was varied at a time, using what was felt to be the optimum values for the other parameters. After all the parameters had been investigated, some minor investigations were made to see if the optimum choices were stable, i.e., uninfluenced by the choices of other parameters. The contrast sensitivity or frequency-weighting characteristic was first studied with the nonlinearity fixed at $u = f(i) = \log(1 + i)$ (i

---

[1] Although these references are for the case of a random process $U(t)$, the results for the random process extend directly to random fields using an extension of a theorem of Kač, Murdock, and Szegö (Sakrison, 1969).

[2] Note that this distribution is the one generated by an optimum quantizer *whenever* the Shannon lower bound holds; it is not then dependent on the source distribution. The only error is that the rate given by Eq. (56) is true only for a Gaussian source and does not reflect the dependency of the source distribution on $f(\cdot)$.

taking on integer values, 0 to 255). The contrast sensitivity or error-frequency-weighting function was taken to be of the form

$$A(f_r) = [c + (f_r/f_0)] \exp[-(f_r/f_0)^k] \qquad (58)$$

in which $f_r = (f_x^2 + f_y^2)^{1/2}$; this function is thus isotropic or circularly symmetric. This function gives a good fit to the contrast sensitivity function of Fig. 2-4 for $c = 0$, $f_0 = 4$ cycles/degree, and k between 1 and 2.

The peak frequency f_0 was varied first. The value that gave the best subjective ratings depended to a limited extent on the image and the rate R. It was always between 6 and 12 cycles/degree with 8 cycles/degree being the value having the highest rating for most rates and images. Further the rating for $f_0 = 8$ was only slightly below the best rating in those cases for which it was not the best rating. Varying the parameter f_0 makes quite noticeable changes in image appearance; low values of f_0 lead to a blurred appearance, while a high value of f_0 leads to a "blotchy" appearance because of the presence of excessive low-frequency noise components.

Variation in the parameters c and k were less important and produced noticeably degraded results only when adjusted well away from their optimum values. The resulting best choice for the frequency weighting was[3]

$$A(f_r) = 2.6[0.192 + f_r/8] \exp[-f_r/8] \qquad (59)$$

Finally for the above choice of $A(f_r)$, four different nonlinearities were investigated:

$$f_1(i) = i, \qquad f_2(i) = i^{0.7}, \qquad f_3(i) = i^{0.33}, \qquad f_4(i) = \log(1 + i) \quad (60)$$

These functions are all monotone increasing convex ∩ and are listed in order of increasing convexity. The function f_3 consistently gave the best subjective appearance with f_4 a close second. The other two functions produced notably poorer images with washed-out appearance and noise very visible in the dark areas.

For numerical values of the ratings and other details, the reader is referred to Mannos and Sakrison (1974). The degree to which the model influences the appearance is illustrated in Fig. 2-10, which shows simulated encoding of an image of a moon rock at rate 0.5 bit/pixel. Figure 2-10a is the original (512 × 512 pixels at 6 bits/pixel), while Fig. 2-10b is the encoded image which is optimum under a standard mean-square-error criterion, $f(i) = i$, $A(f_r) \equiv 1$. Figure 2-10c is the encoded image which is optimum under the best choice determined by the experiments: $u = f(i) = i^{0.33}$ and $A(f_r)$ as given by Eq. (59). The difference is muted by

---

[3] In fact $k = 1.1$ was the optimum determined by the rating, but the improvement over $k = 1.0$ is too insignificant to warrant the added analytic complexity.

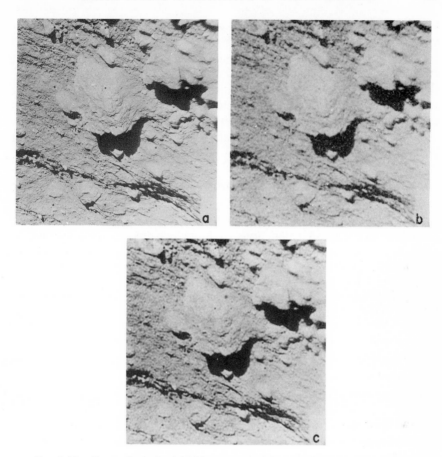

FIG. 2-10.   Comparison of original image (6 bits/pixel) and images optimally encoded at 0.5 bit/pixel under two different distortion criteria. (a) Original; (b) encoded under minimum-mean-square error; (c) encoded under minimum-mean-square frequency-weighted error of cube-root intensity.

the lithographic reproduction process, but there is a clear difference between the two: Figure 2-10c has notably more contrast and resolution than Fig. 2-10b (note some of the holes quite visible in Fig. 2-10c that are indistinct in Fig. 2-10b) and less granular noise than Fig. 2-10b. Figure 2-10b also has very objectionable noise in the dark regions.

2.4.2   Extension to Encoding of Color Images

Frei (1974) had studied color vision and as a consequence proposed a generalization of the log-intensity, frequency-weighted square-error criterion used by Stockham and Mannos and Sakrison. This generalization is based on the Wh − B, R − G, and Y − B three-component system. Let $z(x, y)$, $c_1(x, y)$, and $c_2(x, y)$ represent the responses of these three systems as in Eq. (40); i.e., they are combinations of the log responses of the L, M, and S spectral characteristics. Let $t_i(x, y)$, $i = 1, 2, 3$, denote, respectively, the responses z, c_1, and c_2 after linear filtering with their appropriate spatial frequency contrast sensitivity function (e.g., the function relating t_1 and z is the one discussed for achromatic images). Then the distortion measure considered is

$$d(u - u) = \sum_{i=1}^{3} \int\int dxdy[t_i(x, y) - t_i(x, y)]^2 \qquad (61)$$

To corroborate this model, Faugeras did some experimental work analogous to the experiments done by Stockham for achromatic images. He added white uniform noise of a fixed spectral density to five points in the model:

(1) to the R, G, B components used in scanning and generating the original image;

(2) to the Y, I, Q NTSC television transmission primary components;

(3) to the L^*, M^*, S^* log Wh − B, R − G, and Y − B components

(4) to the z, c_1, c_2 components; and

(5) to the t_1, t_2, t_3 components.

For all five sets of images, the distortion measure $d(\cdot)$ of Eq. (6) was calculated, and subjects were asked to rate the quality of the resulting images. The results are shown in Table 2-2 for one image "Becky." A second image "carport" had similar ratings and distortion levels, and observers gave consistent and nearly unanimous ratings. Note that the dis-

TABLE 2-2

DISTORTION AND RATINGS OF IMAGES WITH
NOISE ADDED TO DIFFERENT
MODEL LOCATIONS[a]

Location	$d(\mathbf{u} - \tilde{\mathbf{u}})$	Rating
1	19.61	4
2	23.04	5
3	16.18	3
4	13.21	2
5	12.59	1

[a] Faugeras (1976).

tortion levels and ratings are montonically related. This work contributes to establishing the validity of the distortion measure of Eq. (61); however results are limited by the number of types of errors (5) used in the study.

Frei and Baxter (1977) have simulated optimal encoding under the distortion criterion of Eq. (61) to further corroborate this choice of distortion measure. As did Mannos and Sakrison, they added noise to the image with the same distribution that would be added by the optimum quantizer or encoder and calculated the encoding rate assuming a Gaussian source. They assumed independence of the Z_1, C_1, C_2 components. Their published work contains only the original and one encoded image, encoded at a bit rate of 1.0 bit/pixel. Encoding according to only a single criterion unfortunately does not allow cross comparison to provide corroboration of a model or determination of its parameters. Their encoded image does, however, provide a very striking example of the good quality that can be obtained at a low bit rate by making use of the model.

2.5 CONCLUSIONS

This chapter has considered why a distortion measure is useful in designing an "optimum" image-encoding system and the primary properties that determine when an error pattern is detectable in an image.

The state of knowledge concerning the detectability of patterns on a uniform (gray) image is quite advanced and seems more than adequate for the objective of encoding. However, the state of knowledge concerning masking effects is rather rudimentary. The masking functions used to date have been chosen on a rather ad hoc basis, and the work done involving masking has consisted of finding the best fit of a small number of parameters of such ad hoc functions. More basic work is needed here. The primary justification for such work should be a healthy curiosity about the functioning of the visual system per se; the author is skeptical that such additional knowledge would lead to a nonnegligible improvement in encoder performance.

It is worth evaluating in some detail the extent to which this knowledge of the visual system can lead to tractable distortion measures that improve encoder design. To clarify just how far such a point of view can go before the complexity is overwhelming, it will be useful initially to ignore the masking effects. Further, rather than consider arbitrary distortion levels and have to try to resolve the viewers' relative displeasure with different distortion levels, consider just the performance at the threshold level of distortion. In this restricted situation, the distortion constraint is expressed quite accurately by the set of inequalities

$$r_k \leq d^*, \qquad k = 1, 2, \ldots \text{ (all channels)} \qquad (62)$$

in which the r_k are the response variables defined by Eq. (38). Equations (41)–(43) consider various scalar-valued distortion measures of differing complexity. The simplest of these is Eq. (43) with $p = 2$

$$d(u - \tilde{u}) = \int\int dxdy \, v^2(x, y) \qquad (63)$$

To simplify the mathematics, assume a raster of samples (say 512×512), denoted by the vector $\mathbf{u}$. Looking back to the discussion on the Shannon lower bound, recall that one wishes to maximize $H(\mathbf{U} - \tilde{\mathbf{U}})$ subject to the fidelity constraint. The constraint of Eq. (63), $E\{d(\mathbf{U} - \tilde{\mathbf{U}})\} \leq d^*$, leads to a distribution on $\mathbf{U} - \tilde{\mathbf{U}}$ that

(a) is Gaussian,
(b) is stationary, and
(c) possesses a spectrum dictated by the contrast sensitivity function. (The spectrum of $V(x, y)$, the error filtered by the contrast sensitivity function, would be constant within the band where the filtered source signal had more power than this constant.)

It has not been possible to determine the distribution that maximizes $H(\mathbf{U} - \tilde{\mathbf{U}})$ subject to the constraint of Eq. (62): all $r_k \leq d^*$ with probability 1. It would not be Gaussian; indeed its density would be zero in any region violating the constraints of Eq. (62). However it would be stationary and its frequency distribution would not differ greatly from (c) above. The author asserts, but cannot prove, that the two distributions [maximizing H under the constraints of Eqs. (63) and (62), respectively] are nearly similar in the following sense. For a raster sufficiently large to contain a representative sample of the source (sample averages approximate ensemble averages), the typical regions in which the densities of $\mathbf{u} - \tilde{\mathbf{u}}$ are nearly constant and have total probability near 1 are of rather similar shape, and the log of their volumes (and hence their entropies) are very nearly the same. If one accepts this statement as true, then the analytically simple distortion constraint of Eq. (63) leads to the design of an encoder with nearly the same error distribution (and hence the same performance) as the visual criterion expressed by the formidable set of Eq. (62). These two distortion criteria would also rank error distributions *similar to this optimal error distribution* nearly equally. But error distributions considerably dissimilar from this optimum distribution might be such that the distribution would give only a very small distortion level according to Eq. (63) but just barely satisfy Eq. (62).

There is another limitation in employing Eq. (63) as a distortion criterion that is worth stating explicitly. If one assumes a stationary Gaussian random field as an image source, then the distortion measure of Eq. (63) dictates that a block transform code with block size equal to the raster is very nearly optimum. But this in fact leads to a quite nonoptimum solution on actual images for the following reason. Any realistic source model will not be a Gaussian random field, and any realistic sample image will have regions of varying "activity." Suppose a sample image possesses a region A with a number of sharp changes in contrast and/or active texture and a region B with no edges and flat texture. (Note that such an image is quite compatible with a *stationary* source model as long as A and B do not have preferred locations in the raster.) A raster-block transform code yields an error distribution with an rms level much greater in region A than in B. It thus will not be stationary *and* Gaussian (it might well be stationary if A and B have no preferred locations). It differs considerably from the error distribution of (a)–(c) above, will have considerably less entropy, and hence will be quite suboptimum. One way of correcting this is to divide the image into subblocks of size comparable to the size of such regions. The number of coefficients used in each subblock is then chosen to yield a (nearly) constant error level in each subblock (Algazi and Sakrison, 1969). Adaptive subblock transform codes, which estimate the source activity (Chen and Smith, 1977) in each subblock, approximate such behavior. If the size of regions of nearly homogeneous activity is such that such regions contain representative sample characteristics, this spatial control of errors on subblocks is not incompatible with frequency control of the errors. If these regions are too small, simultaneous spatial and frequency control is not possible, and a near-optimum error distribution is not easily determined.

Thus the correct use of the distortion constraint of Eq. (63) is as a guide to the distribution of optimum encoding errors; in other situations one should look to see if this distortion constraint is leading to the same conclusions as might be obtained from Eq. (62).

While the above remarks are more qualitative than one would like, they still contribute quantitatively to near-optimum encoder design. *However*, they ignore the masking effect. When one considers the complexity of the situation and that the above discussion was forced to depend on certain judgments rather than on tight analysis, then one appreciates the considerably greater difficulty of incorporating masking effects into encoder design. What is required is to examine existing (albeit imperfect) knowledge concerning the masking effect and try to arrive at some description concerning the optimum distribution of encoding errors. While this is a difficult problem, it is the next large step forward in attempting to make use of the viewer's distortion criteria in a rational approach to encoder optimization. While this remains an interesting, challenging, and profitable research task, the author personally feels that greater gains in performance can be made by exploiting better models of image sources.

ACKNOWLEDGMENT

The amount of effort contributed by the editor of a collection of contributions such as this varies drastically and is somewhat transparent to the reader. I wish to thank Bill Pratt first for inviting me to do this, for I had considerable initial misgivings about the use of time. However, I learned a great deal from this enterprise. Second, I wish to acknowledge his thorough reading of both the original and corrected versions. His care and thoughtful comments greatly improved the quality (such as it is) of the chapter.

REFERENCES

Algazi, V. R., and Sakrison, D. J. (1969). *In* "Computer Processing in Communications," pp. 85–100. Polytechnic Institute of Brooklyn, New York.
Berger, T. (1971). "Rate Distortion Theory, A Mathematical Basis for Data Compression." Prentice-Hall, Englewood Cliffs, New Jersey.
Brown, W. R. J., and MacAdam, D. L. (1959). *J. Opt. Soc. Am.* **39**, 808–834.
Campbell, F. W., and Green, D. G. (1965). *J. Physiol. (London)* **181**, 576–593.
Campbell, F. W., and Robson, J. G. (1968). *J. Physiol. (London)* **197**, 551–566.
Candy, J. C., and Bosworth, R. H. (1972). *Bell Syst. Tech. J.* **51**, 1495–1516.
Chen, W.-H., and Smith, C. H. (1977). *IEEE Trans. Commun.* **com-25**, 1285–1291.
DeValois, R. L. (1971). *Vision Res.* **11**, 383–396.
DeValois, R. L., and DeValois, K. K. (1975). *In* "Handbook of Perception" E. C. Carterette and M. P. Friedman, eds.), Vol. 5, pp. 117–166. Academic Press, New York.
Faugeras, O. D. (1976). "Digital Color Image Processing and Psychophysics within the Framework of a Human Visual Model," Rep. UTEC-CSc-77-029. Computer Science Dept., University of Utah, Salt Lake City.
Frei, W. (1974). "A Quantitative Model of Color Vision," Rep. 540, pp. 69–83. University of Southern California, Image Processing Institute, Los Angeles.
Frei, W., and Baxter, B. (1977). *IEEE Trans. Commun.* **com-25**, 1385–1392.
Gallager, R. G. (1968). "Information Theory and Reliable Communication." Wiley, New York.
Goblick, T. J., Jr., and Holzinger, J. L. (1967). *IEEE Trans. Inf. Theory* **it-13**, 323–326.
Hammerly, J. R., Quick, R. F., Jr., and Reichart, T. A. (1977). *Vision Res.* **17**, 201–208.
Limb, J. O. (1973). *Bell Syst. Tech. J.* **52**, 1271–1302.
Mannos, J. L., and Sakrison, D. J. (1974). *IEEE Trans. Inf. Theory* **it-20**, 525–536.
Mostafavi, H., and Sakrison, D. J. (1976). *Vision Res.* **16**, 957–968.
Netravali, A. N. (1977a). *IEEE Trans. Inf. Theory* **it-23**, 360–370.
Netravali, A. N. (1977b). *IEEE Trans. Commun.* **com-25**, 503–507.
Netravali, A. N., and Prasada, B. (1977). *Proc. IEEE* **65**, 536–548.
Openheim, A. V., Shafer, R. W., and Stockham, T. G., Jr. (1968). *Proc. IEEE* **56**, 1264–1291.

Pearson, D. E. (1972). *In* "Picture Bandwidth Compression" (T. Huang and O. Tretiak, eds.), pp. 47–95. Gordon & Breach, New York.

Ratliff, F. (1965). "Mach Bands: Quantitative Studies on Neural Networks in the Retina." Holden-Day, San Francisco, California.

Roberts, L. G. (1962). *IRE Trans. Inf. Theory* **it-8**, 145–154.

Sakrison, D. J. (1969). *IEEE Trans. Inf. Theory* **it-15**, 608–610.

Sakrison, D. J. (1970). "Notes on Analog Communication." Van Nostrand-Reinhold, New York.

Sakrison, D. J. (1975). *IEEE Trans. Inf. Theory* **it-21**, 301–309.

Sakrison, D. J. (1977). *IEEE Trans. Commun.* **com-25**, 1251–1266.

Shannon, C. E. (1948). "The Mathematical Theory of Communication," originally appeared in *Bell Syst. Tech. J.,* but also available as a book, Illini Books, Urbana, 1964, and *in* "Key Papers in the Development of Information Theory" (D. Slepian, ed.). IEEE Press, New York, 1973.

Stockham, T. G., Jr., (1972). *In* "Picture Bandwidth Compression" (T. Huang and O. Tretiak, eds.), pp. 417–442. Gordon & Breach, New York.

Weale, R. A. (1968). "From Sight to Light." Oliver & Boyd, Edinburgh and London.

Predictive Image Coding

HANS GEORG MUSMANN

*Lehrstuhl für Theoretische Nachrichtentechnik
und Informationsverarbeitung
Technische Universität
Hannover, Germany*

Among those image-coding techniques that reduce the date rate of picture or video signals, predictive coding techniques have the special advantage of a relatively simple implementation. Furthermore, predictive coding techniques, such as differential pulse-code modulation, can generate a uniform or nonuniform output bit rate and achieve a bit-rate reduction comparable to that of competing transform coding techniques when high picture quality is required. These essential features substantiate the important role of predictive coding for image coding.

In this chapter, the fundamentals of predictive coding are presented along with the significant advances in the field during the last five years. Section 3.1 introduces the basic principles of predictive image coding, and a historical summary of work in the field of predictive image coding is presented in Section 3.2. One of the most attractive predictive coding systems is differential pulse-code modulation. The basic structure of such a system is described in the first part of Section 3.3. Two subsections deal with predictor and quantizer optimization based on mean-square error and subjectively weighted error criteria. Extended differential pulse-code-modulation systems with adaptive predictors and adaptive quantizers utilizing spatial masking are discussed in detail in Section 3.4. Section 3.5 is devoted to the principles of information-preserving predictive coding and Section 3.6 explores the concepts of predictive color coding, including separate and composite coding of the color signal components. Transmission error effects are considered in Section 3.7. The summary in Section 3.8 provides a survey of the main results achieved with predictive coding.

3.1 BASIC PRINCIPLES

If no perceptible degradation of picture quality is allowed, pulse-code-modulation (PCM) coding of high-quality gray-tone pictures requires uniform quantization with at least 256 quantizing levels corresponding to $\log_2(256) = 8$ bits per picture element (pel). One of the most practical encoding schemes for reducing the number of bits per transmitted picture element is predictive coding. Rather than the value of a sample representing the luminance level of a picture element being transmitted, in predictive coding the difference between a prediction for that sample value and the actual sample value is coded and transmitted. If this difference or prediction error is quantized and coded, the predictive coding scheme is called differential pulse-code modulation (DPCM). Delta modulation (DM) is a particular form of DPCM with a two-level quantizer. Normally, fixed-length code words are used to encode the quantized prediction errors. Since the prediction value for each sample is calculated only from the past history of the encoded picture signal, the prediction value is available to both the coder and the decoder. To reconstruct a sample or picture element at the decoder, the corresponding transmitted prediction error is added to the prediction value of that sample.

Whenever the input picture signal is in analog form, the predictive encoding procedure includes some kind of amplitude quantization as in PCM. Amplitude quantization produces an inevitable information loss and signal distortion. This distortion can be measured from the generated quantization error, sometimes called quantizing noise, and, under certain conditions, can be observed as a degradation in picture quality. Since this quantization process is irreversible, the user of the transmitted picture has to specify the maximum allowable distortion by a fidelity criterion.

The irreversible operation has to be matched to this criterion in order not to exceed the maximum allowable distortion. If the input picture signal is digital, as in a PCM representation, then instead of irreversible coding, a reversible or information-preserving predictive coding scheme without a quantizer can be applied, and no signal distortion or picture quality degradation is produced.

Predictive coding technique takes advantage of the picture signal statistics on the one hand, and of the human viewer on the other, for reducing the bit rate. In general, the sample values of spatially neighboring picture elements are correlated. In television signals, there also is a temporal correlation between picture elements in successive frames. Correlation or linear statistical dependency indicates that a linear prediction of the sample values based on sample values of neighboring picture elements will result in prediction errors that have a smaller variance than the original sample values. One-dimensional prediction algorithms make use of the correlation of adjacent picture elements within the scan line. Other more complex schemes also exploit line-to-line and frame-to-frame correlation and are denoted as two-dimensional and three-dimensional prediction, respectively. Owing to the smaller variance of the signal to be quantized, coded, and transmitted, in a predictive coding system, the amplitude range of the quantizer can be diminished, the number of quantizing levels can be reduced, and fewer coding bits per picture element are required than in a PCM system without decreasing the signal-to-quantizing-noise ratio. By adapting the nonuniform spacing of the quantizing levels to the noise masking of the human visual system, properties of the human viewer can be taken into account, and a further reduction of the bit rate can be achieved. Although quantizing noise is increased by this technique, picture quality is not degraded if the increased noise does not exceed visibility thresholds determined by the masking effects of the eye.

Sometimes human viewing is not a primary objective, but rather recovery of scientific data in the picture. One example is that of pictures of the earth's surface taken by satellites to monitor natural resources. For digital computer processing, these pictures are converted into a PCM representation, and no additional irreversible coding operation beyond the uniform amplitude quantization of the PCM quantizer is permissible. In this case, a reversible predictive coding technique without a quantizer can be applied to the PCM picture signal to reduce the average bit rate per sample. Since the input sample values and prediction values are digital, the prediction errors to be coded are also digital. Although the set of possible digital prediction errors is greater than that of the input samples, a bit saving can be reached by use of an entropy coding scheme with variable-length code words. The lower bound for the average number of bits per prediction error or per input sample required for this coding technique is given by the entropy of the prediction error.

The design and application of a predictive coding technique must consider also other factors influenced by special properties of the picture source and the transmission channel. An important factor is the sensitivity of a predictive coding algorithm to channel errors. Since the transmitted differences are integrated in the decoder, a transmission bit error generates a sequence of erroneously reconstructed samples with a decay of the error amplitude corresponding to the impulse response function of the decoder. The error pattern in the reconstructed picture can propagate along an image line and from line to line, depending on the prediction algorithm of the coder. Furthermore, with variable-length codes, word synchronization can be lost for the remainder of the picture unless self-synchronizing codes or some kind of error protection is provided.

If the transmission channel requires a constant input bit rate, predictive coding techniques with variable-length codes must be applied with a buffer to smooth the nonconstant bit rate. Problems of buffer overflow and underflow then arise. The buffer and its problems can be avoided, provided there is a possibility of controlling the scanning and sampling frequency of the source by the variable-length coder so that a constant coder output bit rate is generated. These complications do not occur with DPCM coders using fixed-length code words.

The bit saving achieved with predictive coding compared to that with PCM depends on the type of pictures to be transmitted, on the picture quality requirements of the user, and on the coding algorithm. If error protection must be provided, these savings are reduced by the share of bits per picture element used for transmission error detection and correction.

3.2 HISTORY

The first theoretical and experimental approaches to encoding picture signals by methods of linear prediction began in 1952 at the Bell Telephone Laboratories (Oliver, 1952; Kretzmer, 1952; Harrison, 1952). Concurrently with this work, a theory of reversible predictive coding for PCM signals was developed at the Massachusetts Institute of Technology (Elias, 1955). The concepts of differential pulse-code modulation (DPCM) and delta modulation (DM) also originated in the early 1950s (Cutler, 1952; DeJager, 1952). In the coding system proposed by Cutler, quantized differences of successive samples are transmitted. By incorporating a linear predictor into that system and using a nonuniform quantization, which is tailored to the observer's perception, a promising coding technique for video signals was found (Graham, 1958). Much effort has been expended since that time toward improving this initial DPCM system. It is interesting to note that although Graham emphasized the important role of the observer's perception in the design of the DPCM quantizer, subsequent designs used the minimum-mean-square quantization error or the signal-to-quantizing-noise ratio (SNR) as a criterion for optimization. It was almost 15 years before the viewer's ability to detect or to mask differential quantization errors was studied in more detail.

Nevertheless, this intermediate period was important for the development of DPCM systems. During this time an algorithm for designing a quantizer with minimum-mean-square quantizing noise was developed (Panter and Dite, 1951; Max, 1960). By using this algorithm and the theory of optimum linear prediction for minimum-mean-square prediction error (Wiener, 1949), the signal-to-quantizing-noise ratio of a DPCM system for television pictures could be calculated. The coding gain of DPCM is about 14 dB in SNR when compared to PCM (O'Neal, 1966, 1967).

It is known that the spectral parts of quantization noise are weighted differently by the eye (Barstow and Christopher, 1962). In order to exploit the frequency-dependent noise-weighting function for picture coding, scientists investigated coding systems consisting of a preemphasis filter and a quantizer with quantizing error feedback (Kimme and Kuo, 1963; Brainard and Candy, 1969; Musmann, 1971a). These systems are closely related to DPCM systems. It can be shown that under certain conditions they are even equivalent to DPCM systems, although their structure looks different (Cattermole, 1969).

In some papers of that time, practical DPCM coding systems for video signals were described, aspects of implementation were discussed (Limb and Mounts, 1969), and the signal impairments resulting from the quantizing process of a DPCM coder were analyzed in detail in connection with the quantizer design (Millard and Maunsell, 1971). Whenever the number of quantizing levels is restricted to less than 16 levels, then these impairments lead to conflicting requirements in the quantizer design, which can only be met by a compromise between the different types of impairments or by extensions of the DPCM system.

Several proposals have been made for extending DPCM to reduce quantizing effects. One of the most effective extensions of DPCM is the use of a two-dimensional spatial predictor (Connor *et al.*, 1971). The subjective improvement of picture quality obtained with two-dimensional prediction is much higher than expected from the calculated 3-dB SNR increase. A further improvement can be achieved by supplying the DPCM system with an adaptive quantizer. The sliding-scale quantizer expands the quantizing range whenever the amplitude of the prediction error exceeds a predetermined threshold (Brown, 1969). An additional code word must be transmitted to inform the receiver that the quantizer has switched to the expanded range. However, no switching information is required if the quantizer is controlled as a function of previously transmitted code words and reconstructed picture elements (Musmann, 1971b). For optimizing these adaptive quantizers, the signal-to-quantizing-noise ratio was used as a quality criterion (Musmann, 1972). A coding gain between 3 and 4 dB in SNR was measured (Kummerow, 1973). Among the adaptive quantizers, the reflected quantizer represents a solution that is very simple to implement and is very effective for DPCM systems using 32 or more quantizing levels (Bostelmann, 1974). The reflected quantizer technique permits encoding of two quantizing levels by one code word and decoding of the code word without ambiguity, thus increasing the SNR by almost 6 dB. Another possibility for improving the signal-to-noise ratio by about 3.4 dB is adaptive contour prediction (Cohen and Adoul, 1976; Yamada *et al.*, 1977). Results obtained by computer simulation indicate that this coding gain is valid only for contours with short transitions of one or two picture elements (Zschunke, 1977).

Through the work of Candy and Bosworth (1972), the optimization of the DPCM quantizer characteristic for video signals was based on the more appropriate criterion of subjective evaluations of the signal impairments than on the SNR. A technique for measuring the visibility of edge busyness as a function of the signal slope was developed, and a method for designing DPCM-quantizers from this visibility function was described (Candy and Bosworth, 1972). If no visible impairments are allowed, then instead of the visibility function, the visibility threshold of the quantizing noise should be used for designing the quantizer (Thoma, 1974). The visibility threshold can be interpreted as the maximum allowable quantizing noise that is masked by the eye. A systematic investigation of the masking effects, also considering masking originating from the luminance detail surrounding a picture element to be coded, was the next essential step (Netravali and Prasada, 1977). Two algorithms were developed for obtaining the quantizing characteristic from the visibility threshold function (Sharma and Netravali, 1977). One algorithm minimizes the number of quantizing levels for fixed-word-length coding; the other algorithm minimizes the entropy of the quantized output for variable-word-length coding. At the same time, an experimental DPCM system with adaptive quantizer for broadcast television, which also exploits effects of spatial masking, was first built (Musmann and Erdmann, 1977).

This system provides excellent broadcast quality using 25 quantizing levels and 4-bit code words. To assess the picture quality, the grading scale of the International Radio Consultative Committee, as defined in Table 3-1, was applied (CCIR-Recommendations 500, 1974).

Studies of predictive coding for color signals started about 1970. The coding schemes for color broadcast television can be divided into two groups, component- and composite-coding methods. In component coding the three components of a color television signal, the luminance signal and the two chrominance signals, are encoded separately, while in composite coding the composite color television signal consisting of the luminance signal and the modulated subcarrier of the two chrominance signals is encoded as a single signal. In component coding, the chrominance signals I and Q of an NTSC signal can be sampled with a reduced sampling frequency, which is about one-third and one-sixth, respectively, that of the luminance signal Y. For a color video telephone signal with 1-MHz luminance bandwidth, acceptable picture quality has been achieved using previous element prediction and only 7 quantizing levels for I and 5 levels for Q (Limb *et al.*, 1971). For NTSC broadcast signals, a 5-bit quantizer for Y and 4-bit quantizer for I and Q has been proposed (Golding, 1972). In the case of SECAM or PAL color television signals, sampling frequencies of 8.8 MHz for Y and 2.2 MHz for the chrominance signals $R - Y$, $B - Y$ have been considered adequate (Federal Republic of Germany, 1977). Using previous element prediction, a 4-bit quantizer is necessary for the chrominance signals to produce a good picture quality (Sabatier, 1976). A two-dimensional predictor reduces the power of the prediction error by 7 dB and results in a remarkable improvement of picture quality (Pirsch and Stenger, 1977). For predictive coding of chrominance signals, adaptive quantizers exploiting effects of noise masking have also been investigated. It was found that masking by the luminance

TABLE 3-1

FIVE-POINT IMAGE QUALITY AND
IMPAIRMENT SCALE

Quality	Impairment
5 Excellent	5 Imperceptible
4 Good	4 Perceptible, but not annoying
3 Fair	3 Slightly annoying
2 Poor	2 Annoying
1 Bad	1 Very annoying

slope is greater than by the chrominance slope, and therefore, the switching of the chrominance quantizers should be controlled by the luminance slope (Netravali and Rubinstein, 1977). For a system operating at video telephone rates, as described above, adaptive uniform quantizers were compared with nonadaptive uniform quantizers, and an advantage in entropy of about 10% was measured. These results may be improved with adaptive nonuniform quantizers. Adaptive prediction of the chrominance signals based on luminance provides a coding gain in entropy of about 20% (Netravali and Rubinstein, 1978).

Two papers presenting a detailed statistical analysis of color video telephone and color television signals for entropy coding have been published (Rubinstein and Limb, 1972; Pirsch and Stenger, 1977). It was recognized that joint encoding of the components of a color signal brings only little advantage (Rubinstein and Limb, 1972). In the case of digital broadcast television signals, where each component is coded with 8-bit PCM, reversible predictive coding provides a remarkable reduction of the average bit rate resulting in entropies of 4.29, 2.82, and 2.46 bits for Y, $R - Y$, and $B - Y$ (Pirsch and Stenger, 1977).

Predictive composite coding started with intraline prediction algorithms and sampling frequencies at either three times or twice the subcarrier frequency f_{sc} (Thompson, 1972; Devereux, 1973). Thus, in an area of uniform hue, the third or second previous sample, respectively, has the same subcarrier phase and can be used for prediction. Since this is not valid for SECAM signals, only NTSC and PAL signals were considered for composite coding. It was found that the sampling frequency in composite coding need not be an integer multiple of the subcarrier frequency, and more flexibility for matching the bit rate of the coder to the transmission rate of the channel was given (Iijima and Ishiguro, 1973; Iijima and Suzuki, 1974). However, even with $3f_{sc}$ sampling and 6-bit quantization, impairments were still perceptible (Devereux, 1975a). Therefore, two-dimensional prediction schemes were developed (Thompson, 1974; Devereux, 1975b). The combination of two-dimensional prediction and a 5-bit reflected quantizer proved to be very useful, providing excellent picture quality according to the CCIR quality scale (Thompson, 1975).

Relatively little work on three-dimensional prediction for interframe component and composite color coding has been published until now. Some of these techniques are discussed in Chapter 6 (Iinuma *et al.*, 1975; Ishiguro *et al.*, 1976).

Experimental as well as theoretical studies have been concerned with the problem of channel errors in predictive picture coding. Transmission errors in DPCM picture signals with previous element prediction produce annoying visible streaks along the line. The length of these streaks can be reduced by transmitting PCM code words after a block of DPCM code words (Limb and Mounts, 1969), or by a leaking prediction (Kersten and Dietz, 1973). It was found that replacement of an erroneous line by an average of adjacent lines results in a marked improvement of picture quality (Connor, 1973). An erroneous line can be detected with a parity check or with an error pattern detector (Lippmann, 1973). Transmission errors occurring even at a low bit error probability of 10^{-6} are much more annoying in television signals than in a photograph, since the locations of the error patterns change from frame to frame. Two-dimensional prediction exhibits less visible error patterns than previous element prediction (Connor, 1973). These observations were confirmed by a theoretical analysis of the error patterns (Jung and Lippmann, 1975). Besides the prediction algorithm, the code word assignment for the representative quantizing levels also influences the visibility of the transmission errors (Lippmann, 1977). For reducing the error streaks of one-dimensional prediction, a combination of DPCM and PCM coding called hybrid D-PCM was introduced in 1978 (van Buul, 1978) and later extended for DPCM systems with two-dimensional prediction (Brüders et al., 1978).

3.3 DIFFERENTIAL PULSE-CODE MODULATION

Among predictive coding systems with quantizers, differential pulse-code modulation (DPCM) can be considered as the basic system. A block diagram of a digital DPCM system is shown in Fig. 3-1. The input signal x_N of the digital DPCM system is a PCM video signal representing one picture or a sequence of succeeding television frames. Samples of this PCM signal are quantized with a uniform quantizing characteristic and are coded by 8-bit binary numbers. For every input sample x_N, the linear predictor generates a prediction value $\hat{x}_N$ which is calculated from $N - 1$ preceding samples according to the relation

$$\hat{x}_N = \sum_{i=1}^{N-1} a_i x_{N-i} \tag{1}$$

Only preceding transmitted samples are used for prediction, so that the receiver is also able to calculate $\hat{x}_N$. The coefficients a_i are optimized to yield a prediction error

$$e_N = x_N - \hat{x}_N \tag{2}$$

TRANSMITTER

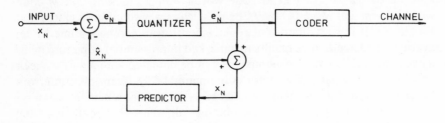

RECEIVER

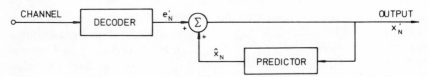

FIG. 3-1.   Block diagram of a digital DPCM system.

with minimum variance. The prediction error e_N is then quantized with a nonuniform quantizing characteristic, which is optimized to produce a minimum-mean-square quantizing error or is matched to the observer's perception of quantizing noise. Assuming a quantizer with K quantizing levels, each quantized prediction error e_N' is coded with $\log_2(K)$ bits and transmitted. By adding $\hat{x}_N$ to the quantized prediction error e_N', the picture element x_N' is reconstructed at the receiver and at the transmitter. The value x_N' again is represented by a binary number of 8 bits, but differs from the original sample x_N by the quantization error

$$q_N = e_N - e_N' = x_N - \hat{x}_N - (x_N' - \hat{x}_N) = x_N - x_N' \qquad (3)$$

For displaying the transmitted reconstructed video signal on a monitor, the decoder output x_N' must be converted into an analog signal. Figure 3-2 illustrates the performance of a DPCM system using a 10-MHz sampling frequency, previous sample prediction, and 4-bit/sample coding. The original 8-bit-PCM television picture is shown in Fig. 3-2a and the reconstructed 4-bit-DPCM picture in Fig. 3-2b. The prediction error and the quantizing error q_N multiplied by a factor of 8 are presented in Figs. 3-2c and d, respectively. The positive and negative errors are represented by white and black picture elements, while a zero error is gray. From Fig. 3-2c, it can be recognized that this one-dimensional predictor works well on horizontal edges but produces large prediction errors on vertical edges.

A completely digital DPCM system, as shown in Fig. 3-1, enables perfect tracking between the transmitter and receiver, which is very important for a correct reconstruction of the pictures. Tracking is more difficult to maintain with analog processing of the samples (Limb and Mounts, 1969). In the following two subsections, optimization of the predictor and the quantizer is described in more detail.

3.3.1 Predictor Optimization

Theoretically, the predictor and the quantizer should not be optimized separately, since there is a complex dependency of the visible quantizing

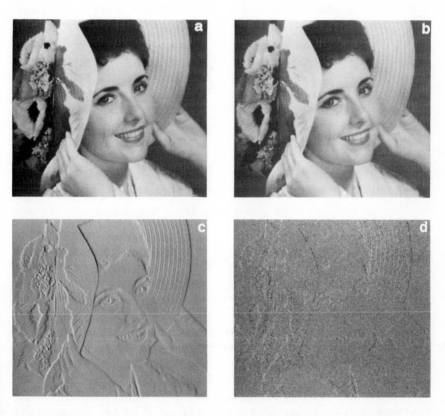

FIG. 3-2. Television pictures processed with a PCM and DPCM system using 10-MHz sampling frequency. (a) Original 8-bit PCM picture; (b) reconstructed 4-bit DPCM picture; (c) prediction error; (d) quantization error magnified by a factor of 8.

error upon the probability distribution of the prediction error. But in the case of a mean-square-error criterion, it can be shown that the mean-square value of the quantizing noise $E[q_N^2] = \sigma_q^2$ is approximately proportional to the mean-square value of the prediction error $E[e_N^2] = \sigma_e^2$ (O'Neal, 1966). The relationship is given by

$$\sigma_q^2 = (9/2K^2)\sigma_e^2 \qquad (4)$$

Therefore, under this approximation, independent optimization of the predictor is allowed. Then, the best estimate of x_N is that value of $\hat{x}_N$ for which the expected value of the squared prediction error

$$\sigma_e^2 = E[e_N^2] = E[(x_N - \hat{x}_N)^2] = E[(x_N - \sum_{i=1}^{N-1} a_i x_{N-i})^2] \qquad (5)$$

is minimum. To find the prediction coefficients a_i that satisfy this condition, the partial derivatives of σ_e^2 with respect to each a_i are taken and set equal to zero. Thus

$$\frac{d\sigma_e^2}{da_i} = -2E[(x_N - \sum_{i=1}^{N-1} a_i x_{N-i})x_{N-i}] = 0 \qquad (6)$$

for $i = 1, \ldots, N - 1$. The optimum prediction coefficients can be calculated from Eq. (6) if the autocovariances $E[x_N x_{N-i}]$ are known. Furthermore, using the best linear prediction $\hat{x}_N$, it follows from Eq. (6) that

$$E[(x_N - \hat{x}_N)\hat{x}_N] = 0 \qquad (7)$$

and the minimum-mean-square prediction error becomes

$$\sigma_e^2 = E[(x_N - \hat{x}_N)^2] = E[(x_N - \hat{x}_N)x_N] \qquad (8a)$$

or

$$\sigma_e^2 = E[x_N^2] - a_1 E[x_{N-1}x_N] - a_2 E[x_{N-2}x_N] - \cdots - a_{N-1} E[x_1 x_N] \qquad (8b)$$

The autocovariances of various kinds of video signals have been measured (O'Neal, 1966; Habibi, 1971).

In Table 3-2, results obtained with DPCM color television signals are presented (Pirsch and Stenger, 1977). The sampling frequencies are 10 MHz for the luminance signal Y and 2 MHz for the chrominance signals $R - Y$, $B - Y$. Each sample is uniformly quantized with 256 levels. The positions of the picture elements used for prediction of x are shown in Fig. 3-3. For the luminance signal, the best two-dimensional predictor reduces the variance of the prediction error by a factor of 2 when compared to a one-dimensional predictor. According to the Eq. (4), this factor corresponds to an improvement of the signal-to-quantizing-noise ratio (SNR) of

TABLE 3-2

PREDICTION ALGORITHMS AND PREDICTION ERRORS OF TELEVISION
LUMINANCE AND CHROMINANCE SIGNALS

Video signal	Prediction coefficients			σ_e^2	σ^2/σ_e^2
	a_A	a_B	a_C		
Y	1	—	—	53.1	33.2
	1	$-\frac{1}{2}$	$\frac{1}{2}$	29.8	59.1
	$\frac{3}{4}$	$-\frac{1}{2}$	$\frac{3}{4}$	27.9	63.2
	$\frac{7}{8}$	$-\frac{5}{8}$	$\frac{3}{4}$	26.3	67.0
R − Y	1	—	—	22.6	7.5
	—	—	1	6.8	25.0
	$\frac{1}{2}$	$-\frac{1}{2}$	1	4.9	34.7
	$\frac{5}{8}$	$-\frac{1}{2}$	$\frac{7}{8}$	4.7	36.1
B − Y	1	—	—	13.3	6.8
	—	—	1	3.2	28.2
	$\frac{1}{2}$	$-\frac{1}{2}$	1	2.5	36.1
	$\frac{3}{8}$	$-\frac{1}{4}$	$\frac{7}{8}$	2.5	36.1

3 dB. The different prediction errors of a one-dimensional and two-dimensional predictor are shown in Fig. 3-4. Positive and negative errors are represented by white and black picture elements, while a zero error is gray. The two-dimensional predictor reduces the prediction error on vertical edges, but increases the prediction error on horizontal edges when compared to one-dimensional prediction. The subjective improvement of picture quality obtained with two-dimensional prediction is greater than expressed by the 3-dB gain in signal-to-quantizing-noise ratio. Results achieved with the chrominance signals indicate that a one-dimensional predictor using x_C instead of x_A for prediction reduces σ_e^2 by a factor of 4 or increases the SNR by 6 dB.

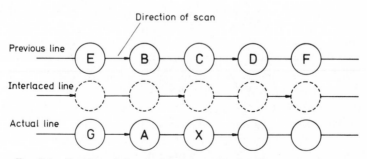

FIG. 3-3. Position of picture elements used for prediction of element x.

FIG. 3-4.   Prediction error of a television picture processed with a 4-bit DPCM system using (a) one-dimensional prediction $(a_A = 1.0)$ and (b) two-dimensional prediction $(a_A = 0.75, a_B = -0.5, a_C = 0.75)$.

A few attempts have also been initiated to consider the observer's perception in optimizing the predictor (Thoma, 1974; Pirsch and Stenger, 1977). In all cases, the predictor was optimized independently of the quantizer. Thoma tried to match the predictor algorithm to the pel spread function of the eye and to distribute equally the prediction error on all edges independently of their direction. Pirsch and Stenger wanted to reduce the annoying effect of edge busyness, which is produced by large prediction errors. To give more weight to these prediction errors, they minimized $E[e_N^4]$ and $E[e_N^6]$ instead of $E[e_N^2]$. However, all of the prediction algorithms they found were very similar to the optimum predictors with minimum $E[e_N^2]$ in Table 3-2.

3.3.2   Quantizer Optimization

In this section two methods for optimizing the quantizer will be described in more detail. With the first method, a quantizer that minimizes the mean-square quantizing error for a given number K of quantizing levels is obtained and with the second method, the number of quantizing levels K is minimized for a quantizer that keeps the quantizing error below a given visibility threshold function.

The algorithm for designing a K-level quantizer with minimum-mean-square quantizing error was developed by Max (1960). Let e_1, $e_2, \ldots, e_k, \ldots, e_K$ be quantizer reconstruction levels and d_1, $d_2, \ldots, d_k, \ldots, d_{K+1}$ be quantizer decision levels; then the quantizer output will be e_k if

$$d_k < e \le d_{k+1} \tag{9}$$

for $k = 1, \ldots, K$. The quantization error is $(e - e_k)$. Assuming a continuous input signal e, the mean-square quantizing error is

$$\sigma_q^2 = \sum_{k=1}^{K} \int_{d_k}^{d_{k+1}} (e - e_k)^2 p(e)\, de \tag{10}$$

where $p(e)$ is the probability density function of e. For minimizing σ_q^2, the following conditions must be satisfied (Max, 1960):

$$\int_{d_k}^{d_{k+1}} (e - e_k)^2 p(e)\, de = 0 \tag{11}$$

for $k = 1, \ldots, K$ and

$$d_k = {}^1\!/_2 (e_{k-1} + e_k) \tag{12}$$

for $k = 2, \ldots, K$. According to Eq. (12), the decision levels d_k are always placed in the middle between two adjacent reconstruction levels e_{k-1}, e_k. To solve Eqs. (11) and (12), an iterative procedure must be carried out.

Sometimes it is useful to have a mathematical formula that describes the mean-square quantizing error σ_q^2 in a closed form. Such a formula has been developed by Panter and Dite (1951). However, the derivation is based on two assumptions: that the input signal probability is constant in each quantizing interval, and that the reconstruction levels are situated in the middle of the quantizing intervals. These assumptions are justified for an approximation of σ_q^2 if the quantization is relatively fine or if K is greater than 8. The mean-square quantizing error then is given by

$$\sigma_q^2 = \frac{1}{12K^2} \left\{ \int_{d_1}^{d_{K+1}} [p(e)]^{1/3}\, de \right\}^3 \tag{13}$$

This formula was used by O'Neal (1966) for evaluating σ_q^2. In the case of picture signals, the input probability density function $p(e)$ may be approximated reasonably well by the Laplacian density function

$$p(e) = \frac{1}{(2)^{1/2} \sigma_e} \exp \left[-\frac{2^{1/2}}{\sigma_e} |e| \right] \tag{14}$$

Assuming peak values of the prediction error $-d_1, d_{K+1} \gg \sigma_e$, it follows from Eq. (13) that

$$\sigma_q^2 = (9/2K^2)\sigma_e^2 \tag{15}$$

According to Eq. (15), the mean-square quantizing error of a well-designed DPCM system is a function of σ_e^2 and K^2. The mean-square prediction error σ_e^2 is minimized by use of an optimum predictor according to Eq. (5). Then the number of quantizing levels K can be adjusted to meet the picture quality requirements given by the maximum allowable distortion σ_q^2 or by the required signal-to-quantizing-noise ratio

$$S/N = 10 \log_{10}(\sigma^2/\sigma_q^2) \qquad (16)$$

Using fixed-length code words, the transmission bit rate is $R = \log_2(K)$ bits per picture element.

If the available transmission channel capacity restricts K to values less than 16, the optimized quantizer can still produce visible quantization distortion in the reconstructed picture depending on the picture material to be coded and on the number of quantizing levels K. The principal impairments are:

1. Quantizer overload error, which is produced if the prediction error to be quantized is greater than the largest quantizer reconstruction level. The overload reduces the resolution of the picture.

2. Granular noise, which is determined by the size of the two smallest reconstruction levels of the quantizer oscillating in low-detail regions of the picture.

3. Contouring patterns, which occur in long sloping regions of the video signal if the quantizing steps for small prediction errors are too large.

4. Edge busyness, which is generated from frame to frame at edges in a still picture if the quantizing steps for great prediction errors are too large.

These impairments lead to conflicting requirements in the quantizer design. The quantizer resulting from the above-described optimization procedure generally shows less granular noise in smooth areas but more slope overload at sharp edges than those that are optimized using subjective distortion criteria (Pirsch and Stenger, 1977).

Since the mean-square-error criterion does not adequately consider the human observer and special properties of visual perception, this distortion measure can only be used with restrictions when subjective fidelity criteria are given. A typical example for such a subjective criterion is coding without producing visible quantization distortion. This criterion is of special interest in cases where a relatively high picture quality of an original analog picture must be preserved as in digital broadcast television coding.

To design a quantizer for monochrome television signals that maintains the quantization error below a certain visibility threshold, Thoma (1974) measured the visibility threshold of the quantization error as a function of the prediction error. He found that the results vary to a certain extent with the kind of prediction algorithm and picture material used in the measurement. In Fig. 3-5a, the visibility threshold function obtained with a predictor ($a_A = 1.0$, $a_B = -0.5$, $a_C = 0.5$) and critical television pictures is shown (Erdmann, 1978). This visibility threshold function is valid for positive and negative prediction errors and can be interpreted as the amount of quantization error at a picture element which is masked by the signal slopes at that point represented by the prediction error. The diagram of Fig. 3-5a indicates that with an increasing prediction error, a larger quantization error can be tolerated.

Now, there shall be derived a quantizer characteristic that minimizes the number K of quantizing levels on the one hand and that keeps the quantization error below the given threshold function on the other. This problem was solved by Sharma and Netravali (1977). The algorithm for finding the reconstruction levels and the decision levels of this quantizer is illustrated in Fig. 3-6 for even K. In this case, $e = 0$ is a decision level, and the geometric procedure starts at the corresponding point on the visibility threshold function with a dashed line of inclination $-45°$. The intersection of this line with the abscissa gives the first reconstruction level. From this point, a dashed line of inclination $+45°$ is drawn. Its intersection with the visibility threshold function gives the next decision level,

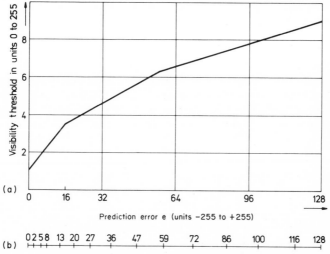

FIG. 3-5 (a).   Visibility threshold of quantization error as a function of prediction error; (b) quantizer reconstruction levels derived from the threshold function of (a).

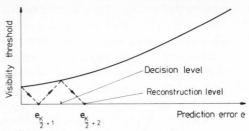

FIG. 3-6.   Illustration of the quantizer design procedure for an even number K of reconstruction levels (from Sharma and Netravali, 1977).

and so on. This procedure is continued until the last $+45°$ line exceeds the amplitude range of e. The number of points in which this path meets the abscissa is the minimum number of levels of the desired quantizer. The resulting dashed zigzag line represents the magnitude of the quantization error as a function of the quantizer input signal e.

If K is odd, then the procedure starts with a reconstruction level at $e = 0$. Using the visibility threshold function of Fig. 3-5a, the described algorithm leads to a quantizing characteristic as shown in Fig. 3-5b. Since the quantizing characteristic is symmetrical with respect to $e = 0$, only the positive reconstruction quantization levels are represented. To encode a monochrome television signal with excellent picture quality, 23 to 25 levels are required for typical television pictures, while 32 levels are necessary for artificial test patterns (Thoma, 1974).

3.4   EXTENDED DIFFERENTIAL PULSE-CODE MODULATION

Several proposals have been made to extend differential pulse-code modulation to improve picture quality or to reduce the number of required quantization levels. These proposals are essentially based on a substitution of adaptive components for time-invariant predictors and quantizers.

3.4.1   Adaptive Prediction

The aim of adaptive prediction algorithms is to reduce the prediction error and thus to decrease the quantization error at picture contours where invariant predictors generally produce the largest prediction errors. There are mainly two types of adaptive predictors.

In a technique proposed by Yamada *et al.* (1977), the prediction value of a conventional two-dimensional predictor ($a_A = 0.75$, $a_D = 0.25$) is multiplied by an adaptive coefficient $k = 1.0 \pm p$ to give the prediction $\hat{x}_N$. The coefficient k is chosen according to the following rule:

$$
\begin{aligned}
k &= 1.0 + 0.125 && \text{if} \quad e_{N-1}' = e_K \\
k &= 1.0 && \text{if} \quad e_1 < e_{N-1}' < e_K \\
k &= 1.0 - 0.125 && \text{if} \quad e_{N-1}' = e_1
\end{aligned} \tag{17}
$$

where e_1, e_K are the maximum negative and positive reconstruction levels. With this relatively simple adaptive technique, the rise time of the step response in DPCM systems using 3 bits or less can be improved for both horizontal and vertical direction.

A somewhat more complicated adaptive predictor has been proposed by Cohen and Adoul (1976). This so-called contour predictor is similar to an algorithm published by Zschunke (1977). The contour prediction aims at selecting that one of the neighboring picture elements x_A, x_B, x_C, or x_D in Fig. 3-3 as prediction value $\hat{x}$ which is most similar in amplitude to the actual picture element x to be coded. The two proposals cited for contour prediction only differ in the selection algorithm. Assuming that the direction of a contour crossing the scan does not change significantly going from x_A to x, then the contour direction can be determined with reference to x_A by searching for that point E, B, or C that gives the minimum difference $|x_A - x_E|$, $|x_A - x_B|$, or $|x_A - x_C|$. The neighboring picture element to the right of this point is taken as the contour prediction value $\hat{x}$. If the signal slope $|x_A - x_G|$ decreases in flat areas below 10% of the total signal range, then $\hat{x} = x_A$ is used instead of a contour prediction.

Results obtained by computer simulation of single frames have shown that contour prediction provides a 3.4-dB gain in signal-to-quantizing noise when compared to fixed prediction. But these results are valid only for contours with short and steep signal slopes (Zschunke, 1977). In the case of television coding, it still is necessary to investigate whether a DPCM system with contour prediction generates annoying quantization impairments, such as edge busyness, which becomes visible only in processing successive picture frames.

Another type of adaptive prediction for television coding is being investigated at the present time (Pearson *et al.*, 1977). Only in stationary areas of a television picture three-dimensional prediction is more favorable than two-dimensional prediction. Therefore, conditional three- and two-dimensional predictors for stationary and nonstationary areas, respectively, might improve the prediction and coding efficiency. This adaptive predictor requires a detector for stationary and nonstationary areas and a frame memory (Wendt, 1973).

3.4.2   Adaptive Quantization

In Section 3.3.2, it was explained that the different quantization impairments generally lead to conflicting requirements in the quantizer optimization. A quantizer that keeps the quantization error below a visibility threshold ensures that no impairments of the picture quality are visible if at least 25 to 32 quantizing levels are provided. Such a quantizer will produce slope overload and edge busyness but no granular noise or contouring if the quantizer reconstruction levels for large prediction errors are omitted in order to achieve a lower bit rate. The resulting annoying impairments can be reduced to a certain extent by use of adaptive quantizers. In this section, two adaptive quantizers, which are based on different strategies, will be described. The first quantizer exploits residual redundancy inherent in DPCM coding. Visual masking effects of the human observer are utilized in the adaptation strategy of the second.

In a DPCM system, the quantizing characteristic is always shifted in such a way that the zero level of the quantizer is positioned at the prediction value $\hat{x}$, as illustrated in Fig. 3-7 by an example. The shape of the quantizing characteristic remains the same. Further, it should be recognized that the quantizer becomes overloaded by the actual prediction error e. On the other hand, the levels $+14$ and $+24$ are redundant since they cannot appear in the shown state of $\hat{x}$. The quantizer could reduce the quantizing error q by substituting two additional negative reconstruction levels for the two redundant levels (Musmann, 1971b). In a DPCM system proposed by Bostelmann (1974), this is accomplished adaptively

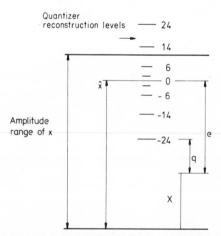

Fig. 3-7.   Graphical representation of the shifted quantizing characteristic of a DPCM quantizer.

TABLE 3-3

Example of a 2^n-Complement
Representation for Negative Numbers
Where $n = 8$

+255	11111111	-1
+254	11111110	-2
+253	11111101	-3
z ↑		$\bar{z} = 256 - z$ ↓
+3	00000011	-253
+2	00000010	-254
+1	00000001	-255
0	00000000	

in a very elegant way. This so-called reflected quantizer uses the 2^n-complement for representing negative numbers inside the DPCM coder. Table 3-3 gives an example for $n = 8$. According to this binary notation, a positive prediction error $e = +2$ is represented by the same binary code word 00000010 as the negative $e = -254$. The ambiguity is eliminated by a special symmetrical structure of the quantizing characteristic, as shown in Fig. 3-8. Depending on the actual prediction value $\hat{x}$ in this quantizing characteristic, the possible range of e always covers a fixed number of levels with a unique set of code words. In Fig. 3-8, the amplitude ranges of

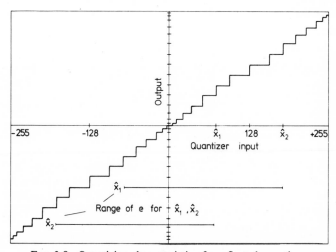

FIG. 3-8 Quantizing characteristic of a reflected quantizer.

e are drawn in for two states of $\hat{x}$. In this way, 64 quantizing levels can be encoded with code words of 5-bit length instead of 6 bit, saving 1 bit per code word.

The reflected quantizer is especially efficient for DPCM picture coding with 5 or 4 bits per picture element, providing excellent picture quality, except in monochrome television coding where the picture quality of the 4-bit version is only between good and excellent. Because of the special binary notation, the size of the quantizing intervals of the reflected quantizer is the same for small as for large prediction errors. Owing to this restriction, the reflected quantizer becomes less efficient when the code word length is reduced below 4 bits per picture element. A special advantage of this adaptive quantizer is that it requires no additional hardware.

It is well known that the luminance sensitivity of a human observer decreases in picture areas with high-contrast detail. With decreasing sensitivity, larger quantization errors are masked by the eye. In Section 3.3.2, the optimization of a fixed quantizer, which utilizes a special part of this masking for minimizing the number K of quantizing levels was described. In that design, the quantizing characteristic is based on the masking caused by the magnitude of the prediction error at a picture element x to be coded. In this case the prediction error is used as a simplified measurement of the amount of picture detail. To include also the spatial masking caused by the picture detail surrounding the picture element x, Netravali and Prasada (1977) introduced a mathematical model for describing and measuring the amount of detail by the luminance activities M. Hypothesizing that the visibility of the quantizing noise is related to M, Netravali and Prasada call M the masking function. The value of M at a picture element x is defined by the weighted sum of the luminance slopes at x and at the neighboring picture elements. Let Δ_i^H and Δ_i^V be the horizontal and vertical slopes of the luminance intensity at these points i; then M is given by

$$M = \sum_i \alpha^{|\delta_i|} \frac{1}{2} (|\Delta_i^H| + |\Delta_i^V|) \qquad (18)$$

where δ_i is the Euclidean distance between x and point i normalized by the distance between horizontally adjacent picture elements and α is a factor equal to 0.35. Since α is smaller than 1, according to Eq. (18) exponentially decreasing weights are assigned as the distance from x increases. The authors point out that the choice of the value α, although based on psychovisual tests, should be considered as a first trial. To find a relationship between the luminance accuracy required by the viewer and the masking function M, the visibility of noise added to a picture element is measured by an experimental method similar to that of Candy and Bosworth (1972). The value of the visibility function is generally high at low values of the masking function M, and vice versa, as shown in Fig. 3-9. From this visibility function, the adaptive quantizer is constructed in the following way. The picture is divided into segments of approximately constant visibility, and an individual quantizer is designed for each segment. The segmentation is controlled by the value of M, as indicated in Fig. 3-9. The resulting adaptive quantizer provides a subjectively equal-weighted quantizing noise throughout the picture.

The approach of Musmann and Erdmann (1977) can be considered as a simplified version of this masking model. However, another type of adaptive quantizer, which keeps the quantization error below a visibility threshold associated with the value of M is derived. It is assumed that the main spatial masking affecting a picture element x is contributed by the maximum prediction error at the neighboring picture elements A, B, C, D according to Fig. 3-3. Therefore M is defined as

$$M = \max\{|e_A|, |e_B|, |e_C|, |e_D|\} \qquad (19)$$

For this M, the visibility threshold is measured using Thoma's (1974) technique. Figure 3-10a shows the results obtained with a two-dimensional predictor ($a_A = 1.0$, $a_B = -0.5$, $a_C = 0.5$) for typical television pictures. The adaptive quantizer derived from this visibility threshold function is based on the quantizing characteristic found in Section 3.3.2 and plotted once more at the top of Fig. 3-10b. In this quantizing characteristic, the masking at point x caused by the prediction error e_x is considered. To encode the prediction error with 4-bit code words, a subset of 16 quantizing levels from the basic characteristic is always used. The spatial masking M contributed from the surrounding luminance activities is neglected for $M < 20$. In this case, the 16 inner quantizing levels are taken according to characteristic I. If M increases to $M \geq 20$, then Fig. 3-10a indicates that quantization errors up to 3.5 units are masked,

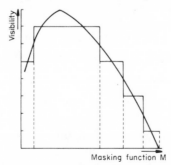

FIG. 3-9. Sketch of a typical visibility function versus masking function M and approximation by a piecewise constant function (from Netravali and Prasada, 1977).

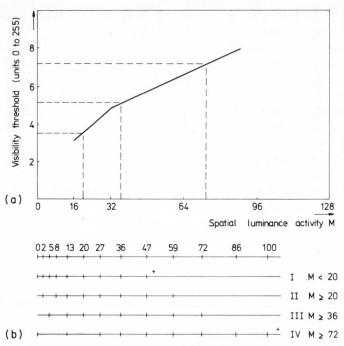

FIG. 3-10 (a)   Visibility threshold of the quantization error as a function of the spatial luminance activity: $M = \max\{|e_A|, |e_B|, |e_C|, |e_D|\}$. (b) quantizing characteristics derived from the threshold function of (a) for an adaptive 4-bit quantizer. +: only positive level available.

and therefore the reconstruction levels 0 and 5 can be omitted in favor of additional levels at the outer part of the quantizing characteristic, as illustrated with characteristic II. This algorithm can be extended to the adaptive quantizer with four quantizing characteristics of Fig. 3-10b. No switching information must be transmitted to the receiver. Since the quantizing characteristics are derived from one basic characteristic, no noise due to switching of the characteristics is visible. The considerable improvement of the picture quality achieved with this adaptive quantizer is demonstrated in Fig. 3-11 using a critical television test picture. An examination of monochrome television pictures according to the CCIR-Recommendations 500 (1974) showed a grading between excellent and good according to the grading scale of Table 3-1. Lippmann developed similar adaptive quantizers for DPCM coding of photographs. Figure 3-12 shows two examples of the picture quality obtained with 3-bit and 1-bit coding. In pictures coded with 3 bits per picture element, distortion is detectable at edges of high contrast. At a bit rate of 1 bit per picture element, granular noise in flat areas of the picture is also visible.

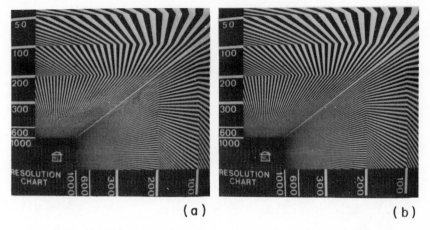

(a)   (b)

FIG. 3-11. Television test pictures processed with a DPCM system using two-dimensional prediction ($a_A = 1.0$, $a_B = -0.5$, $a_C = 0.5$) and a 4-bit quantizer. (a) Fixed quantizer with the quantizing characteristic I of Fig. 3-10b; (b) adaptive quantizer with quantizing characteristics of Fig. 3-10b.

Comparing the two strategies for designing adaptive quantizers using spatial masking, the first strategy is more favorable for those applications where superthreshold quantization is intended. The second strategy, based on a visibility threshold function, provides a technique for optimizing a quantizer with a minimum number of quantizing levels for applications where high picture quality without visible quantization degradations must be preserved.

Finally, it should be mentioned that any adaptive predictor can theoretically be interpreted as an adaptive quantizer. This can also be recognized from Fig. 3-7 where different adaptive strategies of the predictor result in different shifts of the quantizing characteristic. More details of these relations can be taken from the description of the general model of a switched quantizer (Musmann, 1974).

3.5 INFORMATION-PRESERVING PREDICTIVE CODING

Often in applications where digital picture data are interpreted by various kinds of scientific measurements, only reversible information-preserving coding is allowed for saving channel or storage capacity. In these cases differential pulse-code modulation cannot be applied because of the additional quantization errors introduced by the DPCM quantizer. Nevertheless, it is possible to use predictive coding for reducing the bit rate. Figure 3-13 shows the block diagram of a predictive coder that pro-

FIG. 3-12. Photographs processed with DPCM systems using a two-dimensional predictor and adaptive quantizer. Picture resolution is 8×8 picture elements/mm². (From Lippmann, 1978, unpublished). (a) Coding with 3 bits per picture element; (b) coding with 1 bit per picture element.

duces no information loss. The structure of this coder is similar to that of a DPCM system without a quantizer. However, the fixed-word-length coding is replaced by a Huffman coder using variable-length code words. Generally, variable-word-length coding complicates the data handling.

According to the block diagram of Fig. 3-13, a digital prediction value $\hat{x}_N$ is subtracted from the PCM-coded input signal x_N to give a prediction error e_N. If $\hat{x}_N$ and x_N are encoded by binary numbers of 8 bits, then e_N is represented by a number of 9 bits including the sign bit. So the set of possible samples to be coded has expanded at this step. Owing to the more peaked probability distribution of e_N, a Huffman code applied to e_N is more efficient than when applied to x_N. This was proved for television signals measuring the entropies $H(X)$ and $H(E)$ of an optimized predictor, which minimizes

$$H(E) = -\sum_{e_N} P(e_N) \log_2[P(e_N)] \tag{20}$$

(Pirsch and Stenger, 1977). These entropies represent a lower bound for the average bit rate per picture element of Huffman coding.

In all measurements, the original input signal was represented by 8-bit samples. The comparison of $H(X)$ and $H(E)$ in Table 3-4 shows that predictive coding combined with Huffman coding reduces the bit rate by a factor of about 2. Since $H(E)$ is even smaller than the conditional entropies $H(X|X_A)$ and $H(X|X_C)$, the predictive coding technique described is also superior to complex conditional Huffman coding of x_N, which would

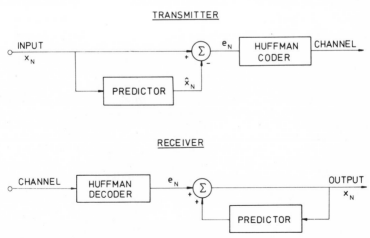

FIG. 3-13. Block diagram of an information preserving predictive coder.

TABLE 3-4

ENTROPY IN BITS PER PICTURE ELEMENT OF VIDEO SIGNALS

Video signal	$H(X)$	$H(X\mid X_A)$	$H(X\mid X_C)$	a_A	a_B	a_C	$H(E)$
					Predictor		
Y	7.34	4.66	4.85	$\frac{7}{8}$	$-\frac{1}{2}$	$\frac{5}{8}$	4.29
R − Y	5.57	3.76	2.96	$\frac{3}{8}$	$-\frac{1}{4}$	$\frac{7}{8}$	2.82
B − Y	5.24	3.75	2.93	$\frac{3}{8}$	$-\frac{1}{4}$	$\frac{7}{8}$	2.46

be necessary to achieve the conditional entropy. The position of the picture elements corresponding to x_A and x_C can be taken from Fig. 3-3.

3.6 PREDICTIVE CODING OF COLOR SIGNALS

In color television, colors are represented by the luminance signal Y and the two chrominance signals R − Y, B − Y. The choice of this special set of color coordinates meets the requirement that color television be compatible with monochrome television when only the luminance component Y is transmitted.

Here only predictive coding of color broadcast television signals will be considered. To avoid a repetitive description of the coding differences among the television standards of the National Television System Committee (NTSC) system, Phase Alternating Line (PAL) system, and Sequential Couleur à Mémoire (SECAM) system, the explanations will be restricted to the basic concepts of predictive coding in component and composite color television coding.

3.6.1 Component Coding

In component coding, the luminance signal Y and the chrominance signals R − Y, B − Y are encoded separately. The sampling frequencies are matched to the individual Nyquist rates of the components. In the case of PAL signals, sampling frequencies of 8.8 to 10.0 MHz for Y and 2.2 to 2.5 MHz for R − Y, B − Y are required.

To encode the luminance signal Y, a DPCM coding technique, as described in Section 3.4.2, can be applied. Using a two-dimensional predictor ($a_A = 1.0$, $a_B = -0.5$, $a_C = 0.5$) and an optimized adaptive quantizer that keeps the quantization noise below a visibility threshold function, excellent broadcast quality is obtained with 4 bits per sample and a

10-MHz sampling frequency (Musmann and Erdmann, 1977). By exploiting the line-blanking interval, this luminance coder generates a transmission rate of 32 Mbits/sec.

According to the results of Pirsch and Stenger (1977) in Table 3-2, the predictor ($a_A = 0.5$, $a_B = -0.5$, $a_C = 1.0$) appears to be a practical and advisable solution for DPCM coding of the chrominance components $R - Y$, $B - Y$. For optimizing the quantizers, visibility density functions of edge noise are known, but no visibility threshold functions have been measured until now. Results obtained by Netravali and Rubinstein indicate that chrominance quantization errors are better masked by luminance slopes than by chrominance slopes. This can be recognized from Fig. 3-14, which shows for the example of $B - Y$, that the measured visibility of chrominance edge noise is less for a masking function M based on the luminance slopes $M = \Delta Y$ than on the chrominance slopes $M = \Delta(B - Y)$. From these results, it can be concluded that adaptive chrominance quantizers should be controlled by the luminance slopes or luminance activities, as illustrated in Fig. 3-15. It is not yet known how many quantization levels are required for an adaptive chrominance quantizer to provide broadcast picture quality without visible quantization distortions. For a fixed quantizer and two-dimensional predictor, 16 quantizing levels appear to be sufficient (Pirsch and Stenger, 1977). Using a

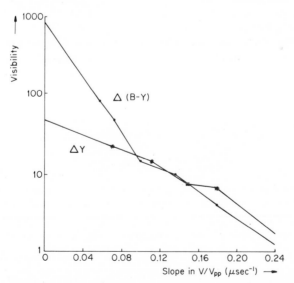

FIG. 3-14.   Visibility of chrominance edge noise at $B - Y$ versus slope of the chrominance signal $\Delta(B - Y)$ and slope of the luminance signal ΔY (from Netravali and Rubinstein, 1977).

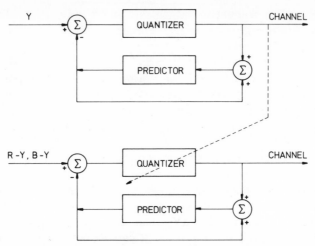

FIG. 3-15   Block diagram of a DPCM system with an adaptive chrominance quantizer controlled by the luminance activity (from Netravali and Rubinstein, 1977).

sampling rate of 2.5 MHz and 4 bits per sample, a transmission rate of 10 Mbits/sec results for each chrominance component. Again, by exploiting the horizontal blanking interval and transmitting the R − Y, B − Y lines alternatively, a transmission rate of 8 Mbits/sec is generated by this chrominance coder. In this way, a total transmission rate of 40 Mbits/sec is required for component coding.

In comparison to composite-coding techniques, which are described in the next section, component coding results in lower bit rates. This can be explained by the individual matching of the sampling frequencies, prediction algorithms, and quantizers to a single component which is not possible in composite coding. By this means, each component can be encoded in a manner best suited to the properties of the human observer.

3.6.2   Composite Coding

A DPCM system, as described for monochrome television in Section 3.3, performs poorly for a composite color signal, since the modulated subcarrier perpetually overloads the quantizer. There results from this overload a severe loss of color saturation in the reconstructed picture. To overcome this problem of composite coding in which a subcarrier is always included in the signal to be coded, the sampling frequency must be locked to the subcarrier frequency f_{sc}. Furthermore, to avoid a prediction considering the phase of the subcarrier frequency, the sampling frequency can be chosen as an integer multiple of the subcarrier frequency. On the other hand, the sampling frequency should be higher than the Nyquist rate to avoid aliasing. The lowest sampling frequency that meets these requirements is three times the color subcarrier frequency. If $3f_{sc}$ sampling is applied, as illustrated in Fig. 3-16, a prediction $\hat{S}_1 = S_4$, using the third previous sample, will be ideal in areas of constant chrominance and luminance. However, at luminance changes, this system performs rather poorly since the prediction value S_4 is three times further away than in previous sample prediction. The severe slope overload obtained on large luminance edges can be reduced by using two-dimensional prediction. But consideration must then be given to the line-by-line reversal of the modulated R − Y component V in PAL signals.

Thompson (1975) proposed the following planar predictor for NTSC signals:

$$\hat{S}_1 = S_2 - S_{10} + S_9 \tag{21}$$

For PAL signals, the effect of the V-axis switch is canceled by locking the sampling frequency to the subcarrier phase, so that one sample out of three, for example, S_1 in Fig. 3-16, lies along the V-axis, and by cycling through a sequence of three prediction algorithms

$$\hat{S}_1 = S_2 + S_8 - S_9 \tag{22a}$$
$$\hat{S}_2 = S_3 + S_{10} - S_{11} \tag{22b}$$
$$\hat{S}_3 = S_4 + S_9 - S_{10} \tag{22c}$$

An analysis of the prediction value $\hat{S}_1$, for example, shows that the chrominance components of S_2 and S_8 cancel while S_9 is in antiphase of S_1. Therefore, $\hat{S}_1$ gives an ideal prediction in areas of uniform hue and also across edges parallel to both $S_1 - S_2$ and $S_9 - S_2$. Thompson (1975) combined these prediction algorithms with a reflected quantizer using 5 bits per pic-

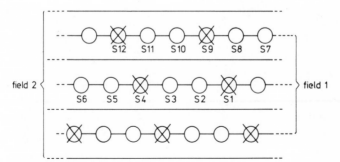

FIG. 3-16. Position of picture elements in the PAL 625 line raster sampled at $3f_{sc} = 13.3$ MHz. Neglecting the operation of the PAL switch, the crossed elements have identical subcarrier phase (from Thompson, 1975).

ture element to encode PAL television signals. The resulting coder provides excellent picture quality using a transmission bit rate of 69 Mbits/sec.

Although a lower bit rate can be obtained by more sophisticated component-coding techniques, composite coding might be of interest in applications where the separation of the components is difficult. An example is the cascading of several codecs in a connection of analog and digital links in which a repetitive separation of the components might produce accumulating distortions.

3.7 Influence of Transmission Errors

In this section the influence of transmission errors in DPCM systems will be considered. In contrast to DPCM speech coding, where transmission errors are less perceptible than in PCM systems, transmission errors in DPCM picture coding produce error patterns in the reconstructed picture that are much more annoying than those of PCM coding.

In DPCM coding, a transmission bit error changes the magnitude of a coded prediction error. The erroneous prediction error enters the decoder and produces a pattern corresponding to the impulse response of the decoder. In Fig. 3-17, these error patterns are shown for a one- and two-dimensional prediction scheme in an area of uniform luminance. In general, two-dimensional prediction algorithms generate less annoying error patterns than one-dimensional algorithms, as can be seen from Fig. 3-18. The decay of the error response is a function of the prediction coeffi-

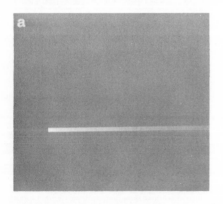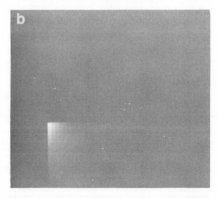

Fig. 3-17. DPCM responses to one transmission error in an area of uniform luminance (a) for one-dimensional prediction ($a_A = 0.97$) and (b) for two-dimensional prediction ($a_A = 0.74$, $a_B = -0.59$, $a_C = 0.82$).

FIG. 3-18. Transmission error effects in a photograph processed with 3-bit DPCM systems. Picture resolution is 8×8 picture elements/mm². (a) One-dimensional prediction ($a_A = 1.0$), bit error rate 10^{-4}; (b) two-dimensional prediction ($a_A = 0.74$, $a_B = -0.59$, $a_C = 0.82$), bit error rate 10^{-4}. (From Lippmann, 1978, unpublished.)

cients. For one-dimensional prediction, the decay can be reduced by decreasing the prediction coefficient a_A. But this leads to a less efficient prediction (Kersten and Dietz, 1973). A theoretical detailed analysis of the conditions for convergence of the error response has shown that for the practically important case $a_A \geq 0$, $a_B \leq 0$, $a_C \geq 0$, and $|a_A a_C| \geq |a_B|$, the following inequalities must be satisfied:

$$|a_A| - |a_B| + |a_C| \leq 1 \tag{23a}$$
$$|a_A|, |a_B| \quad \text{and} \quad |a_C| < 1 \tag{23b}$$

On the basis of the energy in the error signal, it has been analytically verified for a group of prediction algorithms that the visibility of error patterns decreases significantly when the sum of the weighting coefficients is only slightly reduced below the limit of convergence (Jung and Lippmann, 1975).

An interesting proposal for reducing the error sensitivity of DPCM coding was made by van Buul (1978). To achieve a rapid decay of the error patterns, additional PCM information is incorporated into the transmitted prediction errors. To avoid transmitting extra information, this technique is implemented in a DPCM system with a reflected quantizer using the 2^n-complement representation for negative numbers, as demonstrated in the block diagram of Fig. 3-19. From the preceding reconstructed picture element x_{N-1}', the most significant bits are taken and are added in modulo-2 addition to the coded prediction error e_N'. The additional quantizer of this so-called hybrid DPCM coder adapts the number

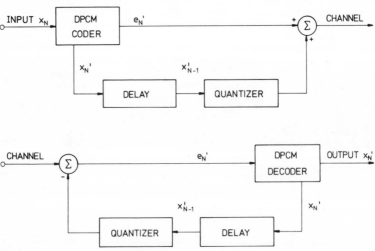

FIG. 3-19.   Block diagram of a hybrid DPCM coder and decoder.

of bits for x_{N-1}' to that of the code words for e_N'. At the receiver, x_{N-1}' is substracted again before usual DPCM decoding. Assuming a positive transmission error in e_N', then x_N' will be larger at the decoder than at the coder. Thus, by the subtraction of x_N' at the decoder in the next step, a decay of the error response is achieved.

For PCM-coded television signals, a bit error rate of less than $5 \cdot 10^{-6}$ is required to provide broadcast quality with imperceptible error patterns. In the case of DPCM-coded television signals, the required bit error rate must be less than 10^{-9} for a DPCM system with one-dimensional prediction and a reflected quantizer, and less than 10^{-7} for DPCM systems with two-dimensional prediction. Experiments have shown that the hybrid DPCM technique provides an additional subjective improvement corresponding to a reduction of the error rate by a factor of about 10 (Brüders et al., 1978).

Assuming a bit error rate of about 10^{-6} for standard digital transmission systems, PCM-coded television signals might be transmitted without error protection techniques; however, DPCM-coded television signals must be protected. Using an error-correcting code of only 3% redundancy for DPCM television coding, a reduction of the bit error rate from 10^{-6} to 10^{-9} has been achieved and appears to be sufficient (Brüders et al., 1978).

For the case of a very high bit error rate of 10^{-2}, Fig. 3-20 shows the improvement obtained by protecting the two most significant bits of a code word by an error-correcting code. Owing to the high bit error rate, however, 25% redundancy is required in this case (Lippmann, 1977).

3.8 SUMMARY

Table 3-5 presents a summary of the bit rates and picture qualities obtained with DPCM coding of gray-tone photographs and monochrome and color television pictures. The grading scale used for the picture quality assessment corresponds to that of the International Radio Consultative Committee and is defined in Table 3-1 (CCIR-Recommendations 500, 1974).

With gray-tone pictures such as photographs, the saving varies in a relatively wide range, mainly depending on the required picture quality and on the picture resolution. Using a DPCM coder with two-dimensional prediction and an adaptive quantizer, which is not the simplest, but still a practical coding system, very high picture quality requirements can be met with 4 bits per picture element. In pictures coded with 3 bits per picture element, distortion is detectable at edges of high contrast. At a bit

FIG. 3-20. Photograph processed with 3-bit DPCM and two-dimensional prediction demonstrating the effect of error protection. (a) Bit error rate 10^{-2}, no error protection; (b) bit error rate 10^{-2}, with error protection of the two most significant bits. (From Lippmann, 1978, unpublished.)

rate of 2 bits or 1 bit per picture element, granular noise in flat areas of the picture is visible. Because of these quality degradations, the lower bit rates will only be of interest for special applications. Degradations become less annoying when the spatial resolution of the picture is increased.

In monochrome broadcast television, a stationary picture is displayed

TABLE 3-5

CODING BITS PER SAMPLE AND PICTURE QUALITY OF DPCM
CODING USING FIXED-LENGTH CODE WORDS

Picture signal	Sampling frequency	Coding bits per sample	Picture quality	Reference
Photographs	8 × 8 picture elements/mm	4	Excellent	From Lippmann,
		3	Good	1978,[a] as used in
		2	Fair	this chapter
		1	Poor	
5-MHz color TV component coding				
Luminance	10 MHz	4	Excellent	Musmann and Erdmann, 1977;
Chrominance	2.63 MHz	4	Good	Sabatier, 1976
		3–4	Good	Netravali and Rubinstein, 1977[b]
5-MHz color TV composite coding	Twice subcarrier frequency	6	Good	Devereux, 1975[a]
	Three times subcarrier frequency	5	Excellent	Thompson, 1975

[a] Unpublished.
[b] Obtained with videotelephone signals.

in the form of a sequence of frames. Owing to camera noise, the quantizing error at a single picture element may change from frame to frame and may produce "busy edges." The human eye is relatively sensitive to these temporarily changing quantizing errors, so that for critical pictures with narrow oblique lines, such as test pictures, a DPCM coder with a two-dimensional predictor and a 32-level quantizer corresponding to 5 bits per picture element is necessary to achieve the same picture quality as with PCM (Thoma, 1974). For encoding natural pictures, the number of quantizing levels can be reduced to 25 levels. Equivalent results have been obtained with an adaptive 4-bit quantizer utilizing spatial masking (Musmann and Erdmann, 1977).

For coding low- and medium-resolution monochrome video telephone signals of 1- or 4-MHz bandwidth, where the quality constraints are less stringent, predictive coders are incorporated into frame replenishment systems to increase the coding efficiency of the frame replenishment technique. These special predictive coding schemes are treated in connection with frame replenishment coding in Chapter 6.

Coding schemes for color broadcast television can be divided into two groups: the component- and the composite-coding methods. In component coding, the three components of a color television signal, the luminance signal and the two chrominance signals, are encoded separately, while in composite coding, the composite color television signal consisting of the luminance signal and the modulated subcarrier of the two chrominance signals is encoded as a single signal. The luminance signal corresponds to the monochrome television signal, and can be encoded with the above-mentioned 4-bit DPCM coder (Musmann and Erdmann, 1977). This coder almost meets the relatively high quality requirements of color broadcast television. For encoding the two chrominance signals, good broadcast quality has been obtained with DPCM coders using one-dimensional prediction and a 4-bit quantizer (Sabatier, 1976). From computer simulations, it can be concluded that two-dimensional prediction will result in almost excellent picture quality (Pirsch and Stenger, 1977). Investigations with adaptive quantizers for the chrominance signals, which are controlled by the luminance signal, indicate that for color broadcast television it also may be possible to reduce the number of coding bits per chrominance sample below 4 bits without decreasing picture quality (Netravali and Rubinstein, 1977). In composite coding, the sampling frequencies are locked to the color subcarrier frequency. Using twice subcarrier frequency sampling and a simple second-previous-element predictor, good picture quality can be achieved with 6-bit quantization (Devereux, 1975a). With three times subcarrier sampling, two-dimensional prediction, and a 5-bit quantizer, broadcast quality can be provided (Thompson, 1975).

Finally, it should be mentioned again, that in general, the bit saving achieved with predictive coding compared to that with PCM depends on the type of pictures to be transmitted, on the picture quality requirements of the user, and on the coding algorithm. If error protection must be provided, the savings are reduced by the share of bits per picture element used for transmission error detection and correction.

References

Barstow, J. B., and Christopher, H. N. (1962). *AIEE Trans. Commun. Electron.* **63**, 313–320.

Bostelmann, G. (1974). *Nachrichtentech. Z* **27**, 115–117.

Brainard, R. C., and Candy, J. C. (1969). *Proc. IEEE* **57**, 776–786.

Brown, E. F. (1969). *Bell Syst. Tech. J.* **48**, 1537–1553.

Brüders, R., Kummerow, T., Neuhold, P., and Stamnitz, P. (1978). "Ein Versuchssystem zur digitalen Übertragung von Fernsehsignalen unter besonderer Berücksichtigung von Übertragungsfehlern." Festschrift 50 Jahre Heinrich-Hertz-Institut, Berlin.

Candy, J. C., and Bosworth, R. H. (1972). *Bell Syst. Tech. J.* **51**, 1495–1516.

Cattermole, K. W. (1969). "Principles of Pulse Code Modulation," Iliffe, London.

CCIR, XIIIth Plenary Assembly (1974). Vol XI, Recommendation 500, Int. Telecommun. Union, Geneva.

Cohen, P., and Adoul, J. P. (1976). *Natl. Telecommun. Conf. Rec.* pp. 6.1-1–6.1-5.

Connor, D. J. (1973). *IEEE Trans. Commun.* **com-21**, 695–706.

Connor, D. J., Pease, R. F., and Scholes, W. G. (1971). *Bell Syst. Tech. J.* **50**, 1049–1061.

Cutler, C. C. (1952). U. S. Patent 2,605,361.

DeJager, F. (1952). *Philips Res. Rep.* **7**, 442–466.

Devereux, V. G. (1973). *BBC Res. Rep.* **1973/6**.

Devereux, V. G. (1975a). *BBC Res. Rep.* **1975/4**.

Devereux, V. G. (1975b). *BBC Res. Rep.* **1975/20**.

Elias, P. (1955). *IRE Trans. Inf. Theor.* **it-1**, 16–32.

Erdmann, W. D. (1978). Dissertation an der Universität Hannover.

Federal Republic of Germany (1977). "Bandwidth and Sampling Rates of Colour-Television Signal Components Considered for Digital Modulation." Contribution to CCIR Question 25-1/11 Standard for Television Systems Using Digital Modulation.

Golding, L. S. (1972). *Proc. Int. Conf. Digital Satellite Commun., 2nd, 1972* pp.384–397.

Graham, R. E. (1958). *IRE WESCON Conv. Rec.* Part 4, pp. 147–157.

Habibi, A. (1971). *IEEE Trans. Commun. Technol.* **19**, 948–956.

Harrison, C. W. (1952). *Bell Syst. Tech. J.* **31**, 764–783.

Iijima, Y., and Ishiguro, T. (1973). *IECE (Jpn.) Commun. Syst. Study Group Monog.* CS73–44.

Iijima, Y., and Suzuki, N. (1974). "Experiments on Higher Order DPCM for NTSC Color Television Signals," report. NEC Cent. Res. Lab.

Iinuma, K., Iijima, Y., Ishiguro, T., Kaneko, H., and Shigaki, S. (1975). *IEEE Trans. Commun.* **com-23**, 1461–1466.

Ishiguro, T., Iinuma, K. Iijima, Y., Koga, T., Azami, S., and Mune, T. (1976). *Natl. Telecommun. Conf., 1976* Vol. 1, pp. 6.4-1–6.4-5.

Jung, P., and Lippmann, R. (1975). *Nachrichtentech. Z.* **28**, 431–436.

Kersten, R., and Dietz, W. (1973). *Int. Elektron. Rundsch.* **27**, 8–12.

Kimme, E. G., and Kuo, F. F. (1963). *IEEE Trans. Circuit Theory* **10**, 405–413.

Kretzmer, E. R. (1952). *Bell Syst. Tech. J.* **31**, 751–763.

Kummerow, T. (1973). *Tagungsber. NTG-Fachtagung "Signalverarbeitung"* pp. 425–439.

Limb, J. O., and Mounts, F. W. (1969). *Bell Syst. Tech. J.* **48**, 2583–2599.

Limb, J. O., Rubinstein, C. B., and Walsh, K. A. (1971). *IEEE Trans. Commun.* **19**, 992–1006.

Lippman, R. (1973). *Proc. Int. Conf. Commun., 1973* pp. 48-12–48-18.

Lippmann, R. (1977). *Acta Electron.* **19**, 289–294.

Max, J. (1960). *IRE Trans. Inf. Theory* **it-6**, 7–12.

Millard, J. B., and Maunsell, H. I. (1971). *Bell Syst. Tech. J.* **50**, 459–497.

Musmann, H. G. (1971a). *Nachrichtentech. Fachber.* **40**, 13–27.

Musmann, H. G. (1971b). *Nachrichtentech. Z.* **24**, 114–116.

Musmann, H. G. (1972). *Natl. Telecommun. Conf. Rec.* pp. 27E-1–27E-6.

Musmann, H. G. (1974). *Proc. Int. Zürich Semin. Digital Commun. 1974,* pp. C1(1)–C1(7).

Musmann, H. G., and Erdmann, W. D. (1977). German Patent Appl. No. P 2740945.6.

Netravali, A. N., and Prasada, B. (1977). *Proc. IEEE* **65**, 536–548.

Netravali, A. N., and Rubinstein, C. B. (1977). *Proc. IEEE* **65**, 1177–1187.

Netravali, A. N., and Rubinstein, C. B. (1978). To be published.

Oliver, B. M. (1952). *Bell Syst. Tech. J.* **31**, 724–750.

O'Neal, J. B. (1966). *Bell Syst. Tech. J.* **45**, 689–721.

O'Neal, J. B. (1967). *Proc. IEEE* **55**, 287–292.

Panter, P. F., and Dite, W. (1951). *Proc. IRE* **39**, 44–48.

Pearson, D. E., Dennis, T. J., and Brown, M. A. (1977). *Abstr. Pict. Cod. Symp., 1977* pp. 129–130.

Pirsch, P., and Stenger, L. (1977). *Acta Electron.* **19**, 277–287.

Rubinstein, C. B., and Limb, J. O. (1972). *IEEE Trans. Commun.* **com-20,** 890–899.

Sabatier, J. (1976). *Acta Electron.* **19**, 245–253.

Sharma, D. K., and Netravali, A. N. (1977). *IEEE Trans. Commun.* **com-25,** 1267–1274.

Thoma, W. (1974). *Proc. Int. Zürich Semin. Digital Commun. 1974* pp. C3(1)–C3(7).

Thompson, J. E. (1972). *IEEE Conf. Publ.* **88,** 26–32.

Thompson, J. E. (1974). *IEEE Trans. Commun.* **com-22,** 1106–1113.

Thompson, J. E. (1975). *Proc. Int. Conf. Digital Satellite Commun., 3rd, 1975* pp. 315–321.

van Buul, M. C. W. (1978). *IEEE Trans. Commun.* **com-26,** 362–368.

Wendt, H. (1973). *Int. Elektron Rundsch.* **27,** 2–7.

Wiener, N. (1949). "Extrapolation, Interpolation and Smoothing of Stationary Time Series." MIT Press, Cambridge, Massachussetts.

Yamada, K., Kinukaba, K., and Sasaki, H. (1977). *Int. Conf. Commun. Rec.* **1,** 76–80.

Zschunke, W. (1977). *IEEE Trans. Commun.* **com-25,** 1295–1302.

Transform Image Coding

ANDREW G. TESCHER

Engineering Sciences Operations
The Aerospace Corporation
Los Angeles, California

Transform image coding was invented in the late 1960s and early 1970s. Initial concepts were based on the Fourier transform (Andrews and Pratt, 1968; Anderson and Huang, 1971; Woods and Huang, 1972), the Hadamard transform (Pratt *et al.*, 1969; Pratt and Andrews, 1972); the Karhunen–Loeve (K–L) transform (Habibi and Wintz, 1971); and the cosine transform (Ahmed *et al.*, 1974). Since then many transform coding algorithms have been developed and analyzed; however, practical implementations have been considered only recently.

The primary purpose of this chapter is to review the progress to date on transform image coding. This is accomplished, in part, through a critical review of research developments in the field. Since a transform coding algorithm requires a relatively complicated implementation, hardware design is also considered. In addition to reviewing the field as it exists, an attempt is made to extrapolate into the future with regard to potential implementation.

Transform techniques are more complex than other conventional and classical data compression algorithms. One should expect excellent performance given the complexity of transform algorithms. It will be demonstrated that, for nonadaptive transform technique implementations, only small future advances are expected. Further additional advances are expected primarily in adaptive techniques.

This chapter consists of four sections. Section 4.1 discusses the basic concepts of transform coding. In Section 4.2, the various adaptivity concepts are developed. Actual adaptivity implementations are described in Section 4.3. The last section provides conclusions.

4.1 Basic Transform Coding Techniques

Several excellent reviews on basic transform image-coding concepts and background material are available (Huang, 1972; Pratt, 1978; Huang and Tretiak, 1972; Huang *et al.,* 1971; Pearson, 1975; Schreiber, 1967; Tescher, 1975, 1976; Wintz, 1972). Consequently, this section is limited to a critical review rather than a comprehensive discussion of all aspects of transform coding. The primary subjects addressed are the actual transform and the quantization and coding of transform coefficients.

4.1.1 Basic Concepts

Transform or block coding is a data compression technique by which a set of source elements is coded as a unit. The term "transform" indicates that the original set of elements is first processed by an invertible mathematical transformation prior to encoding. Figure 4-1 contains the basic block diagram representation of a transform coding–decoding system. The coding unit consists of a reformatting memory followed by the transformation and, finally, the actual coding process. The receiver is the mirror image of the decoder. Motivation for this system is provided by the statistical characterization of typical pictures.

Several recent papers have analyzed the theoretical concepts associated with transform coding (Jain, 1976). However, the original paper by

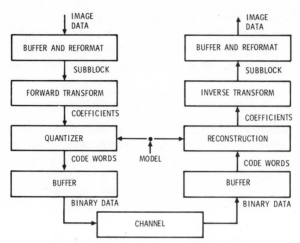

FIG. 4-1.   Basic transform coding system.

Huang and Schultheiss (1963) is still an excellent basic reference for a description of the advantages of certain transformations prior to encoding. The authors demonstrate that for a correlated Gaussian source, optimum encoding consists of two steps. These are the decorrelation process followed by the application of a memoryless quantizer on the output of the transformation. If the Gaussian assumption can be extended to image sources, then the optimum encoding should always first involve a decorrelation procedure. For Gaussian sources, decorrelation implies statistical independence (Papoulis, 1965).

The optimum transform for decorrelation is usually identified as the Karhunen–Loeve or Hoteling transformation (Habibi and Wintz, 1971). Thus, the early concepts indicated the desirability of a decorrelating transform and provided motivation for transform coding.

Other coding aspects can be related to the relationship between compression rate and distortion. Again, the available literature is quite extensive. The primary and obvious consideration is that transform coding introduces a distortion that is a function of the desired compression rate. The understanding of the trade-off between rate R and distortion D will lead to practical procedures; i.e., for an at least locally stationary procedure, the relationship between rate and distortion leads to useful algorithms. It is demonstrated that the rate-versus-distortion formalism is fundamental in the proper design of a highly adaptive coding system. The appropriate formalism is developed as needed for the appropriate adaptive techniques.

Unfortunately, most of the research work has directly related to transform algorithms and not to what should be done once the transformation is accomplished. In the opinion of this author, the emphasis on the transform algorithm, essentially at the expense of the coding procedures, has resulted in a suboptimum level of progress for transform coding.

4.1.2   Review of Classical Techniques

Early research on transform coding primarily concentrated on the transform algorithms. The Fourier transform was found to be a good approximation to the K–L transform. However, the early problem with Fourier techniques involved another classical behavior of Fourier analysis which has been referred to as the Gibbs phenomenon (Bracewell, 1965). This term really refers to a particular behavior of the Fourier transform as a method for the approximation of functions with discontinuities. The Fourier transform, when used for approximation (interpolation), replaces a discontinuity with the average value of the neighborhood of the discontinuity. The discretized implementation of the Fourier transform creates difficulties related to the Gibbs phenomenon.

The Fourier integral is defined over the entire real axis. However, the discrete Fourier series is defined over a finite interval. In application of the Fourier series, it is assumed that the function to be approximated is periodic over the finite interval of the Fourier series. The practical implication is that the numerical Fourier transform assumes that the first and the last points of the basic interval are neighbors. Since the Gibbs phenomenon is applicable to the Fourier series, the discontinuity between beginning and end of the basic period is approximated by the Fourier series with appropriate average values.

In the practical sense, the discontinuity problem of the discrete Fourier transform in early applications of transform coding has been significant. The Fourier transform approximation when used over small blocks produces undesirable blocking effects. Several attempts have been made to minimize this blocking problem (Anderson and Huang, 1971).

In recent years it was realized that significant improvement can be obtained in eliminating the blocking problem by introducing forced symmetry. The basic solution is rather simple. The original subblock is replaced by its symmetrized version, as shown in Fig. 4-2. The Fourier transform is applied to this new larger subblock. Since only the even terms are nonzero, the number of nonzero output elements is identical to the number of input elements. Moreover, this larger subblock has no discontinuities between the appropriate boundary points. Consequently, the modified block structure does not eliminate the Gibbs phenomenon but rather the original discontinuity that creates the Gibbs phenomenon.

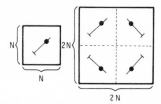

FIG. 4-2. Demonstration of cosine transform symmetry.

It is surprising that this symmetrized approach to Fourier coding was discovered only recently (Ahmed *et al.*, 1974). Recent studies further demonstrate that the cosine transform is virtually identical to the K–L transform for numerous practical conditions for which the Markovian-type source assumption is valid (Jain, 1976).

The cosine transform, unlike the K–L transform, can be implemented numerically through a "fast" transform. More important, the cosine transform virtually approaches the K–L transform performance with neither utilization nor knowledge of the source correlation. For the K–L transform, the source covariance model must be available to derive the actual transform matrix.

The cosine transform is a strictly deterministic transform. Conversely, the K–L transform is a class of transformation, and for each application it is a function of the appropriate covariance matrix. It is a significant practical benefit that the single deterministic transformation closely approaches in performance the entire class of theoretical optimum transformations.

The considerable amount of past research effort involving the various types of transforms appears to be of somewhat questionable value. Early techniques included utilization of several transforms, including the slant, Hadamard, and a large class of transforms that can be derived from the first two transforms (Dail, 1976; Pratt *et al.*, 1974; Andrews, 1975). Earlier discovery of the cosine transform would have likely reduced interest in other transform types.

The transform research may be summarized by two conclusions: (1) No deterministic transform has equaled the performance of the cosine transform; (2) no theoretical justification was offered in the first place as to why the "other" transforms should be beneficial.

When this author attempted, at an earlier date, to produce a theoretical justification for the Walsh functions, the only reason he could find was that these functions were similar to the Fourier basic functions (Tescher, 1973). Thus, the Hadamard/Walsh techniques succeed as essentially ad hoc approximations to the Fourier/cosine techniques. A further fundamental observation is that, unlike the Fourier transform, the various other transforms will not asymptotically approach the K–L transform performance with increasing transform sizes.

Two other considerations of transform algorithms are computability and size. Under computability, the complexity of the potential device for implementation of the transform is defined. Fortunately, except for the general K–L transform, most of the useful transformations are implementable via fast algorithms such as the fast Fourier transform algorithm (Cooley and Tukey, 1965). The suboptimal Hadamard and Haar can be implemented without multiplication. For specialized applications, a computationally more efficient transform, even at the expense of performance loss, may be preferred. For example, the significantly suboptimal Haar transform can be implemented through a fast algorithm without any multiplication. On the other hand, various hybrid implementations for the cosine transform, e.g., through charge-coupled-device (CCD) technology, minimize the advantages of the suboptimal transform (Whitehouse et al., 1975).

Transform size is an important practical consideration. The argument is often made that no benefit is obtained by choosing transforms larger than the image correlation distance, assuming that it is known. This approach is artificial and ignores the fact that a transform decorrelates only the pixels within a subblock. It will not decorrelate pixels among subblocks. A typical subblock consists of 8×8 or 16×16 pixels. The appropriate reasoning is that the image correlation is not likely to exceed 8 or 16 pixels, respectively. Although this reasoning has not been challenged, it is not valid. Even if all pixels within the transform block become decorrelated via the transformation, the pixels on the border remain correlated with respect to pixels on the borders of adjacent subblocks. Consequently, the argument against using large subblocks to achieve improved image decorrelation is not proper, as it is based on the correlation distance. Recent work with relatively large-size (256×256) transforms has demonstrated significant performance gains over small-size implementations (Tescher, 1973; Tescher and Andrews, 1974). However, for practical reasons, it is advantageous not to exceed 16×16 or 32×32 size.

An additional argument against the larger size is the concept of adaptivity. It is still an unresolved question how to optimize the transform size both to achieve maximum decorrelation and yet include adaptivity consideration dependent on local image structure. These two concepts are contradictory, and the solution is not at all obvious. To obtain maximum decorrelation, increasing block size is beneficial. Conversely, to adapt to the local image structure, a smaller block size is preferred. In addition, the overhead associated with an adaptive transform algorithm is likely to become more important with decreasing transform block sizes.

In summary, three primary considerations relate to transform size. Larger sizes minimize block-to-block correlation. Adaptive procedures are likely to favor smaller sizes. Finally, the overhead information per subblock should not exceed a reasonable fraction of the available bandwidth.

Another potential study relates to the (spatial) shift variance impact of the transform. In general, transform coding is a shift-variant procedure. The degree of shift variance is a function of the transform size as well as of the local image origin. Consideration of the shift variance problem has been generally ignored. An example of a simple shift-variant filtering is the removal of the visually undesirable blocking introduced at extreme compression rates. The required filter will only smooth block boundaries without much processing within blocks.

The general effect of quantization of the source is a primary consideration for all source-coding procedures. Quantization is the noninvertible mapping from the analog source to its quantized equivalent. Thus, the originally continuous parameters will be represented by integers. In general, the quantizer is the major error source in image coding. All other error sources, such as numerical round-off, are negligible in most instances. If not, they can be minimized or even eliminated by increasing register sizes and by using integer arithmetic. However, quantization is a fundamental distortion, and in most cases it is unavoidable.

A quantizer is a mapping from the continuous variable domain of transform coefficients into the domain of integers. These integers become the code words that are transmitted through the channel (O'Neal, 1971). An alternative superior approach is a two-phase coding technique in which the integers are the secondary input into an entropy coding processor. The output of this coder generates the final code words to be transmitted through the channel. The two-phase coding approach has not been pursued, except for the work of Tasto and Wintz (1971). Practical difficulty with entropy coding is that it is an open-loop procedure.

The quantizer output is an integer that is also the code word for one-step coding. The relevant optimization procedure is the minimization of mean-square error between original and quantized coefficients. Since all practical transform coding systems utilize unitary transforms, the mean-square error is preserved under the transformation. Thus, quantizer optimization in the transform domain guarantees optimum spatial domain performance in the minimum-mean-square-error sense.

For a given transform domain model, the quantization parameters are easily obtained via the Max (1960) quantizer algorithm. Knowledge of the probability density function of the random variable for a specified number of quantization bins permits computation of the required thresholds and reconstruction levels through the Max algorithm or approximations (Panther and Dite, 1951).

The actual coefficient quantization is performed in two steps: (1) the coefficient is normalized by its estimated variance; (2) the normalized variable is processed by the optimum quantizer based on the modeled probability density function of unit variance. The number of bits for a quantized coefficient is determined by relating the assumed prequantized variance to distortion. The result can be derived through several different ways, including formal rate distortion theory (Habibi, 1975b). To maintain equal distortion for each quantized coefficient, the required number of quantization bins should be proportional to the standard deviation of the quantity to be quantized. Thus, the appropriate bit assignment procedure follows directly from this argument. The coefficients are generally assumed to be Gaussian random variables. In recent experiments, the exponential density function has been found more appropriate (Tescher and Cox, 1976).

It should be noted that the Max quantizer minimizes the global error between input and output, usually mean-square error. A more difficult problem is accurate determination of the prequantizer normalization factor. This problem reduces to the establishment of a transform domain statistical model. Most investigators assume the Markov correlation model for the image from which the generalized power spectral density is derived. This model is convenient and only requires either one or two parameters. For the two-parameter case, the image correlation in orthogonal directions is assumed to be different. The required normalization factors also can be obtained directly from a class of images through a learning procedure in which the appropriate transform coefficients of one or several images are averaged in the root-mean-square sense. This approach is found to be superior to the Markov model, and it produces the required normalization parameters directly.

A disadvantage of the second approach is that transmission of the normalization parameters may significantly tax the available bandwidth. For a separate training set, a mismatch may develop between the training set and the image to be coded. The logistics of determining the normalization parameters for different image classes may become substantial.

An alternative technique by Tescher (1973) requires no *a priori* development of normalization parameters. The necessary parameters are obtained recursively from previously quantized transform coefficients and may be determined in real time. Although the early work was promising, it has not been pursued by other researchers primarily because of its complexity. The implementation was over large transforms. It was also an open-loop procedure; thus, the actual compression rate could not be specified in advance. These early problems have been resolved, and the procedure is discussed in Section 4.2.4.

Since the recursive model is attractive for image compression, its theoretical advantages should be discussed. The previous two quantization models (the Markov and the training set model) are utilized in deterministic fashion. In contrast, the recursive model considers the normalization parameters to be a set of highly correlated random variables. The recursive model generates the normalization parameters from the values already decoded. Thus, the recursive approach to transform image coding allows an improved utilization of the transform domain without any overhead and prior model assumptions.

Several additional considerations should be mentioned. Clearly, the mathematical complexity has increased for the recursive technique. Both the estimation procedure and the determination of the number of bits for each coefficient require real-time computation. The same hardware must also be included in the decoder since it performs the same recursive computation. The results of the computation in the decoder must be identical to that of the coder; otherwise, synchronization loss may develop. This requirement implies not only performance of the identical estimator procedures, but also implementation of the appropriate algebraic steps in the identical order. The potential problem is that the round-off error may produce different bit assignments between the coder and decoder. This technique, like all variable-rate adaptive techniques, is sensitive to channel errors. Thus, potential propagation of catastrophic errors must be avoided by periodic resynchronization.

Thus far in the discussion, no attempt has been made to specify the transformation. However, one could argue that the quantization model and its subsequent utilization are at least as important as the transform itself. The various quantization models are equally applicable to all transformations.

The importance of the proper quantization procedure cannot be overemphasized. The cosine transform decorrelates most practical types of imagery. Both theoretically and practically, the cosine transform closely approximates the K–L transform performance for reasonable block sizes of 8×8 pixels or greater. Thus, little, if any, additional gain can be obtained by the optimization of the transform itself. The real gain is in the modeling and the appropriate quantization strategy (Reader, 1975; Reis *et al.*, 1976). Entropy coding (Huffman, 1952) and/or carefully designed quantization strategy is more important than optimization of transforms.

A practical difficulty with conventional entropy coding is that it does not guarantee a specific rate. It may not even achieve bandwidth compression. The generalized adaptive coding strategy is also applicable to entropy coding. Conventional open-loop entropy coding can be converted into a closed-loop system through the generalized adaptive model.

For historical completeness, the threshold coding system should be mentioned (Anderson and Huang, 1971). In this system, only those coefficients that exceed a fixed threshold are quantized. Unfortunately, threshold coding possesses many undesirable features. It is open loop and highly error sensitive. Its coefficient modeling is poor, since each coefficient is processed by the same quantizer if it is above the threshold. Also, specification of the coefficients to be transmitted requires considerable overhead. Threshold coding approximates entropy coding in complexity, without benefits of the latter technique.

4.1.3   Image Quality Degradation

For image coding, in general, and transform coding, in particular, image quality measures that quantitatively correlate well with subjective judgments of perceived image degradation introduced by the coder are unavailable. Conventional measures, such as the mean-square error and its derivatives (e.g., the weighted mean-square error), are helpful for comparison purposes. However, these measures are limited, in an absolute sense. Even without useful quantitative measures, degradation associated with transform coding can be discussed.

Three classes of degradations can be identified: (1) transform coefficients are replaced by their quantized equivalent; (2) some of the coefficients are replaced by zero (in effect, a great deal of the bandwidth compression is the result of this low-pass filtering); (3) the transform coding procedure is not shift invariant. The processing is performed over adjacent blocks, which may produce visually undesirable blocking effects. If a new global origin is chosen for the process, the results are different.

Visually, these effects can be separated in most instances. Coefficient quantization introduces apparent additional image noise. Replacement of coefficients by zero in the decoder is a low-pass-filtering effect. The decoded image compared with the original image may lose some of its details. Low-pass filtering is rather noticeable at low data rates. Although this effect is transform dependent even for the cosine transform at low rates, the visual blocking at the transform boundaries is clearly undesirable. The term "low bit rate" indicates that only a small fraction of coefficients, say 10%, will be transmitted. The same problem is further magnified with suboptimal transforms. For the Fourier transform, the

Gibbs phenomenon was discussed earlier in the chapter. The cosine transform is less sensitive to this blocking effect. However, in the limit, it also introduces blocking.

Although reliable mathematical measures are not available, techniques that indicate image quality degradation in the decoded image in comparison with the original are available. The "error image" consisting of the absolute value of the difference between the original image and the decoded image is useful. For display purposes, the error image is usually scaled by a factor of from 10 to 40. If the information loss is small, the information present in the error image should also be small. For a high-quality coding system, the error image will appear to be white noise.

4.1.4   Implementation Consideration

In order to establish a framework within which several different and possibly competing designs can be compared, it is necessary to define certain evaluation criteria. It is attempted here to present a somewhat simplified by practical demonstration of various theoretical information concepts. The concepts are presented as subsequent aids for trade-off analyses of various designs. The following three primary quantities or parameters are considered: cost C, distortion D, and rate R. Of these quantities, only the rate is well defined; it will always refer to the appropriate channel operation rate.

The term "distortion" is somewhat ambiguous. Frequently, this parameter is defined as the mean-square error. In subsequent discussions in this chapter, the distortion parameter provides the mechanism by which the rate is controlled.

The "cost" is difficult to define. It can be defined in several different, although related, ways. Cost may imply financial investment in the design and hardware complexity. In many cases, an adaptive technique by itself may not be too complicated. However, the required channel protection necessitates added complexity which must be factored into the overall design.

To be meaningful, the distortion measure should be related to image quality. In general, reasonable correlation exists between distortion and what appears to be a perceived image quality measure. The following conclusion may be drawn. Regardless of cost, with coding at a fixed rate, the attainable distortion or, equivalently, image quality is restricted to a certain range. In order words, only limited gain is achieved by going to more complex designs. Equivalently, for a desired image quality and rate, the design may be rather expensive. It suffices to say that the cost aspects are complex and numerous. A fair portion of cost analysis to date is either of questionable value because of the rapidly changing hardware technology or irrelevant because of the context in which it was made. For example, in transform coding, it is necessary to reformat the image into blocks inasmuch as the normal ordering of picture elements (pixels or pels) follows the conventional raster scan. The input requirement by the transform coder necessitates a block ordering. This consideration is unimportant for a video-type implementation. However, the appropriate memory consideration for reformatting becomes a major cost factor in the case of large-size image formats.

Technology advances in terms of special-purpose analog devices and general digital equipment have created a significant change in the attitude of designers as to what is reasonable to compute in a practical device. It was only a few years ago that implementation of a sinusoidal type of transform for a practical device was totally unacceptable, primarily on the basis of cost. But, based on current technology, the same computation may represent only a fraction of the cost associated with complicated coding equipment. The complexity associated with reformatting is probably more demanding for large-size image formats.

4.1.5 Implementation Concepts

Up to this point, the design constraints introduced have been in terms of basic parameters of the coding process. It is important also to consider building blocks of the coding device from the standpoint of both general availability and hardware complexity. In general, the following device considerations apply: memory, arithmetic operations, control units, and auxiliary operations. Superficially, these concepts also would be utilized for the design of a computer.

The similarity is not really surprising. An image-coding algorithm implemented in the digital domain is functionally a special-purpose computer. However, fundamental laws of information theory also explicitly apply for a data compression device. Thus, despite the willingness to apply high-speed arithmetic operations, the potential performance gain in additional compression may not be too significant. On the other hand, basic concepts associated with the compression device can be functionally described in terms of computer terminology, such as memory management and arithmetic operations.

Another general concept of significant importance is the relative complexity between the compressor and the expander. For most implementations, the compressor is likely to be more complicated than the decoder. The reasons are fundamental. The decoder is slaved to the coder; it can make no independent decisions. Conversely, the coding device has not only the same information available to the decoder, it has access to the original source. Consequently, it has the option of making decisions based on the availability of the original image.

The distinction in complexity between coder and decoder is not particularly significant for nonadaptive algorithms. It becomes rather important for adaptive procedures. For more complex and sophisticated compression schemes, the coder is likely to be significantly more complex than the decoder. Although this observation is useful for the design of image-coding systems, it is unfortunate that for most difficult image-coding problems, the coder is more constrained than the decoder. The usual constraints are hardware utilization, power consumption, etc. Two obvious examples are satellite applications, such as Landsat and the remotely piloted vehicle. For these applications, the coder complexity is severely limited. Conversely, the decoding process can allow for relatively greater complexity (Habibi, 1975a; Habibi and Samulon, 1975).

For completeness, analog transform implementation should be mentioned. The CCD technology allows analog implementation of various transform types (Buss *et al.*, 1975). This interesting development is beneficial to data-processing applications involving large-size transforms. For realistic transform coding algorithms, the benefits are marginal, since large transform sizes and the associated high number of arithmetic operations are not justified. For specialized implementations with stringent power and weight requirements, an analog approach might be appropriate.

4.1.6 Fundamental Limitations of Nonadaptive Transform Coding

Various degradations associated with transform coding are described in previous sections. For a nonadaptive technique with a specified rate, the degradations are essentially unavoidable. Except for changing the bit rate, these degradations are deterministic. A nonadaptive algorithm is designed to be a fixed coding algorithm operating identically for all images and all image regions.

For a nonadaptive technique, the image to be coded is assumed to be a stationary source. Were the stationarity assumption valid, a nonadaptive coder could be an optimal image coder. In general, the stationarity assumption is poor.

Images usually have different statistical structures, both from image to image as well as within an image. Image nonstationarity results not only from scene nonstationarity but also from the imaging process itself. An imaging device projects a three-dimensional scene onto a two-dimensional plane. Consequently, those parts of the image in focus require high fidelity and, equivalently, a substantial portion of the available bandwidth. Those segments that are out of focus (say, the background) appear to be blurred, thus requiring only a small fraction of the bandwidth.

This qualitative discussion suggests that the stationarity model for image coding might be a severe design limitation. In his review, Wintz (1972) indicated that nonadaptive transform coding is of little, if any, benefit over other conventional but simpler image-coding techniques (Habibi, 1971). The real gain is in adaptivity. Unfortunately, research advances obtained to date are limited. In the next section, primary concentration is on nonstationary models, algorithm implementations, and relevant concepts.

4.2 TRANSFORM CODING ADAPTIVITY CONCEPTS

Several years ago, Wintz (1972) urged the implementation of adaptive techniques. In this review, over five years later, it would be pleasing to report that numerous algorithms and implementations dealing with adaptivity now exist. Unfortunately, this situation has not developed. Most systems that have been designed are nonadaptive.

In this section, the principles of adaptivity are reviewed and various implementation methods are discussed. Unfortunately, the available literature on which to base this analysis is rather limited, and the following discussion is heavily based on the author's own research.

4.2.1 Nonstationary Image Model Considerations

Here, the assumption is made that imagery as a source should be modeled as a nonstationary representation. Consequently, coding procedures, which to a large extent freeze the algorithm, are not appropriate. In the following discussions, the image-coding model is part of the information to be utilized by the decoder. This fact does not necessarily indicate that new or additional modeling information must be transmitted to the decoder. For an efficient system, the modeling information can, and should, be derivable from previously decoded information.

The basic assumption is made that the image-coding procedure is the transmission of fluctuation information about a preassigned model. However, this model is part of the information to be transmitted. Ideally, the model would permit local changes through parameterization. More important, it would assist in meaningful redistribution of the available bandwidth among partitions of the image.

Before proceeding with various adaptive algorithms, it is necessary to review the impact of a realistic communication system model as a constraint.

4.2.2   Communication Model as a Practical Constraint

Although image coding is applicable for nonreal-time applications such as storing pictorial information on magnetic tape, the primary application is real-time image transmission through communication channels. Thus, the image coder must be consistent with the constraints of a realistic communication model.

With increasing adaptivity, the coder output will fluctuate in rate if the adaptivity permits a variable-rate compressor. The relevant problem is how to interface the variable-rate compressor with the fixed-rate channel. For a variable-rate compressor, communications model constraints become a necessary consideration. In principle, the solution is simple. The compressor (source encoder) must be interfaced with the communication channel through a rate-equalizing buffer. This buffer permits the deviation in bits from the average rate as required. However, the practical solution is somewhat involved.

Another practical consideration for a communication channel relates to channel errors. The various applicable channel coding techniques can be classified into two groups: In one case, through algebraic coding, channel errors are essentially eliminated. In the other case, a fixed, nonnegligible rate of channel errors, including catastrophic errors, is permitted. However, periodic reinitialization of the algorithm is performed.

In general, it is difficult to evaluate the impact of channel errors for adaptive procedures. Erroneous bits may be significantly important, particularly for overhead information. On the other hand, erroneous bits that result only in incorrect reconstruction of a single transform coefficient may result in relatively minor image degradation. Consequently, the primary impact of a communication system is the need to interface the inherently fixed-rate transmission system with a locally fluctuating-rate source-encoding system. The appropriate problem is to design a global fixed-rate system that is highly rate adaptive locally.

4.2.3   Types of Adaptivity

Adaptivity procedures can be classified into two broad categories. For the first, the source-coder rate is constant. However, various other coder parameters are changing. For the second, in addition to other parameters, the local compression rate is also variable. The second adaptivity category involves implementation difficulty because of the varying rate.

In addition to classification according to rate, other considerations are appropriate. For a highly adaptive system, the degree of adaptivity or the number of different ways the coder can operate may be either a large number or essentially a continuous parameter. In this case, the overhead information needed by the decoder to determine the operation mode should be decodable from previously decoded data. Otherwise, the transmitted overhead would require a greater fraction of the available bandwidth.

A somewhat simplified adaptivity procedure may allow a few operational modes, say four, and within each class the appropriate coding algorithm may be considered to be a nonadaptive procedure. This type of approach has several advantages despite its limitations. Basically, for a small number of algorithm modes, one designs several independent coding algorithms corresponding to the different classes, Thus, except for determining within which class the algorithm currently operates, the decoder is essentially nonadaptive.

The appropriate modeling is similar to a Markov chain. For each subblock, the source corresponds to one of the states of the Markov chain, and the coder processes the data according to the same state classification. For the four-class example, two bits must be allocated for overhead per subblock. Consequently, the available bandwidth is primarily utilized for the transmission of transform coefficients for any reasonable-size transform block, say 8×8 or larger.

4.2.4   Buffering Concepts

Variable-rate source-coding techniques require rate-equalizer buffers. Since the communication channel operates at a fixed rate, the source-coder rate fluctuation must be absorbed.

A general model of a variable-rate system is shown in Fig. 4-3. The rate-equalizing buffer is implemented between the source coder and the channel. The important consideration is how the source-coding system controls gross parameters of the decoder. In a realistic system the source coder cannot operate at variable rates without some externally controlled mechanism. An open-loop source-coding system is not acceptable. This statement is consistent with the assumed philosophy of nonstationarity. Even for a variable-rate system, image nonstationarity may be more extreme than what the rate-equalizer buffer could allow without an additional controlling mechanism.

In any transform coding system (Fig. 4-1) some form of a "pre buffer"

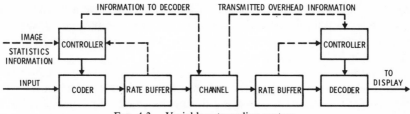

Fɪɢ. 4-3.   Variable-rate coding system.

is required to perform the image reformatting into subblocks. For a variable-rate system, an additional buffer is required to accommodate source-coder fluctuations. The basic problem is to determine how to control the overall coding parameters in terms of utilization of the various buffers. Two general solutions are available. The first approach uses the reformatting buffer to control the coding parameters, while the second approach uses the rate-equalizer buffer in a feedback loop. The two techniques are not equivalent. The first technique is logically easy to understand; however, it is less efficient. Here, the reformatting buffer serves as a control mechanism. Although general designs are deferred to Section 4.3.3, the principle of buffer control is introduced here.

It is assumed that the adaptivity procedure is not applied to the entire image, but is restricted to only that portion of the image that instantaneously resides in the reformatting buffer. Consequently, each image segment corresponding to the prebuffer is transmitted at a fixed rate corresponding to the required channel rate.

Larger reformatting buffers result in more adaptive systems. For conventional raster-type image structure, the transform blocks are $N \times N$ subblocks. Thus, the minimum prebuffer size is N lines. For a 512×512 image, with 16×16 transform subblocks, adaptivity is implemented over 32 subblocks. The result is a significant redistribution of the available bandwidth over a reasonable image size. If each image segment corresponding to the prebuffer is coded at the channel rate, the coding system operates at the appropriate channel rate.

The logical operational approach is to code the entire prebuffer and to place the output into the "postbuffer." By design, the postbuffer is filled if the ratio of memory sizes is equal to the appropriate ratio associated with the image compression. The compressed data may be transmitted through the channel at its fixed rate. A short delay will develop corresponding to coding the image segment that fills the prebuffer. For a practical implementation, two memories could be used. While compressed data are transmitted from the equalizer buffer, another compressor operates on another identical prebuffer. The delay is also a result of the finite time required for classification. The reformatting operation time can be minimized. Each line segment can be placed in the proper location of the prebuffer in real time. Thus, after the last segment is available, the coder can immediately begin its operation.

However, the controller must examine the entire image region residing in the reformatting buffer in order to arrive at the correct control parameter. Hence, the engineering design must take into consideration two types of delays. One delay is associated with image line reformatting into subblocks; additional delays are required by the controller. Thus, the controller should be fast, because during the operation additional buffering arrangement must be made to accept incoming data.

Increasing the region over which the algorithm is adaptive can be accomplished only by increasing the reformatting buffer. For example, to double the adaptivity area, the prebuffer size must also be doubled. It should be noted that the prebuffer contains the image in full resolution. An increase in prebuffer size refers to the original image representation. The smallest prebuffer size is determined by the minimum needed for reformatting. It is N lines for an $N \times N$ transform coder.

The general concept of prebuffering may be understood by referring to Fig. 4-4. Several nonoverlapping image segments, which reside one at a time in the prebuffer, are shown with appropriate D-versus-R figures. For each image segment, a distortion measure is associated with the compression rate. The distortion parameter may be considered as a global parameter for that image region. This parameter controls the algorithm to yield the required rate for the particular segment. For a nonstationary model, the appropriate D-versus-R curves are different for various regions. The

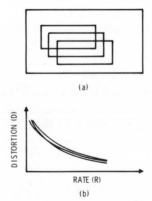

(a)

(b)

Fig. 4-4.   Effect of nonoverlapped segments on distortion-rate function. (a) Segments; (b) function.

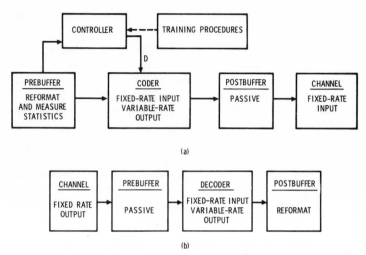

(a)

(b)

FIG. 4-5. Variable-rate coding system utilizing prebuffering. (a) Coder; (b) decoder.

controller must determine for the image segment residing in the prebuffer the corrected D parameter that yields the required global rate. Specific designs are considered in Section 4.3.3. A schematic representation of a prebuffer-based coding–decoding system is shown in Fig. 4-5.

A potentially negative aspect of prebuffer utilization is the effect of image quality discontinuity between adjacent image segments. This statement is more understandable through a specific simple example. In Fig. 4-6, a small area A, corresponding to a transform block, may be present in two different image regions which occupied the reformatting buffer at different times. By assumption, one region is "busy" and the other one is "quiet." In the busy region, fewer bits will be available for A than in the quiet image region. If the same subblocks are also adjacent to each other, the apparent image quality associated with them will be significantly dif-

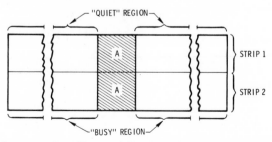

FIG. 4-6. Demonstration of image quality discontinuity effect in prebuffering variable-rate coding system.

ferent because in one case the coder allocated more bits to the equivalent
subblock than it did in the other case.

The prebuffer segments the image into nonoverlapping regions corresponding to the reformatting buffer size or its multiple. It performs a
rate-controlling function for each nonoverlapping region. A controller design through a reformatting buffer is inflexible. This system is heavily
image format dependent. Furthermore, it is not easily adaptable to an
image-coding application for varying image sizes. The prebuffering concept eliminates the difficulties associated with an open-loop operation.
However, difficulties and disadvantages remain with a prebuffer utilization. Another buffering approach, postbuffering, eliminates most of these
disadvantages.

A postbuffer control communication system utilizing adaptive transform coding is illustrated in Fig. 4-7. It should be noted that although advantages are highly applicable to transform coding, this approach to adaptive coding is general. Thus, the same concept is equally applicable to
transform and other coding procedures where "feedback" is implemen-

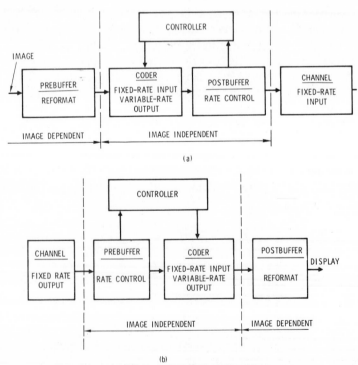

FIG. 4-7.   Variable-rate coding system utilizing postbuffering. (a) Coder; (b) decoder.

table. Utilization of a rate-equalizer buffer with feedback is not a new concept; however, the mode of feedback mechanism implementation is novel.

The necessary solution involves modification of the distortion parameter based on an image region that previously resided in the equalizer buffer. The representation of the D-versus-R curve earlier introduced will be utilized. Figure 4-8 provides an example for the case of overlapped image segments. The controller constantly adjusts the appropriate distortion parameter to yield the required rate.

The basic problem is how to deal with nonstationarity for overlapping image regions. For each region, one must approximate the D-versus-R curve. Subsequently, the correct distortion parameter to yield the appropriate rate is determined. By design, adjacent image regions significantly overlap. For example, two adjacent image regions (say, A and B) contain a common area exceeding 95% of each segment. For this example, the appropriate D-versus-R curves will only vary a small amount between the two segments. This result is expected since, except for a 5% fraction of each segment, the two are identical. One may assume that the appropriate distortion parameter is available for segment A. Within that segment, utilization of the appropriate D parameter yields the required rate. Note that the local fluctuation is not constrained. One attempts to have global control parameters for segment A, which on the average yields the correct rate. For segment B, it is reasonable to utilize the same distortion parameter. Therefore, by design, the controller chooses that distortion term for segment B. The coder will process the input for a small fraction of that segment.

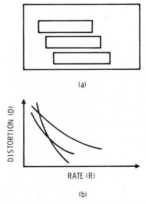

(a)

(b)

FIG. 4-8.   Effect of overlapped segments on distortion-rate function. (a) Segments; (b) function.

At the conclusion of coding of the last small segment, the average rate over the past image segment will differ from the desired rate. Thus, the rate-equalizer buffer acquires a small bias. Consequently, the distortion parameter must be modified to adjust the rate properly. Furthermore, the coder must also be adjusted to counteract the bias in the rate-equalizer buffer.

Operationally, the continuous D-versus-R curve does not exist. But the coder can estimate the desired D value by linear interpolation of D-versus-R data samples based on previous coder operation. Estimation could also be extended to the differential of this curve. The given approach could be implemented by methods of Kalman filtering; however, this has not yet been attempted. The estimation procedure, in general, requires a local estimate of both the distortion parameter and its change of rate with respect to R. Since for a practical communication system the differential will have the same sign, a simplified estimator could be utilized.

The indicated conceptual procedure is a buffering technique that utilizes the important parameters, i.e., the buffer size and its projections into the image. This technique is stable because variations in buffer status are immediately fed back into the control operation.

Before specific implementations are considered, the general usefulness of the discussed approach can be compared with the controlling operation through prebuffering. The coding mechanism via postbuffering is highly flexible. Except for the reformatting buffer, the system is completely format independent. The reformatting buffer performs no controlling operation. Consequently, the coder can be utilized for different image formats by modifying the reformatter. This consideration may be important if a general adaptive transform coder is to be developed. Since this system will be of considerable complexity, it would be desirable to use the same design for various applications, including different image types and formats.

The coder operates with one block of data at one time; therefore, the postbuffering concept can be extended to include several multiplexed coders that utilize a single postbuffer. The postbuffer controls each coder. Each transform block is treated independently by the coder. Similarly, the coder may operate on subblocks in a nonsequential order. The rate fluctuation from block to block will, of course, differ for an alternate ordering; however, the coding efficiency should remain the same. This consideration is not entirely artificial. Transform coding requires a considerable number of arithmetic operations. At video rates, this requirement may be quite demanding. In order to reduce the effective computation rate, several coders may multiplex their output into a single rate buffer.

Another observation is that unlike the case of prebuffer control, no discontinuity in image quality among different image regions develops as a result of adaptive coding. The distortion parameter D is updated continuously. Two similar adjacent subblocks are not likely to be coded differently because of discontinuity in the D parameter. To minimize the problem of image quality discontinuity, the postbuffer should be sufficiently large, say two or more image strips.

Memory utilization is improved through postbuffer control as compared to that with prebuffering. The postbuffer control operates through the compressed image, unlike the prebuffer control. To improve adaptivity with postbuffer control is less demanding, since the necessary buffer increase is in terms of a compressed image.

Another advantage of postbuffer control is parallel controller operation. By design, this function may be simultaneously performed with the coding operation. Consequently, the requirement for additional buffering to permit the controller to determine the appropriate distortion parameter is not necessary.

The controller updates the distortion parameter in parallel significantly less frequently than the actual arithmetic operation rate required for the coder. Thus, the computational requirement for the controlling system is limited. It should also be noted that the buffer control is strictly based on buffer behavior, and the required information is based on previously transmitted data. Since the decoder performs the same function, the entire control operation can be performed with no overhead.

4.2.5 Learning Procedures

Compressional algorithms with separate adaptivity classes require pretraining prior to actual coding. For these algorithms, a parameterization is required in order to relate to local image structure. In order to perform the adaptive coding, it is necessary to develop techniques that meaningfully assign the mode of the image coder to one of the available classes.

In general, it is necessary to develop training procedures that yield the appropriate coding classes. Thus, prior to the actual coding, a training procedure must be implemented. The result of this training of the coder must also be available to the decoder as well. It requires considerable overhead to transmit this information. Consequently, the training procedure is not likely to be performed frequently.

Alternatively, several types of training images may be available to both coder and decoder. When a specific image is coded prior to transmission of the compressed image, the required parameters are specified by indicating the appropriate training image.

Performance variation of an adaptive technique based on classification procedures, which, in turn, are based on "typical" image identification, makes evaluation of the adaptive algorithm difficult. First, one must evaluate the capability and performance of the algorithm. Second, the algorithm sensitivity to the specification of typical image sets should be considered. Thus, an efficient compression algorithm can become suboptimal. The implementation can be significantly degraded if a mismatch develops between the image to be coded and the image that was used for training.

Adaptive techniques with a fixed number of operating modes are attractive. The overall system complexity must include the training procedures, and consequently it becomes rather involved. An equivalent adaptive technique that eliminates the training procedure is discussed in Section 4.3. Although the source-coder complexity increases, the overall system complexity is reasonable. Besides a higher degree of coder adaptivity, the need for training procedures is eliminated.

4.2.6 Classifiers

In this section, the discussion is limited to adaptive techniques that utilize a finite number of classes. For each class, a different coding mode is utilized. The conceptual difference between a classification process, which is a response to local image structure fluctuation over subblock size, and buffer control should be noted. The latter function operates over much larger image regions. It introduces a small perturbation in the coding process to achieve the necessary fixed-rate output averaged over many subblocks.

To perform the classification, the coding algorithm performs some measurement, and through an appropriate deterministic procedure each subblock is assigned to one of the finite number of classes. The considerable amount of research in pattern recognition performed to date has had little or no impact on transform image-coding algorithms.

Two types of simple classifiers have been developed. Only one has been used extensively. The first classification process utilizes the subblock energy as primary input to the classifier algorithm. Tasto and Wintz (1971), as well as Chen and Smith (1976), utilized this local energy concept to perform the classification process. In both cases, the local ac energy (e.g., pixel variance of subblocks) is deterministically mapped onto a small set of integers representing the finite number of classes.

The energy concept appears reasonable. It is indicative of subblock busyness. For a unitary transformation, energy is an invariant parameter. However, energy in the transform domain is primarily represented by a few transform low-order coefficients only. Consequently, an energy-based classification procedure does not properly assign the available bandwidth among the various classes, since the relevant decision is based on the magnitude of a few low-order coefficients.

A recently proposed classification procedure utilizes the sum of the logarithms of coefficient magnitudes (Melzer, 1977). This quantity can be interpreted to be image entropy. Thus, the classification decision is made on local entropy. It should be noted that zero-order entropy in the transform domain closely approximates image entropy, since the coefficients are nearly decorrelated. For this second procedure, the classifier specifies classes in accordance with local entropy.

Classification includes bit allocation as well. The classifier specifies two sets of matrices, representing the normalization factors for coefficients and the appropriate bit assignment. The latter two quantities can be determined independently through training procedures. For a K-class classifier, K normalization matrices and K-bit-assignment matrices are required. Alternatively, first the normalization matrices are obtained. The bit assignment matrices are derived from the normalization matrices according to the standard rule (Habibi and Wintz, 1971). The distortion parameter D is determined such that the required number of bits is achieved. Specific implementations are considered in Section 4.3.3.

Although the concepts discussed are independently straightforward, the various quantities must be related to each other. The classification must be jointly considered with different buffering procedures.

Classification with subblock energy can be performed prior to transformation. Consequently, it can be performed as part of the controlling function for buffer control, using the prebuffering concept.

For classification in the transform domain using local entropy, the same procedure becomes rather involved with the prebuffering concept. The primary problem is to perform buffer control. It is necessary to operate simultaneously on all blocks residing in the prebuffer. Before the controlling function can be implemented, all subblocks must be transformed. Therefore, the requirement develops for another large buffer in which the transform blocks of the prebuffer must be stored.

However, if rate control is achieved by the postbuffering technique, the requirement for the additional large buffer does not exist. Postbuffer control can be equally well implemented through spatial and transform domain classification. For the present discussion, the emphasis is not on arithmetic complexity, but rather on required buffer size.

4.3 IMPLEMENTATION OF ADAPTIVE TRANSFORM CODING SYSTEMS

Previous sections reviewed basic concepts relevant to transform image coding. Specifically, the required concepts for adaptive transform coding were considered. It should be reemphasized that adaptivity is necessary to justify the additional complexity of transform coding. However, to date, only a limited number of transform coding systems have been studied. In particular, no variable-rate transform coding design has been developed to the hardware stage. However, several computer-simulated systems have been studied.

In this section several designs are reviewed, and fully adaptive transform coding procedures with a rate-equalizer buffer are discussed. The emphasis is on implementation concepts. The discussion, here, relates to transform techniques. However, it should be pointed out that the same concepts are general and are also applicable to other coding techniques.

Prior to the discussion of mathematical models for adaptive transform coding, specific definitions of image segmentation are required. Four image region types are considered. The entire image is referred to as the "frame." The smallest grouping of pixels used is a "block." The block is the basic input to the transform coding algorithm. It corresponds to the pixel set over which the transformation is performed. The "strip" refers to a set of blocks, which, in general, corresponds to N image lines for $N \times N$ block size. Transform coding can be implemented with nonsquare blocks. However, to simplify the discussion, only square blocks are considered. The strip also corresponds to the minimum number of subblocks required to perform the reformatting function. The "region" corresponds to a relatively small image area over which the adaptive coder operates without additional control information from the buffer control algorithm. The region size can be a block or several blocks. These image subelements are utilized for adaptivity, adaptivity control, and local transformation.

4.3.1 Memory Architectures

A transform coding algorithm operates over transform blocks. Thus, the conventional image raster format requires reformatting into blocks. For variable-rate adaptivity, in addition to a reformatting buffer, a rate-equalizer buffer is included.

Memory architecture associated with the indicated buffers is simple. For application with large-size images, these buffers may become important. Image compression with large formats also require large-size buffers. While operation complexity remains simple, the large buffers require consideration of expense and reliability. Reliability is particularly important for the equalizer buffer that contains code words. An error within the rate-equalizer buffer is equivalent to a channel error.

The buffer that performs the reformatting function, although not truly random access, requires that memory input and output addressing be performed differently. The rate-equalizer buffer may be considered schematically as a two-sided memory. At the forward side the compressor inputs code words. From the other side the channel, at fixed bit rate, removes code words.

Depending on adaptivity implementation, a control function is associated with one of the two buffers. The information required for adaptivity processing is external to the buffers. For example, the prebuffering concept for adaptivity control requires block energy, which can be determined on input to the memory. Consequently, no memory access is required after the appropriate image area is placed into this buffer.

Similarly, for postbuffer control no requirement exists to access data in the buffer. The buffer control requires the buffer fullness information, which, again, is determined externally to the buffer. The buffer fullness is obtained through monitoring the number of bits into the buffer and into the channel. The difference between the two is the buffer fullness required for adaptivity control.

4.3.2 Specific Designs

In this section, several approaches to adaptive transform coding are discussed. Through these techniques, actual implementation is related to theoretical concepts previously developed.

The discussion begins with a short overview of an adaptive transform coding system developed at the National Aeronautical and Space Administration Research Center in Ames, California. Knauer (1975) and his co-workers at NASA have implemented an adaptive interframe coder based on a relatively simple algorithm proposed by Landau and Slepian (1971). The NASA model, shown in Fig. 4-9, is an adaptive interframe coder utilizing $4 \times 4 \times 4$ Hadamard matrices that operates at a constant rate. The normalization model (i.e., the quantizer) varies according to local activity. The implementation is straightforward since the rate is

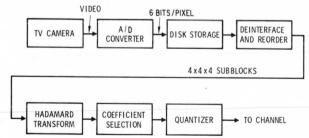

FIG. 4-9. Block diagram of NASA Ames image compression system.

fixed. A frame storage is required for four frames. Two-bit overhead indicates the classification information to the decoder. The system operates at 1 bit per pixel with excellent image quality compared with the original video image. The actual implementation of the algorithm has been performed at regular TV rates.

Determination of different classes is based on temporal activity in the image. Thus, the amount of image motion within four frames determines the allocation of the available bits in the temporal direction. Since the overall rate is fixed, the total number of bits for each $4 \times 4 \times 4$ transform block is constant.

Operation at 1 bit per pixel is probably close to the lowest rate at which the system could operate with acceptable image quality. The basic system limitation is that each three-dimensional transform block utilizes an identical fraction of the available bandwidth. For an interframe coding problem, the local variability, both spatially and temporally, is likely to be significant. The current NASA concept is the only existing real-time transform coding system, either for intraframe or interframe coding.

The NASA design incorporates several diagnostic modes, which also serve an educational purpose by demonstrating various motion types within an image and are also helpful in designing quantizer parameters associated with various classes. Except for the four-frame memory requirement, the system design is straightforward. Implementation through the Hadamard matrices eliminates multiplications.

The discussion on variable-rate adaptive transform coding begins with open-loop techniques. An open-loop transform coding procedure is a fully adaptive algorithm with no requirement to constrain the bit fluctuation within an equalizer buffer. Consequently, there is no deterministic procedure to maintain the algorithm at a specified bit rate. Two techniques have been developed previously. Since these techniques cannot easily operate in a standard communications environment that requires fixed-rate throughput, they are mainly of interest for historical perspective. However, these techniques also serve as a motivation for developing the required modifications that would permit them to operate at fixed rate.

The first open-loop technique, the algorithm of Tasto and Wintz (1971), utilized the K–L transform. Subblocks were partitioned (classified) according to energy. Four classes, each requiring a two-bit overhead, were used. The quantization strategies implemented included a combination of a uniform quantizer with Huffman coding. Algorithm development has not, however, considered training procedures. Both training and coding were performed on the same image. Consequently, the problem associated with maintaining channel rate from one image to another and the mismatch problem were avoided. The results demonstrated that adaptivity is a viable concept.

Another open-loop technique was developed by Tescher (1973). The adaptive coding procedure eliminated the need for classification. The algorithm utilized large transform blocks (256 × 256). The new concept was to derive recursively, on the basis of previously decoded information, both the normalization terms and the bit assignment.

Superficially, this technique is similar to conventional, two-dimensional differential pulse-code modulation (DPCM). However, unlike DPCM, rather than the coded value, its variance is estimated. Thus, the appropriate estimation procedure obtains the standard deviation of the transform coefficient to be coded. Since only previously coded values are used in the estimation, the procedure is fully decodable. The decoder repeats the same steps of the coding process.

This technique is fully adaptive to the transform domain structure. The compression rate is determined on actual image activity. Also, the technique is "self-truncating." When the predicted number of bits for a coefficient falls below unity, no further information is transmitted. This open-loop technique for large transform sizes has been successful for various applications, including monochrome color and interframe coding.

The two fundamental new concepts established deserve to be emphasized. The first result is that a successful adaptive transform coding may be developed without an *a priori* assumed fixed model, such as the Markov model. More important, there has been developed a procedure that permits real-time model identification through which the appropriate bit assignment procedure can also be implemented. Through the second concept, an algorithm was developed that utilizes the available bandwidth according to need. Unfortunately, the algorithm is not feasible. The utilization of large transform sizes and open-loop techniques is inappropriate. The next step was to develop an implementation that is fully adaptive, yet utilizes small transforms. The author extended the early adaptive concepts to more conventional transform sizes.

Basic features of the algorithm are presented in Fig. 4-10. A recursive procedure is utilized. Starting with the largest coefficient, the algorithm recursively predicts the next coefficient standard deviation from which the appropriate number of bits is determined. A simple zigzag scanning process, illustrated in Fig. 4-11, maps a two-dimensional block into one dimension. Since the subdiagonal elements have approximately the same relative importance, the mapping approximately results in a monotonically decreasing set of elements. Several examples are shown in Fig. 4-12. The 2-bit/pixel reconstructed "SITE" image shown in Fig. 4-12a is visually identical to the original. Figure 4-12b contains the absolute error image magnified 30-fold for display purposes. The magnitude display of the cosine transform domain, before and after coding, is shown in Figs. 4-12c and d, respectively, and the 30-fold magnified transform domain

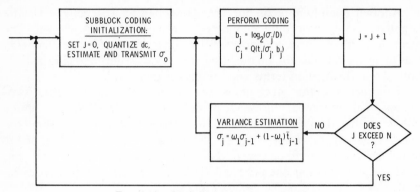

FIG. 4-10.   Variance estimation method.

error is demonstrated in Fig. 4-12e. The image in Fig. 4-12f is derived by "binarizing" Fig. 4-12d. Transmitted transform values are shown in white; dark regions indicate those coefficients replaced by zeros at the receiver. The procedure is fully adaptive. The normalization coefficients and the bit assignment, as well as the total number of bits per block, are adaptively determined. When the predicted number of bits for a coefficient falls below a fixed value, say two, the coding is terminated for that block. Similarly, the receiver duplicates the recursive procedure; thus, the process is decodable.

The outlined procedure appears to be promising. However, its undesirable feature is the open-loop operation. The coding algorithm properly allocates bits according to the relative importance (e.g., image entropy) of

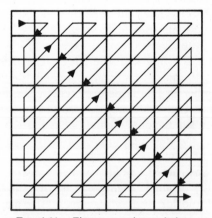

FIG. 4-11.   Zigzag scanning technique.

subblocks. However, channel rate is not considered. The next logical step is to convert the open-loop technique to a closed-loop procedure. Through the utilization of the previously discussed general rate control approach, the solution is straightforward. But first, techniques based on classification procedures should be discussed.

Chen and Smith (1976) developed a closed-loop adaptive procedure that is a simplification of Tasto's technique. The Chen–Smith coder utilizes the cosine transform. On the basis of subblock energy, a four-class partitioning is performed. Prebuffer control maintains the required bit rate.

The concept is as follows. The coefficient energy of subblocks within the reformatting buffer is measured and classified. The four-class classifier requires three thresholds in subblock energy. For each class, subblocks are given a predetermined number of bits. The distribution function for subblock energy is determined. For the proper thresholds, the product of the given class bit rate and the integral of the distribution function summed over the four classes yields the required rate, as shown in Fig. 4-13. Consequently, the number of bits for the various classes permits straightforward computation of the required thresholds. The necessary computation, although simple, must be performed for each data set that resides in the reformatting buffer. For a real-time system, the computation requires additional buffering.

In their paper, Chen and Smith (1976) effectively argued the benefits of adaptive coding. Through various experiments, they identified a "typical" probability distribution for subblock activity. They observed, consistent with this author's experience, that for many image types the indicated probability density is an approximately exponentially decreasing function of energy. This observation indicates that, in general, most subblocks are relatively quiet. Only a small number of subblocks contain significant activity. Consequently, a strong motivation for adaptivity is available. The coding algorithm at relatively low rates is acceptable for a large fraction of image subblocks. A small additional bandwidth is required to accommodate the small number of active subblocks. The coding experiment of Chen and Smith included monochrome as well as color images.

Unlike Tasto and Wintz (1971), Chen and Smith did not consider entropy coding of the transform domain. Tasto and Wintz utilized the appropriate K–L transform for each class. In contrast, the implementation by Chen and Smith utilized the cosine transform for all classes. The probable benefit of a specific transform for each class is marginal.

The techniques of both Chen and Tasto share a common limitation. The classifier uses floating thresholds to arrive at the fixed rate. Consequently, the energy classification is adaptive for each subblock. How a

b

a

FIGS. 4-12 (a)–(f). Examples of adaptive transform image coding. (a) Reconstructed image, 2 bits pixel; (b) absolute error display, image domain.

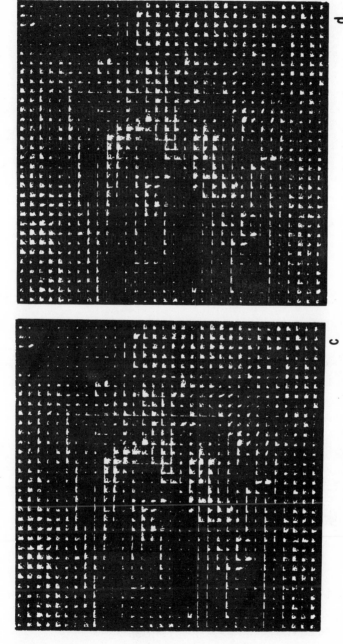

d

c

Fig. 4-12 (c) Cosine transform magnitude before coding, (d) cosine transform magnitude after coding.

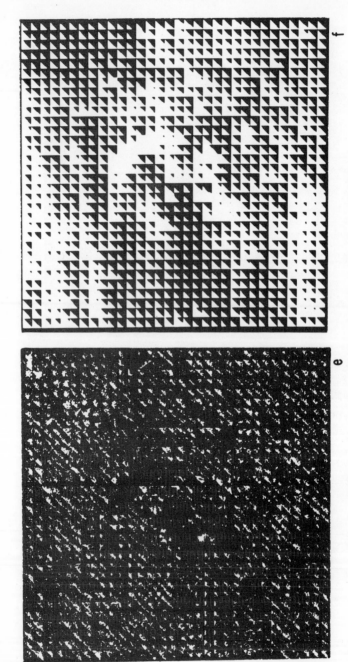

FIG. 4-12. (e) Absolute error display, transform domain, (f) discarded coefficient map.

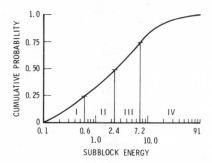

FIG. 4-13. Subblock classification based on energy.

particular subblock is classified depends on the subblock energy distribution for the image region that is utilized for threshold determination.

Cox and Tescher (1976) developed an absolute classification procedure of the closed-loop format. This classifier utilizes fixed preassigned thresholds. Thus each subblock is classified according to its absolute energy without regard to the distribution of neighbor subblocks. To maintain a fixed average channel rate, bit assignment matrices are recalculated for each image strip. Figure 4-14 indicates the appropriate constraints. Determination of the D parameter is made such that summation over all bit assignment matrices results in the total allowed number of bits for that image segment associated with the adaptivity computation. Letting n_k denote the number of subblock classified in the kth class according to absolute energy, the algorithm dynamically determines $b_{i,j}^{(k)}$, the number of bits for coefficient i, j in class k. One could argue the superiority of this technique: An image subblock is paired with the appropriate normalization matrix regardless of the distribution of other subblocks in the adaptivity region.

A major criticism of previous techniques is that classification is based on a single parameter which can provide only limited information on image structure. Subblock entropy utilization should yield superior classification. The problem still remains how to model the normalization matrix for a class.

The next logical approach is to implement the recursive, fully adaptive technique over small subblocks with postbuffer feedback control. The result is a self-consistent transform coding procedure. This technique, developed by this author, is discussed next.

On the basis of the foregoing discussion, the combination of general rate control and the open-loop adaptive transform coding is relatively simple. The procedure is to develop a controller that specifies to the previous open-loop technique the D parameter. In Fig. 4-15, a flowchart is

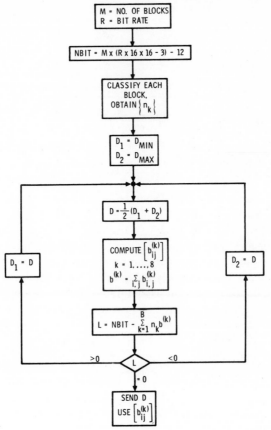

FIG. 4-14.   Flow diagram of absolute classification procedure.

given for the appropriate logic. The following definitions apply: The channel operation rate is $\bar{R}$. The required current rate is $R(t)$. The slope of the D-versus-R curve is $C(t)$. The estimate of D at time t is $\hat{D}(t)$. The buffer size is N. The number of bits transmitted during a cycle time Δ is n. The normalized buffer status is $B(t)$. The initial condition must be separately specified. For the first subblock to be coded, an assumed distortion D_0, which corresponds to the desired average rate, is specified. The algorithm is stable; even for unreasonable initial conditions, the controller rapidly stabilizes at an effectively steady state condition.

Conceptually, the controller attempts to maintain the buffer bias B within the available buffer. Consequently, the maximum deviation from a specified rate is negligible for image sizes much larger than the postbuffer size. The postbuffer control size has a limited impact on performance,

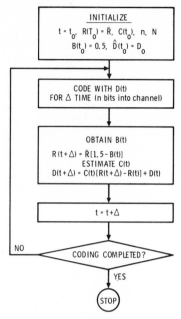

FIG. 4-15. Buffer feedback logic.

although it is small. Computer simulations have indicated a small image quality degradation in terms of mean-square error as the postbuffer size is reduced from two-image strips to one-fourth of an image strip.

As discussed in Section 4.2.4, this technique can utilize parallel computation, and it is flexible in image format. Various examples, including buffer performance behavior, are shown in Fig. 4-16. It should be noted that the various parameters behave reasonably, and no sign of unstable buffer behavior develops. The intermediate controller parameters are also shown. They are the "desired" local rate and the estimated and required D parameters. The estimated parameters represent quantities averaged over large image segments. These parameters change only slowly. The instantaneous rate associated with individual subblocks fluctuates significantly. At two bits per pixel, for example, the instantaneous rate variation is likely to exceed a factor of 4.

The described procedure is highly adaptive to local image structure and is self-terminating. Yet, the procedure behaves in a manner consistent with a communication channel for practical operation. For a lower average bit rate, while more image subblocks operate at a lower instantaneous rate, the coder still assigns a relatively large number of bits to a selected small set.

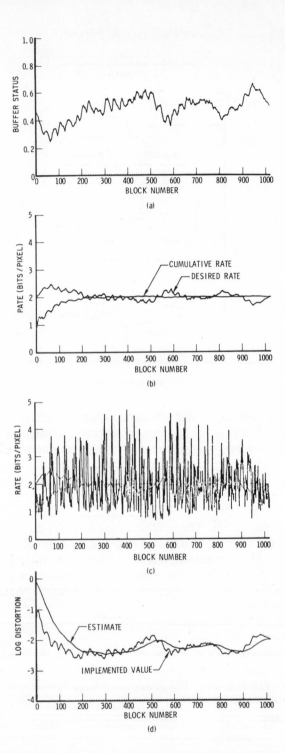

(a)

(b)

(c)

(d)

This technique is particularly beneficial for high-quality imagery with high signal-to-noise properties. For this case, the various image regions are dispersed in a local image structure. The algorithm requires minimal overhead. The coder adapts to each subblock independently. Since possible combinations for different subblocks are essentially infinite, this procedure effectively utilizes an infinite number of classes.

The algorithm can be extended to utilize a two-dimensional predictor. However, the prediction mechanism has to be more complex to follow each transform line of rapidly decaying transform coefficient amplitudes. A major practical advantage of the self-adaptive transform coding algorithm is its capability to operate without any prior training. Thus, the same algorithm can be equally applicable for significantly different image types.

4.3.3   Channel Error Considerations

While consideration of the channel error problem is important, it is a separate problem. Except for Chen and Smith (1976), studies of adaptive transform techniques have not considered channel correction procedures. Chen and Smith performed several experiments to demonstrate, not unexpectedly, that additional channel consideration can effectively minimize the channel error problem.

Channel error sensitivity usually is directly proportional to the degree of adaptivity. In principle, a high sensitivity to channel noise may be taken advantage of in the self-adaptive transform coding algorithm. This can be accomplished as follows. A single channel error causes synchronization loss. Thus, subsequent transform values yield erroneous transform variance estimates. Since the estimated values immediately become obviously unrealistic, it is relatively easy to identify an error. A simple algorithm may monitor the estimated variance or the predicted bit assignment to check if the algorithm is working properly.

For a typical subblock, the estimated bit assignment values over small transform domain regions are constant or decreasing; only occasionally does a small increase occur in the allocated number of bits for the next coefficient. Consequently, if the predicted number of bits begins to increase, a channel error is indicated. Once the error is detected, the decoder may simply ignore the remaining part of the subblock. Since the erroneous bit is closely localized, one may attempt to correct the error by

FIG. 4-16.   Demonstration of typical buffer feedback behavior. (a) Normalized buffer status; (b) cumulative and deferred rates; (c) actual local subblock rate; (d) distortion history.

trial and error and recover the remainder of the subblock. However, this is a conceptual approach yet to be implemented.

4.3.4 Applicability of Adaptivity Concepts to Other Coding Techniques

It is worthwhile to point out that some of the discussed concepts of this section are directly applicable, with little or no modifications, to other coding techniques (Tescher and Cox, 1977). Specifically, the self-adaptive procedure is applicable to hybrid transform/DPCM coding. The generalized buffer feedback procedure is applicable to all image-coding types, as well as to general data compression procedures. In particular, the same feedback logic is useful for entropy coding, as well as for procedures where entropy coding is utilized jointly with another coding technique.

4.4 CONCLUSIONS

This chapter has attempted to demonstrate that transform coding is a valuable and efficient technique for image compression. However, various considerations are necessary before the transform coding procedure can be used in a practical environment. Adaptivity concepts have been reviewed, followed by considerations of variable-rate algorithms with the constraint of the fixed-rate channel.

Several solutions are identified. Some of these solutions are also applicable to other data compression algorithms. Adaptive transform coding procedures are promising. These techniques can and should be implemented through a feedback mechanism to control the rate. The necessary hardware will likely exceed what is needed for a nonadaptive technique. However, the benefits will more than offset the hardware penalty.

The required technology is in existence. The discussed channel error correction procedure, based on the detection of catastrophic failure location, is an interesting problem that would probably be worthwhile to pursue. It should be again emphasized that the most promising problem areas for improved efficiency are not in the development of new transform algorithms but rather in the procedures that follow the transformation.

Several other considerations associated with transform image coding need to be reviewed. Transform coding is a statistical procedure based on the decorrelation property of the transformation. An alternative philosophy based on approximation theory has been proposed recently. Image regions are considered to be two-dimensional segments that the data compression algorithm approximates by some known function set. Therefore, one could claim that an approximation with sinusoidal functions may be suboptimal. The relevant question is whether other functional approximations of image segments may converge faster than the sinusoidal set. This question is discussed with reference to the singular value decomposition technique of image segments which, in the least-squares sense, is optimum(Albert, 1972).

Unfortunately, what may be optimum or attractive in approximation theory does not always result in an efficient coding system. The least-squares approach requires the transmission of the transformation parameters, as well as of the appropriate coefficients. The required bandwidth is likely to become considerable. For a specific type of imagery, such as artificially generated scenes, an approximation theory may be appropriate (Andrews and Patterson, 1976; McCaughey, 1976). However, most imagery can be characterized only in a statistical sense. Therefore, an approximation theory will not yield improvements over statistical transform techniques.

Another area that needs further study and could be potentially useful for transform coding is a better understanding of image quality criteria. The self-adaptive technique approximately performs classification according to transform domain entropy, which is also a measure of image entropy. For large bandwidth compression, transform block classification according to some generalized criteria may be valuable even at the expense of increased distortion. However, it must be remembered that both theoretical and practical limits for an image compression algorithm with negligible distortion are determined by the entropy measure. A highly adaptive transform coding technique closely approximates the actual image entropy.

Future algorithm developments in compression rate reduction are not likely to be dramatic. Most improvements may be accomplished by the implementation of techniques discussed in this chapter. Considerable effort is still required to ensure that the various designs are implemented through practical hardware.

In this chapter, the primary algorithm components that are necessary for implementation are identified. In addition, it was attempted to interface, at least conceptually, some of these components. What are these components? For transform coding, a transform algorithm is needed. Prior to the transform, a reformatting buffer is required. An important new component is the buffer control algorithm.

Hardware implementation for the discussed techniques could benefit from a possible design that is based on independent components. These components can be independently developed and appropriately interfaced for a particular transform coding algorithm. This modular design, in addition to transform coding, is also applicable to other data compression techniques, such as entropy coding through a buffer feedback mechanism.

This author believes that a well-designed adaptive transform coding algorithm represents the most efficient image compression technique for high-quality data. Although conceptual design configurations discussed in this chapter are promising, they are still only in the simulation stage and the actual hardware design is yet to be pursued.

ACKNOWLEDGMENTS

The assistance of several individuals in the preparation of this chapter is greatly appreciated. The suggestions of Professor William K. Pratt were most helpful. Ms. Carolyn Budelier provided expert editorial assistance. Ms. Peggy Ritter typed the earlier versions of the manuscript. The encouragement from The Aerospace Corporation and, in particular, from Mr. Charles J. Leontis to undertake this effort has been most welcome.

REFERENCES

Ahmed, N., Natarajan, T., and Rao, K. (1974). *IEEE Trans. Comput.* **c-23**, 90–93.
Albert, A. (1972). "Regression and the Moore-Penrose Pseudo Inverse." Academic Press, New York.
Anderson, G. B., and Huang, T. S. (1971). *IEEE Trans. Commun. Technol.* **19**, 133–140.
Andrews, H. C. (1975). *Top. Appl. Phys.* **6**, 21–68.
Andrews, H. C., and Patterson, C. L., III (1976). *IEEE Trans. Acoust., Speech, Signal Process.* **24**, 26–53.
Andrews, H. C., and Pratt, W. K. (1968). "Fourier Transform Coding of Images," Hawaii Int. Conf. Sys. Sci., pp. 677–679. Western Periodicals Company, North Hollywood, California.
Bracewell, R. (1965). "The Fourier Transform and Its Applications." McGraw-Hill, New York.
Buss, D. D., Brodersen, R. W., Hewes, C. R., and Teasch, A. F., Jr. (1975). *SPIE Proc.* **66**, 48–56.
Chen, W., and Smith, C. H. (1976). Conference Record, *Int. Conf. Commun. 1976* IEEE Cat. No. 76CH1085-0 CSCB, pp. 47-7–47-13.
Cooley, J. W., and Tukey, J. W. (1965). *J. Math. Comput.* **19**, 297–301.
Cox, R. V., and Tescher, A. G. (1976). *SPIE Proc.* **87**, 239–246.
Dail, J. E. (1976). Conference Record, *Int. Conf. Commun. 1976* IEEE Cat. No. 76CH1084-0, CSCB, pp. 47-14–47-19.
Habibi, A. (1971). *IEEE Trans. Commun. Technol.* **19**, 948–956.
Habibi, A. (1975a). "Study of On-Board Compression of Earth Resource Date," Tech. Doc. Rep. No. 26566. TRW Systems, Redondo Beach, California.
Habibi, A. (1975b). *Natl. Telecommun. Conf. Rec., 1975* IEEE Cat. No. 75CH1015-7 CSCB, pp. 38-16–38-21.
Habibi, A., and Samulon, A. S. (1975). *SPIE Proc.* **66**, 23–35.

Habibi, A., and Wintz, P. (1971). *IEEE Trans. Commun. Technol.* **19**, 957–972.

Huang, J. J. Y., and Schultheiss, P. M. (1963). *IEEE Trans. Commun. Syst.* **11**, 289–296.

Huang, T. S. (1972). *Prog. Opt.* **10**, 1–44.

Huang, T. S., and Tretiak, O. J., eds. (1972). "Picture Bandwidth Compression." Gordon & Breach, New York.

Huang, T. S., Schreiber, W. F., and Tretiak, O. J. (1971). *Proc. IEEE* **59**, 1586–1609.

Huffman, D. A. (1952). *Proc. IRE* **40**, 1098–1101.

Jain, A. K. (1976). *In* "Image Science Mathematics" (O. C. Wilde and E. Barrett, eds.), pp. 201–223. Western Periodicals Company, North Hollywood, California.

Knauer, S. C. (1975). *SPIE Proc.* **66**, 58–69.

Landau, H. J., and Slepian, D. (1971). *Bell Sys. Tech. J.* **50**, 1525–1540.

McCaughey, D. G. (1976). *In* "Image Science Mathematics" (O. C. Wilde and E. Barrett, eds.), pp. 168–175. Western Periodicals Company, North Hollywood, California.

Max, J. (1960). *IRE Trans. Inf. Theory* **it-6**, 7–12.

Melzer, S. (1977). *In* "Sensor Data Characteristics and Data Compression Projects of Future Military Satellite Systems" (R. G. Nishinaga, ed.), Tech. Doc. Rep. No. TOR-0077(2060)-1, App. C. Aerospace Corporation, El Segundo, California.

O'Neal, J. B. (1971). *IEEE Trans. Inf. Theory* **IT-17**, 758–761.

Panther, P. F., and Dite, W. (1951). *Proc. IRE* **39**, 44–48.

Papoulis, A. (1965). "Probability Random Variables and Stochastic Processes." McGraw-Hill, New York.

Pearson, D. E. (1975). "Transmission and Display of Pictorial Information." Wiley, New York.

Pratt, W. K. (1978). "Digital Image Processing." Wiley (Interscience), New York.

Pratt, W. K., and Andrews, H. C. (1972). *In* "Picture Bandwidth Compression" (T. S. Huang and O. J. Tretiak, eds.), pp. 515–554. Gordon & Breach, New York.

Pratt, W. K., Kane, J., and Andrews, H. C. (1969). *Proc. IEEE* **57**, 58–68.

Pratt, W. K., Chen, W., and Welch, L. (1974). *IEEE Trans. Commun.* **com-22**, 1075–1093.

Reader, C. (1975). *SPIE Proc.* **66**, 108–118.

Reis, J. J., Lynch, R. T., and Butman, J. (1976). *SPIE Proc.* **87**, 24–35.

Schreiber, W. F. (1967). *Proc. IEEE* **55**, 320–330.

Tasto, M., and Wintz, P. (1971). *IEEE Trans. Commun. Technol.* **19**, 957–972.

Tescher, A. G. (1973). Ph. D. Dissertation, USCIPT Report 510. University of Southern California, Los Angeles.

Tescher, A. G., ed. (1975). "Efficient Transmission of Pictorial Information," SPIE Proc. 66. Bellingham, Washington.

Tescher, A. G., ed. (1976). "Advances in Image Transmission Techniques," SPIE Proc. 87. Bellingham, Washington.

Tescher, A. G., and Andrews, H. C. (1974). *In* "Applications of Walsh Functions and Sequency Theory" (H. Schreiber and G. F. Sandy, eds.), IEEE Cat. No. 74CH0861-SEMC.

Tescher, A. G., and Cox, R. V. (1976). *Proc. Int. Conf. Coord. Chem., 17th, 1976* IEEE Cat. No. 76CH1085-0 CSCB, pp. 47-20–47-25.

Tescher, A. G., and Cox, R. V. (1977). *SPIE Proc.* **119**, 147–154.

Whitehouse, H. J., Means, R. W., and Wrench, E. H. (1975). *SPIE Proc.* **66**, 36–47.

Wilde, O. C., and Barrett, E., eds. (1976). "Image Science Mathematics." Western Periodicals Company, North Hollywood, California.

Wintz, P. A. (1972). *Proc. IEEE* **60**, 809–820.

Woods, J. W., and Huang, T. S. (1972). *In* "Picture Bandwidth Compression" (T. S. Huang and O. J. Tretiak, eds.), pp. 555–573. Gordon & Breach, New York.

Hybrid Transform/Predictive Image Coding

JOHN A. ROESE

Naval Ocean Systems Center
San Diego, California

The current emphasis on digital communications systems has generated considerable interest in the development of effective techniques for bandwidth compression of digital images. The main emphasis of research in this area has been on intraframe coding of single images. However, recent efforts have extended some of the more effective intraframe coding schemes to include interframe coding of temporal image sequences (Noble *et al.,* 1973; Roese *et al.,* 1975, 1977).

In the design of digital image coding systems, the primary objective is to achieve high-quality receiver image reconstructions with a minimum number of transmitted code bits. Two highly efficient classes of digital image coding techniques have been developed: unitary transform coding and linear predictive differential pulse-code-modulation (DPCM) coding. The approach employed by both techniques is to operate on naturally correlated image data to produce nearly decorrelated signals, which are then separately quantized and coded for transmission over a digital communications channel.

Comparisons of transform and DPCM coding systems have shown that both approaches possess relative advantages and limitations (Rao *et al.,* 1977). With transform image coding, higher image fidelity reconstructions are achieved at low bit rates. Also, transform coding techniques are not as sensitive to variations in image statistics and are less vulnerable to channel error effects. By comparison, use of DPCM predictive coding techniques results in superior coding performance at high bit rates, less complex hardware implementations, and greatly reduced storage requirements.

A significant advance in image coding methodology occurred with the introduction of the concept of hybrid transform/DPCM coding (Habibi, 1974). The basic intraframe hybrid coding system proposed by Habibi employs a one-dimensional unitary transform coder cascaded with parallel DPCM coders. Hybrid coders retain many of the attractive characteristics of both transform and DPCM techniques while maintaining good coding performance. The concept of hybrid transform/DPCM image coders has been augmented by the development of a unifying theory relating transform coding using lower triangular operators and DPCM coders for Markov data (Habibi and Hershel, 1974).

The advent of hybrid transform/DPCM coding, combined with recent technological advances in signal-processing circuitry, has made transmission of intraframe coded digital television imagery practical. Recent and projected future applications areas for hybrid intraframe image coding include bandwidth compression for air-to-ground video links for remotely piloted vehicles (RPV) operating in a jammable environment, video links for space shuttle orbiters, and transmission of satellite imagery such as multispectral LANDSAT scanner pictures. A particularly attractive aspect of hybrid transform/DPCM coders is that the basic operating principles can be extended to include interframe coding of image sequences. Since considerable temporal as well as spatial correlation exists between frames of many types of real-time imagery such as television, hybrid interframe coding appears to be a viable concept. This assertion is supported by high-quality coding results achieved in recent computer simulations using hybrid two-dimensional transform/DPCM coders with time sequences of digital television images (Roese, 1976).

This chapter presents an overview of hybrid transform/DPCM coding techniques. In Section 5.1, hybrid intraframe image coding is discussed. Major topics covered in this section include the mathematical relationships defining the operation of hybrid coders, theoretical coder performance levels based on statistical models of the image data, a spatially adaptive refinement of the basic coder design, and the results of computer simulations that evaluate the coder's performance on actual image data. This section also contains brief descriptions of current hardware implementations for intraframe hybrid transform/DPCM coders. Section 5.2 illustrates the extension of hybrid transform/DPCM techniques to interframe image coding. The major concepts of interframe hybrid image coding are developed in a manner similar to that of Section 5.1. The chapter concludes with a brief performance comparison between hybrid intraframe and interframe image coders.

5.1 INTRAFRAME HYBRID IMAGE CODING

A wide variety of applications exist for intraframe image coders. The unique implementation characteristics and coding performance of intraframe hybrid coders are well suited to many important image coding problems. The basic concepts of intraframe hybrid image coding, as well as theoretical and experimental analyses of coding performance, are presented below.

5.1.1 System Definition

The intraframe hybrid coder exploits horizontal and vertical correlation within an image by the use of cascaded unitary transform and DPCM operators. A simplified system block diagram of the intraframe hybrid coder is presented in Fig. 5-1. In operation, one-dimensional transforms are taken along image rows. One of the banks of parallel DPCM linear

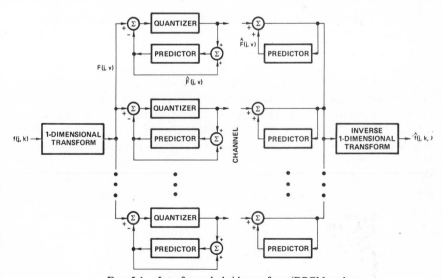

FIG. 5-1.   Intraframe hybrid transform/DPCM coder.

predictive coders is then applied to the set of coefficients at each transform coordinate in a columnwise fashion. (Alternatively, a single timeshared DPCM coder can be utilized.) The resulting sequence of transform coefficient differences is then coded for transmission to the receiver. At the receiver, coefficient differences are used to reconstruct the transform coefficients in each column. Replicas of transmitted images are then obtained by applying inverse one-dimensional transforms to the coefficients along each row.

For actual coder implementations, the pixel amplitudes of the input image $f(j, k)$ are generally partitioned along the image rows to form several smaller image subarrays. Transform processing is applied in the horizontal direction within each subarray, while DPCM coding is applied over the entire vertical extent of the image.

The general forms of the one-dimensional forward and inverse transforms along the image rows are

$$F(j, v) = \sum_{k=0}^{K-1} f(j, k)\phi(k, v) \tag{1a}$$

and

$$f(j, k) = \sum_{v=0}^{K-1} f(j, v)\phi^{-1}(k, v) \tag{1b}$$

where $\phi(k, v)$ is the one-dimensional transform kernel and v is the transform domain row coordinate.

Many different types of unitary transforms, including the Fourier, sine, cosine, Hadamard, slant, and Karhunen–Loeve have been investigated for image coding. One of the most attractive from the standpoint of coding performance and implementation simplicity is the discrete cosine transform. It has been shown that the theoretical mean-square-error coding performance of the cosine transform is nearly equivalent to that obtained for the optimal Karhunen–Loeve transform for Markovian image sources (Ahmed et al., 1974). Furthermore, the cosine transform can be efficiently computed by transversal filtering methods (Means et al., 1974). For these reasons the cosine transform has been adopted for the theoretical and experimental analyses of hybrid coding techniques described in this chapter. Equations (1a) and (1b) assume the following forms for the cosine transform kernel:

$$F(j, v) = \frac{1}{K} \sum_{k=0}^{K-1} f(j, k) \cos\left[\frac{(2k + 1)v\pi}{2K}\right] \tag{2a}$$

$$f(j, k) = \frac{1}{K} \sum_{v=0}^{K-1} F(j, v) \cos\left[\frac{(2k + 1)v\pi}{2K}\right] \tag{2b}$$

The coefficients resulting from unitary transforms taken along the image rows are processed in a columnwise fashion using parallel DPCM coders. For first-order linear predictive coding, the difference signal

$$D(j, v) = F(j, v) - \hat{F}(j, v) \tag{3}$$

between vertically adjacent transform coefficients is formed between $F(j, v)$ and its linear estimate

$$\hat{F}(j, v) = a_1(v)F(j - 1, v) + a_0(v) \tag{4}$$

The weighting coefficients $a_j(v)$ are chosen to minimize the mean-square prediction difference $E\{D^2(j, v)\}$. Under the assumption of a zero-mean random process in each column, the optimum weighting coefficients in Eq. (4) are

$$a_1(v) = \frac{E\{F(j, v)F(j - 1, v)\}}{E\{F^2(j - 1, v)\}} \tag{5a}$$

and

$$a_0(v) = 0 \tag{5b}$$

The difference signals in Eq. (3) are quantized and coded for transmission to the receiver. A zonal coding strategy is used in which the number of code bits assigned to each difference signal is set in proportion to the logarithm of its variance.

Reconstruction of each transmitted image occurs at the receiver, where the transform coefficient difference signals for each column are decoded followed by an inverse transformation along the image rows.

5.1.2 Theoretical Performance Model

To model the performance of the intraframe hybrid coder, the image field is approximated as a stochastic process with zero mean and known, spatially separable autocorrelation function. Under the assumption of a wide-sense stationary Markov process, the covariance matrix $\mathbf{K}_{f_k}$ for pixel amplitudes along each row may be modeled as

$$\mathbf{K}_{f_k} = \sigma_k^2 \begin{bmatrix} 1 & \rho_R & \rho_R^2 & \cdots & \rho_R^{K-1} \\ \rho_R & 1 & \rho_R & & \cdot \\ \rho_R^2 & & 1 & & \cdot \\ \cdot & & & \cdot & \cdot \\ \cdot & & & & \cdot \\ \cdot & & & & \cdot \\ \rho_R^{K-1} & \cdot & \cdot & \cdot & 1 \end{bmatrix} \tag{6}$$

where ρ_R represents horizontally adjacent pixel correlation and $\sigma_k{}^2$ denotes pixel variance along a row.

The covariance matrix of the cosine transform coefficients can be obtained from

$$\mathbf{K}_{F_v} = \mathbf{C}\mathbf{K}_{f_k}\mathbf{C}^{\mathbf{T}} \tag{7}$$

where $\mathbf{C}$ represents the cosine transform kernel in matrix form. The row transform variance vector, $\mathcal{V}_{F_v}$, consists of the diagonal elements of the transform coefficient covariance matrix. That is,

$$\mathcal{V}_{F_v}{}^{\mathbf{T}} = [K_{F_v}(0, 0), K_{F_v}(1, 1), \ldots, K_{F_v}(K-1, K-1)] \tag{8}$$

where the elements of $\mathcal{V}_{F_v}$ are ordered in decreasing magnitude. The columnwise transform coefficient difference variance vector $\mathcal{V}_D$ is related to the row transform variance vector by

$$\mathcal{V}_D = \mathcal{V}_F\{1 - \rho_C{}^2\} \tag{9}$$

where ρ_C is the vertical column correlation of the transform coefficients (Habibi, 1971).

For zonal coding of the transform coefficient differences, the number of code bits allocated for quantization is determined by the modeled coefficient difference variances of $\mathcal{V}_D$. The resulting intraframe coder mean-square error with zonal coding and constant-length binary codes is found to be

$$\mathcal{E} = \sum_{v=0}^{K-1}\left[\mathcal{V}_D(v) - \sum_{n=1}^{2^{b(v)}} R_n{}^2(v)P\{D_n(v) \leq \mathcal{V}_D(v) < D_{n+1}(v)\}\right] \tag{10}$$

where D_n, D_{n+1}, and R_n are quantizer decision and reconstruction levels; $b(v)$ is the number of bits allocated to the $\mathcal{V}$th transform coefficient differences; and $P\{\cdot\}$ is the probability that $\mathcal{V}_D(v)$ lies between decision levels D_n and D_{n+1} (Pratt, 1978). A minimum value for the mean-square quantization error occurs when the decision and reconstruction levels are set according to an optimum quantization strategy, e.g., a Max quantizer, for the assumed probability density of the quantized variable (Max, 1960). The probability density for the dc and higher order transform coefficient differences is generally assumed to be Laplacian. Under this assumption, the mean-square-error expression for intraframe hybrid coders becomes

$$\mathcal{E} = \sum_{k=0}^{K-1}\left\{\mathcal{V}_D(v) - \frac{1}{2}\sum_{n=1}^{2^{b(v)}} R_n{}^2(v)\right.$$
$$\left. \cdot \left[\exp\left(\frac{-(2)^{1/2}D_n(v)}{\mathcal{V}_D(v)}\right) - \exp\left(\frac{-(2)^{1/2}D_{n+1}(v)}{\mathcal{V}_D(v)}\right)\right]\right\} \tag{11}$$

Figure 5-2 contains a plot of the theoretical coding performance of the intraframe hybrid cosine transform/DPCM coder model in terms of the mean-square-error (MSE) percent versus transform vector length for various spatial correlations for Markov source data. Improved coding performance for a given image is to be anticipated for longer transform vector lengths up to a vector length of about 16.

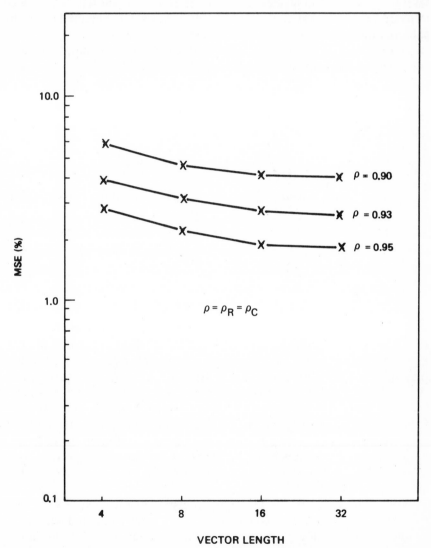

FIG. 5-2. Theoretical performance evaluation for intraframe hybrid coder at 1.0 bit/pixel for zonal coding with Markov data.

5.1.3   Adaptive Intraframe Hybrid Coding

In most intraframe coders using unitary transforms, the image is partitioned into small subarrays because of storage and computational considerations. Conventional hybrid transform/DPCM coders apply quantizer bit assignments which are, in some sense, representative of the entire image to each image subarray. A spatially adaptive hybrid transform/DPCM coder implementation can be formulated in which separate transform coefficient statistics and bit assignments are computed for each subarray of the image.

For adaptive hybrid coding, the statistical measures required for each subarray are the column mean of the transform coefficients,

$$\bar{F}(v) = \frac{1}{J} \sum_{j=1}^{J-1} F(j, v) \tag{12}$$

and the column correlation coefficient,

$$\rho_C(v) = \frac{1}{J-1} \sum_{j=1}^{J-1} F(j, v)F(j-1, v) / \frac{1}{J} \sum_{j=0}^{J-1} F^2(j, v) \tag{13}$$

The column variance of the transform coefficient differences is estimated as

$$\sigma_D^2(v) = \frac{1}{J-1} \sum_{j=1}^{J-1} D^2(j, v) - \left[\frac{1}{J-1} \sum_{j=1}^{J-1} D(j, v) \right]^2 \tag{14}$$

where

$$D(j, v) = F(j, v) - \rho_C(v)F(j-1, v) \tag{15}$$

for $v = 1, 2, \ldots, K - 1$. For each columnwise sequence of transform coefficients, the correlation $\rho_C(v)$ is the gain coefficient of the DPCM predictor feedback loop. The transform coefficient mean $\bar{F}(v)$ provides biasing to achieve a zero-mean input sequence of transform coefficients. A one-dimensional bit assignment is computed for each image subarray from the transform coefficient difference variance $\sigma_D^2(v)$. Thus, the resulting bit assignments, predictor feedback loop gain coefficients, and associated biasing and scaling factors are, in general, different for different image subarrays. Although the subarray bit assignments may vary, the total number of bits available for coding within each subarray is constrained to be equal.

Local adaptation to the measured statistics of each image subarray will normally produce improved coding results when compared with nonadaptive implementations. However, spatial adaptation does result in increased coder complexity.

5.1.4   Experimental Performance Evaluation

Extensive computer simulations have been performed to experimentally evaluate the performance of the intraframe hybrid coder. The hybrid coder is parametric in many variables including choice of separable transforms, coding and quantization strategies, presence or absence of channel noise, transform vector length, and average pixel bit rate.

To evaluate objectively the coding efficiency of the intraframe hybrid coder, two image fidelity criteria measures are used. The first criterion, normalized mean-square error (NMSE), is a measure of the normalized mean-square error between the coder input $f(j, k, l)$ and its output $\hat{f}(j, k, l)$ averaged over the lth frame. Here, j and k are spatial coordinates and l denotes frame number. Normalization is achieved by dividing the mean-square error by the mean signal energy within the frame. The expression for the NMSE at the lth frame is

$$\text{NMSE} = \frac{1}{JK} \sum_{j=0}^{J-1} \sum_{k=0}^{K-1} [f(j, k, l) - \hat{f}(j, k, l)]^2 / \frac{1}{JK} \sum_{j=0}^{J-1} \sum_{k=0}^{K-1} f^2(j, k, l) \quad (16)$$

The second criterion, SNR, measuring the ratio of peak-to-peak signal to rms noise for the lth frame, is defined as

$$\text{SNR} = -10 \log_{10} \left\{ \frac{1}{JK} \sum_{j=0}^{J-1} \sum_{k=0}^{K-1} [f(j, k, l) - \hat{f}(j, k, l)]^2 / Y_{\text{max}}^2 \right\} \quad (17)$$

where Y_{max} represents the maximum luminance value of $f(j, k, l)$, typically 255.

The source data for the experimental evaluation of the intraframe hybrid coder consist of individual frames selected from two multiple-image sequences. These sequences each contain 16 images digitized from sequential frames of 24-frame/sec motion pictures. One sequence, called "Walter," contains images from a fixed-position camera of a moving subject engaged in conversation. The other sequence contains images of a chemical plant photographed from an airplane in a flyby trajectory. Each frame is digitized at a spatial resolution of 256 × 256 pixels with pixel amplitudes linearly quantized to 256 levels. The uncoded version of the sixteenth frame of both data sequences are shown in Fig. 5-3.

Figures 5-4 and 5-5 illustrate intraframe cosine/DPCM coder reconstructions of the sixteenth frame of the "Walter" data base for average bit rates of 2.0, 1.0, and 0.5 bits/pixel with nonadaptive and adaptive coding, respectively. Artifacts arising from the image subarrays of size 256 × 32 can be observed at the lower bit rates.

Application of the same bit rates to the chemical plant data gives subjectively poorer coding results owing, in part, to the higher spatial fre-

FIG. 5-3.   Sixteenth frame of data base image sequences. (a) Walter; (b) chemical plant.

quency content of the source image. Reconstructions of the sixteenth frame of the chemical plant data are shown in Figs. 5-6 and 5-7 for nonadaptive and adaptive coding, respectively. These figures illustrate that improved coding performance is obtained for the adaptive over the nonadaptive implementations of the hybrid intraframe coder.

Performance of the adaptive intraframe hybrid coder in the presence of noise has been investigated by computer simulation of a binary symmetric channel transmission system. The channel operates on each trans-

FIG. 5-4. Experimental coding performance of the intraframe hybrid coder with nonadaptive coding. (a) 2.0 bits/pixel, NMSE = 1.10%; (b) 1.0 bit/pixel, NMSE = 1.33%; (c) 0.5 bit/pixel, NMSE = 2.02%.

mitted bit independently, changing each bit from 0 to 1 or from 1 to 0 with probability P_e and leaving the bit unchanged with probability $1 - P_e$. At the receiver, the encoded picture is reconstructed from the string of bits, including errors, transmitted across the channel.

The effects of channel noise on the adaptive intraframe hybrid coder are illustrated in Figs. 5-8 and 5-9 for the sixteenth frame of the "Walter" and the chemical plant data bases. Probabilities of channel noise simulated are 10^{-2} and 10^{-3}. Subjectively, the image degradations due to

FIG. 5-5.   Experimental coding performance of the intraframe hybrid coder with adaptive coding. (a) 2.0 bits/pixel, NMSE = 0.47%; (b) 1.0 bit/pixel, NMSE = 0.63%; (c) 0.5 bit/pixel, NMSE = 1.17%.

channel noise are not as pronounced in the "Walter" images as they are in the chemical plant scene.

5.1.5   Hardware Implementations

Intraframe hybrid coder implementations are well suited for many system applications for which computational and storage requirements, high data throughput rates, and good coding performance are paramount considerations. As an example, a major Advanced Research Project Agency (ARPA) program to define and implement algorithms for video

FIG. 5-6. Experimental coding performance of the intraframe hybrid coder with nonadaptive coding. (a) 2.0 bits/pixel, NMSE = 0.67%; (b) 1.0 bit/pixel, NMSE = 1.49%; (c) 0.5 bit/pixel, NMSE = 2.43%.

bandwith reduction has been underway since 1972 at the Naval Ocean Systems Center, San Diego. The goal of this program is the development of a small, lightweight, low-power television link with antijam protection for airborne RPV applications.

Current system implementations achieve reductions in video bandwidth by a combination of techniques. These include reducing spatial resolution to 256 × 256 pixels, using low frame rates with multiple-frame refreshing at the receiver, and employing intraframe hybrid transform/DPCM coding techniques. The selection of an intraframe hybrid coder implementation was based on studies performed by the University of

FIG. 5-7. Experimental coding performance of the intraframe hybrid coder with adaptive coding. (a) 2.0 bits/pixel, NMSE = 0.58%; (b) 1.0 bit/pixel, NMSE = 1.33%; (c) 0.5 bit/pixel, NMSE = 2.34%.

Southern California, which indicated that the hybrid cosine transform/DPCM system could achieve the required video bandwidth reduction while preserving acceptable RPV image fidelity (Habibi, 1974).

During the course of this program, both analog and digital hybrid coder implementations were considered. Initially, analog techniques were used for computation of the transform coefficients. The basic Fourier transform chirp-Z algorithm, shown in Fig. 5-10, was adapted to calculate the discrete cosine transform coefficients (Speiser, 1973). This modified algorithm computes the cosine transform as a cascade of a complex multiplication, a complex convolution, and another complex multiplication. An

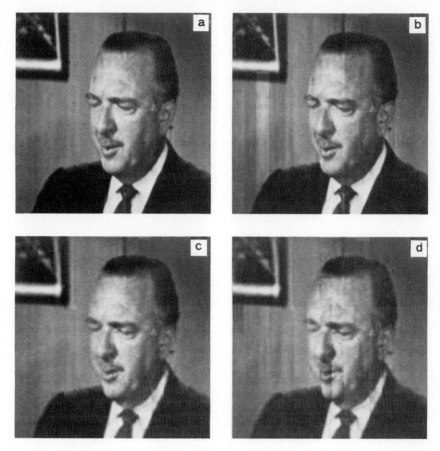

FIG. 5-8. Experimental coding performance of the intraframe hybrid coder with adaptive coding and channel noise. (a) 2.0 bits/pixel, $P_e = 10^{-3}$, NMSE = 0.50%; (b) 2.0 bits/pixel, $P_e = 10^{-2}$, NMSE = 1.09%; (c) 0.5 bit/pixel, $P_e = 10^{-3}$, NMSE = 1.18%; (d) 0.5 bit/pixel, $P_e = 10^{-2}$, NMSE = 1.64%.

attractive feature of the chirp-Z algorithm is that the convolution operation can be implemented with transversal filters.

Both surface acoustic wave and charge transfer devices were investigated for transversal filter hybrid coder implementations. A 63-tap surface acoustic wave transversal filter, shown in Fig. 5-11, was developed to perform the convolution operations for a 32-point discrete Fourier transform (Alsup *et al.*, 1973). The filter has equally spaced taps with weights corresponding to the sine and cosine components of the chirp-Z algorithm. Computation time is proportional to the number of input samples. Advantages of this type of filter are small size and low power re-

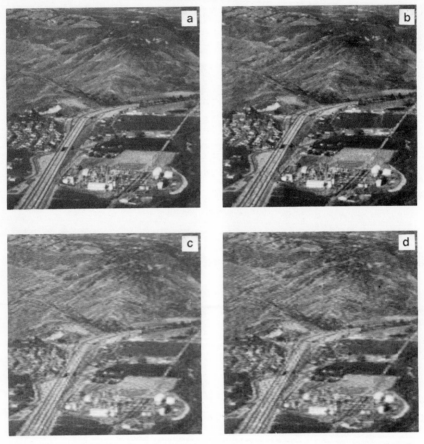

FIG. 5-9. Experimental coding performance of the intraframe hybrid coder with adaptive coding and channel noise. (a) 2.0 bits/pixel, $P_e = 10^{-3}$, NMSE = 0.60%; (b) 2.0 bits/pixel, $P_e = 10^{-2}$, NMSE = 1.05%; (c) 0.5 bit/pixel, $P_e = 10^{-3}$, NMSE = 2.36%; (d) 0.5 bit/pixel, $P_e = 10^{-2}$, NMSE = 2.72%.

quirements. However, because of the high insertion losses and large number of amplifiers required for surface acoustic wave devices, charge transfer transversal filter techniques were also considered for RPV applications. A prototype 63-point charge-coupled-device transversal filter which operated at a 5-MHz clock rate with data rates of up to 1600 kbits/sec was developed. Although this system implementation essentially satisfied the RPV mission requirements for size, weight, power, and data rates, certain hardware limitations were encountered with the analog multipliers. Recent developments employing a new prime cosine algorithm (Speiser, 1976) have shown promise for reducing the hardware

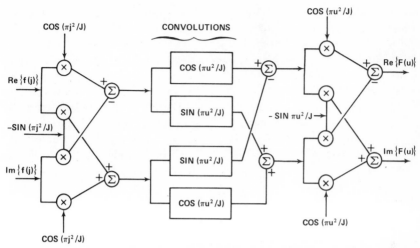

FIG. 5-10. Chirp-Z implementation of discrete Fourier transform.

problems, since the prime cosine algorithm does not use the analog multipliers required by the chirp-Z method. Work in the area of analog transversal filter hybrid coder implementations is continuing under this program.

Other efforts directed toward an all-digital RPV hybrid coder implementation have been undertaken by the Radio Corporation of America.

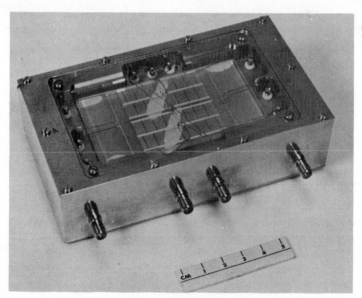

FIG. 5-11. Surface acoustic wave transversal filter.

With the exception of the video A/D converter, the RCA system is all-digital and uses state-of-the-art LSI silicon-on-sapphire technology for multipliers, adders, and other registers. This system also uses intraframe hybrid cosine transform/DPCM coding in conjunction with the bandwidth reduction techniques previously mentioned. The complete RCA airborne encoder system is packaged on the 5 × 9 in. circuit board shown in Fig. 5-12. In this configuration, the encoder circuitry is arranged functionally with the DPCM and discrete cosine transform modules located at the center and right side, respectively, of the circuit board. The complete hybrid cosine transform/DPCM encoder assembly weighs less than 1 lb and dissipates approximately 15 W (Rudnick *et al.*, 1977).

5.2 INTERFRAME HYBRID IMAGE CODING

In high-repetition-rate sequences of images such as those encountered in video transmissions, new information is normally contained in only a relatively small number of pixels. Often, the vast majority of pixels within each frame represent background material that does not significantly change between frames. From a statistical viewpoint, similarity of pixel

FIG. 5-12.   Digital intraframe cosine transform/DPCM encoder assembly (courtesy of RCA).

values from one frame to the next implies high frame-to-frame correlation between temporally adjacent pixel values. The class of transform, predictive, and hybrid transform/predictive techniques developed to exploit spatial correlation within a single image can, in principle, be extended to include interframe correlation, thereby achieving still further reductions in channel bandwidth requirements.

Investigations of three-dimensional Fourier transform coding has indicated that bit rates can be reduced by a factor of 5 by incorporating correlation of the data in the temporal direction (Tescher, 1974). However, a serious drawback of transform interframe coders is the requirement for multiple-frame storage of the transform coefficients. This characteristic of three-dimensional transform coders severely limits their usefulness for implementation in practical interframe coding systems.

In this section, the concept of an interframe hybrid two-dimensional transform/DPCM coder is introduced. This coder is closely related to the intraframe hybrid coder and, when using first-order linear prediction, offers the advantage of requiring only a single frame of storage.

5.2.1   System Definition

A block diagram of the basic interframe hybrid coder is shown in Fig. 5-13. In this coding system, a two-dimensional unitary transform is per-

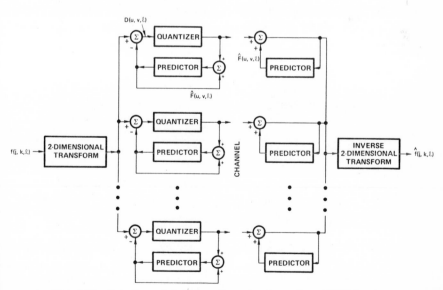

FIG. 5-13.   Interframe hybrid two-dimensional transform/DPCM coder.

formed on spatial subblocks within each image. One of the banks of parallel DPCM linear predictive coders is then applied to each set of transform
coefficients in the temporal direction. The resulting sequences of transform coefficient temporal differences are quantized and coded for transmission. Image reconstruction occurs at the receiver where the transform
coefficient differences are decoded, and a replica of each transmitted image
is reconstructed by a two-dimensional inverse transformation.

A general expression for the spatial domain processing of the interframe hybrid coder can be obtained by letting $f(j, k, l)$ denote a three-
dimensional array of amplitude values for a digital image sequence of L
frames. Also, let $F(u, v, l)$ be the three-dimensional array obtained by
taking two-dimensional transforms in subblocks of size $J \times K$ within each
frame.

Mathematically, this transformation pair can be described in general
form by

$$F(u, v, l) = \sum_{j=0}^{J-1} \sum_{k=0}^{K-1} f(j, k, l)\phi(u, v, j, k) \tag{18a}$$

and

$$f(j, k, l) = \sum_{u=0}^{J-1} \sum_{v=0}^{K-1} F(u, v, l)\phi^{-1}(u, v, j, k) \tag{18b}$$

where j and k are spatial coordinates, u and v are transform domain coordinates, l is the temporal coordinate indicating frame number, and
$\phi(u, v, j, k)$ is a set of two-dimensional orthogonal basis functions.

As in the case of intraframe hybrid coders, the discrete cosine transform has been chosen for the analysis of interframe image coding techniques. Equations (18a) and (18b) assume the following forms for the discrete two-dimensional cosine transform:

$$F(u, v, l) = \frac{1}{JK} \sum_{j=0}^{J-1} \sum_{k=0}^{K-1} f(j, k, l) \cos\left[\frac{(2j + 1)u\pi}{2J}\right] \cos\left[\frac{(2k + 1)v\pi}{2K}\right] \tag{19a}$$

and

$$f(j, k, l) = \sum_{u=0}^{J-1} \sum_{v=0}^{K-1} F(u, v, l) \cos\left[\frac{(2j + 1)u\pi}{2J}\right] \cos\left[\frac{(2k + 1)v\pi}{2K}\right] \tag{19b}$$

The cosine transform kernels in Eq. (19) are separable. Computationally,
transform separability means that the two-dimensional transform of an
image can be computed by applying a one-dimensional transform along

the rows (columns) of the image or image subblock followed by another one-dimensional transform along the columns (rows). Thus, the basic one-dimensional cosine transform operations that are applied to the rows and columns within each image subblock are given by Eq. (2).

At each spatial frequency (u, v), the DPCM coder quantizes and codes the difference signal between temporally adjacent transform coefficients defined by

$$D(u, v, l) = F(u, v, l) - \hat{F}(u, v, l) \tag{20}$$

where

$$\hat{F}(u, v, l) = a_1 F(u, v, l - 1) + a_0 \tag{21}$$

is the first-order, linear, minimum-mean-square-error estimate based on the previous frame. Under the assumption that $F(u, v, l)$ is a zero-mean sequence of transform coefficients, the quantities a_0 and a_1 needed to form the estimate $\hat{F}(u, v, l)$ are given by a generalization of Eq. (5). These equations define the form of the predictors used in each of the parallel DPCM coders shown in Fig. 5-13.

Analogous to the case of intraframe hybrid systems, the difference signal $D(u, v, l)$ is coded using a zonal coding strategy in which the number of code bits assigned to each difference signal is set essentially in proportion to the logarithm of its variance.

5.2.2 Theoretical Performance Model

A theoretical performance model based on a wide-sense stationary Markov source data model has been developed for the class of interframe hybrid coders. Representing the image sequence as a stochastic process of known autocorrelation and zero mean, covariance matrix approximations of the form of Eq. (6) may be made for the column $\mathbf{K}_{f_j}$ and row $\mathbf{K}_{f_k}$ pixel values. For the cosine transform, column and row transform domain covariance matrices $\mathbf{K}_{F_u}$ and $\mathbf{K}_{F_v}$ are computed in the same manner as in Eq. (7). A major difference occurs between the previous model formulation and that of the interframe hybrid coder in that knowledge of the two-dimensional distribution of the transform coefficient variances is now required. This information is contained in the variance matrix

$$\mathbf{V}_F = \mathscr{V}_{F_u} \mathscr{V}_{F_v}^{\mathrm{T}} \tag{22}$$

where vectors $\mathscr{V}_{F_u}$ and $\mathscr{V}_{F_v}$ represent the diagonal elements of covariance matrix models $\mathbf{K}_{F_u}$ and $\mathbf{K}_{F_v}$, respectively.

The relationship between the matrix of transform coefficient variances V_F and the matrix of transform coefficient temporal difference variances V_D for first-order DPCM predictive coding is given by

$$V_D = V_F\{1 - \rho_T^2\} \tag{23}$$

where ρ_T is the temporal correlation of the transform coefficients (Habibi, 1971). Equation (23) permits the matrix V_D to be modeled for interframe hybrid coders using unitary transforms and first-order DPCM predictive coding with specified row, column, and temporal correlation.

A zonal coding strategy is also assumed for the theoretical performance evaluation of the interframe hybrid coder model. In this application of zonal coding, the number of code bits allocated for quantization is different for each zone of the transform coefficient difference variance matrix V_D with coefficient difference variances having zero allocated bits defining the subset of transform coefficient differences not coded for transmission.

Equation (10) gave the general form for mean-square error of zonal coding. For the interframe hybrid coder, the expression for mean-square error is defined in terms of the probability density of the transform coefficient temporal differences, as well as the quantizer decision and reconstruction levels and bit allocations. The form for the probability density of the dc and higher-order cosine transform temporal differences is also assumed to be Laplacian. Under these conditions, the mean-square-error expression for interframe hybrid coders is

$$\mathscr{E} = \sum_{u=0}^{J-1} \sum_{v=0}^{K-1} \left\{ V_D(u, v) - \frac{1}{2} \sum_{u=1}^{2^{b(u,v)}} R_n^2(u, v) \right.$$
$$\left. \cdot \left[\exp\left(\frac{-(2)^{1/2} D_n(u, v)}{V_D(u, v)} \right) - \exp\left(\frac{-(2)^{1/2} D_{n+1}(u, v)}{V_D(u, v)} \right) \right] \right\} \tag{24}$$

where $V_D(u, v)$ is the variance of the transform coefficient differences at location (u, v); D_n, D_{n+1}, and R_n are optimal Laplacian quantizer decision and reconstruction levels; and $b(u, v)$ is the number of assigned bits.

The theoretical performance of the interframe hybrid coder has been evaluated using separable cosine transforms and first-order DPCM predictive coding. Three original images were modeled as a Markov process with equal horizontal, vertical, and temporal correlations of 0.90, 0.93, and 0.95. In these simulations, zonal coding with Max quantizer decision and reconstruction levels was used to achieve an average pixel bit rate per frame of 0.25. The results of the interframe hybrid coder theoretical performance evaluation are presented in Fig. 5-14.

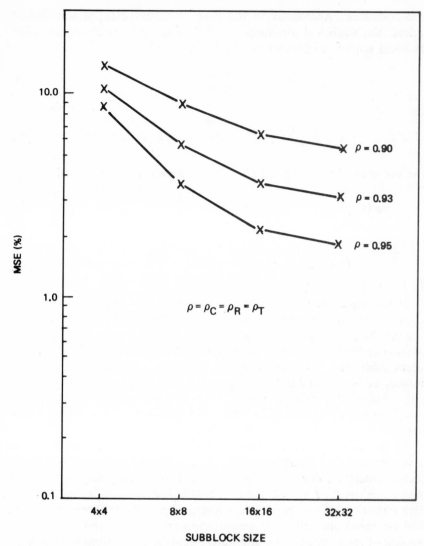

FIG. 5-14. Theoretical performance evaluation for interframe hybrid coder at 0.25 bit/pixel/frame for zonal coding with Markov data.

5.2.3   Adaptive Interframe Hybrid Coding

Significant improvements in coding performance can be obtained by spatial adaptation in the interframe hybrid coder to use calculated statistical measures of the transform coefficient temporal difference signal in each subblock. Analogous to the case of adaptive intraframe hybrid coders, the statistical measures are the mean and correlation for each temporal sequence of transform coefficients defined by

$$\bar{F}(u, v) = \frac{1}{L} \sum_{l=0}^{L-1} F(u, v, l) \qquad (25)$$

and

$$\rho_T(u, v) = \frac{1}{L-1} \sum_{l=1}^{L-1} F(u, v, l)F(u, v, l-1) \Big/ \frac{1}{L} \sum_{l=0}^{L-1} F^2(u, v, l) \quad (26)$$

The variance of the temporal coefficient differences is estimated as

$$\sigma_D^2(u, v) = \frac{1}{L-1} \sum_{l=1}^{L-1} D^2(u, v, l) - \left[\frac{1}{L-1} \sum_{l=1}^{L-1} D(u, v, l)\right]^2 \quad (27)$$

where

$$D(u, v, l) = F(u, v, l) - \rho_T(u, v)F(u, v, l-1) \qquad (28)$$

for $l = 1, 2, \ldots, L - 1$.

In this case, the computed transform coefficient difference variances $\sigma_D^2(u, v)$ are used to generate two-dimensional subblock bit assignments. The resulting bit assignments, predictor feedback loop gain coefficients, and associated biasing and scaling factors are, in general, different for different subblocks. As in the adaptive intraframe hybrid coder, the total number of bits available for coding each subblock is constrained to be equal. Adaptation in the case of the interframe hybrid coder also produces improved coding results when compared with nonadaptive implementations.

In the adaptive coding process described above, the receiver must have the statistical parameters $\bar{F}(u, v)$, $\rho(u, v)$, and $\sigma_D^2(u, v)$ available at each coefficient index (u, v). One approach is to form these statistics at the transmitter for L stored frames, and then quantize, code, and transmit each statistic to the receiver. The disadvantages of this approach include data overhead and effects of quantization error introduced in the transmission of each statistic. An alternative approach is to form the statistics jointly at the transmitter and receiver utilizing the coefficient feedback predicted value $\hat{F}(u, v, l)$ in Eqs. (25)–(28). This scheme requires no channel overhead since the transmitter and receiver coefficient predictions are identical in the absence of channel errors. Furthermore, quantization error of the statistics is reduced by the DPCM feedback process. With either approach, it is necessary to occasionally retransmit the feedback prediction estimate $\hat{F}(u, v, l)$ to correct for accumulated channel error effects.

5.2.4   Experimental Performance Evaluation

The performance of the interframe hybrid coder has been experimentally evaluated using the complete 16-frame "Walter" and chemical plant data bases. In evaluating coder performance levels, the normalized mean-square-error (NMSE) and signal-to-noise-ratio criteria (SNR) defined in Eqs. (16) and (17) are used in conjunction with subjective visual evaluations.

Photographs of reconstructions of the sixteenth frame of the input image sequence are shown in Figs. 5-15 and 5-16 for average coding rates

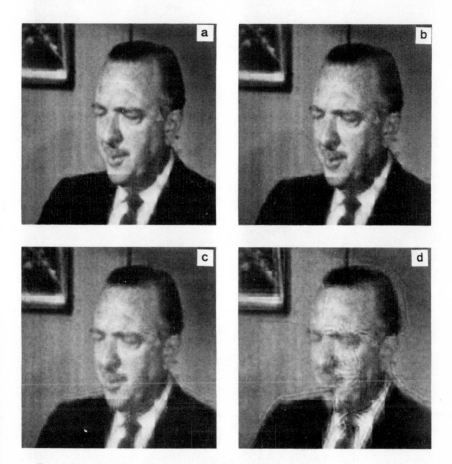

FIG. 5-15. Experimental coding performance of the hybrid transform/DPCM coder without adaptive coding. (a) 1.0 bit/pixel/frame, NMSE = 1.03%; (b) 0.5 bit/pixel/frame, NMSE = 1.23%; (c) 0.25 bit/pixel/frame, NMSE = 1.60%; (d) 0.1 bit/pixel/frame, NMSE = 2.63%.

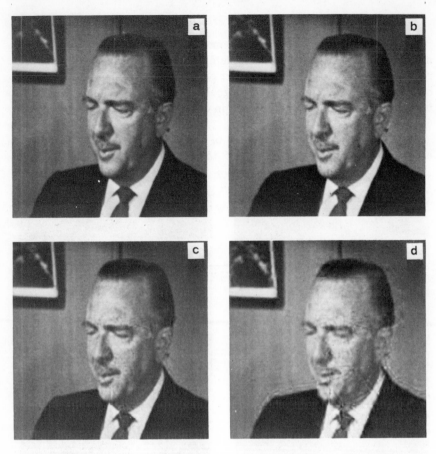

FIG. 5-16. Experimental coding performance of the hybrid transform/DPCM coder with adaptive coding. (a) 1.0 bit/pixel/frame, NMSE = 0.02%; (b) 0.5 bit/pixel/frame, NMSE = 0.07%; (c) 0.25 bit/pixel/frame, NMSE = 0.19%; (d) 0.1 bit/pixel/frame, NMSE = 0.63%.

of 0.1, 0.25, 0.5, and 1.0 bit/pixel/frame for nonadaptive and adaptive coding, respectively. In these experiments the first frame of the sequence is available at both the transmitter and receiver as an initial condition. The transform coefficient statistics in the adaptive coder simulation have been generated from the common feedback predicted coefficient $\hat{F}(u, v, l)$ available at both the transmitter and receiver, and therefore, there is no channel overhead for this form of adaptive coding. Visually, little or no image degradation can be seen for bit rates as low as 0.5 bit/pixel/frame with adaptive coding. Some artifacting effects due to the 16 × 16 sub-block partitioning of the images is apparent at the 0.25-bit/pixel/frame rate. Also, regions outlining the subject's head begin to show degradation at this bit rate because of head motion and the relatively few coefficients assigned to transmit high-frequency coefficients. The observed image degradations are similar in nature, but more pronounced at the 0.1-bit/pixel/frame rate.

Figure 5-17 illustrates MMSE and SNR as functions of frame number for the adaptive interframe hybrid coder at average pixel bit rates from 0.1 to 1.0 bit/pixel/frame with 16×16 subblocks. These graphs indicate that even at the lowest bit rate, stability in coder performance is achieved within the first eight frames. Performance stability occurs much earlier in the frame sequence for higher bit rates. In these simulations the first frame is assumed available at the receiver, and consequently zero NMSE is obtained at the first frame.

The performance of the adaptive interframe hybrid coder has also been investigated in the presence of noise for a binary symmetric channel transmission system. Photographs showing the visual effects of channel noise on the sixteenth frame of the data base are given in Fig. 5-18. The results illustrated are for average pixel bit rates of 1.0 and 0.25 bit/pixel frame, and P_e of 10^{-2} and 10^{-3}. Simulations have also been run with a channel error probability of 10^{-4}. Coding results obtained with $P_e = 10^{-4}$

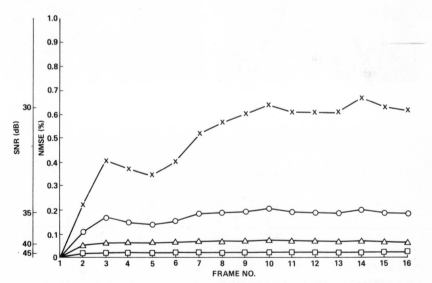

FIG. 5-17. Coding performance as a function of frame number for the interframe hybrid coder with adaptive coding. $\times$, 0.1 bit/pixel/frame; $\bigcirc$, 0.25 bit/pixel/frame; $\triangle$, 0.5 bit/pixel/frame; $\square$, 1.0 bit/pixel/frame.

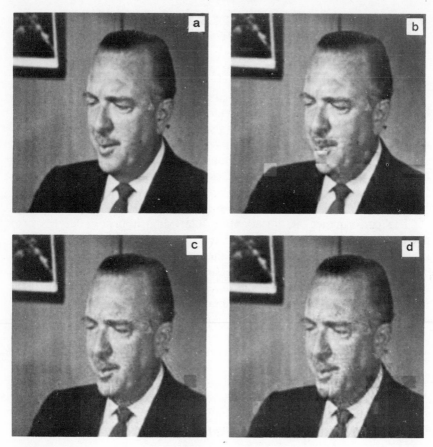

FIG. 5-18.   Experimental coding performance of the interframe hybrid coder with adaptive coding and channel noise. (a) 1.0 bit/pixel/frame, $P_e = 10^{-3}$, NMSE = 0.04%; (b) 1.0 bit/pixel/frame, $P_e = 10^{-2}$, NMSE = 0.28%; (c) 0.25 bit/pixel/frame, $P_e = 10^{-3}$, NMSE = 0.22%; (d) 0.25 bit/pixel/frame, $P_e = 10^{-2}$, NMSE = 0.45%.

are essentially indistinguishable from the case with $P_e = 0$, and therefore are not included.

   An additional series of simulations has been performed to evaluate coding performance as a function of spatial subblock size. Figure 5-19 illustrates NMSE and SNR values versus subblock size for the interframe hybrid coder on frame number 16 of the "Walter" data base. The results of this experiment show a continual improvement in coding performance for increasing subblock size and suggest that the largest subblock size consistent with coder storage and complexity limitations should be employed.

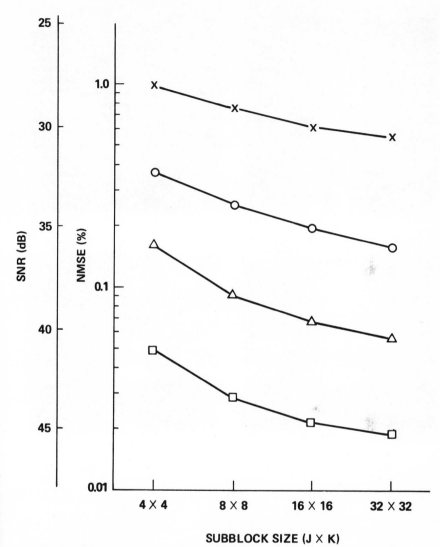

FIG. 5-19. Experimental performance evaluation of the interframe hybrid coder as a function of subblock size. ×, 0.1 bit/pixel/frame; ○, 0.25 bit/pixel/frame; △, 0.5 bit/pixel/frame; □, 1.0 bit/pixel/frame.

5.3   SUMMARY

The concept of hybrid unitary transform/DPCM coding has been investigated for both intraframe and interframe applications. Figure 5-20 compares the performance of the two classes of coders for the "Walter"

FIG. 5-20. Comparison of intraframe and interframe hybrid coders with adaptive coding. Top—Intraframe hybrid coder: (a) 2.0 bit/pixel; (b) 0.8 bit/pixel. Bottom—Interframe hybrid coder: (c) 0.25 bit/pixel/frame; (d) 0.2 bit/pixel/frame.

and chemical plant data bases. The average pixel bit rates selected for this comparison give subjectively equivalent image reconstructions although the nature of the image degradations differs for the two coders. For these data bases, exploitation of temporal correlation using hybrid interframe coding has resulted in a 4:1 or better reduction in average pixel bit rate when compared to hybrid intraframe coding. On the basis of the theoretical and experimental results obtained, it has been demonstrated that exploitation of temporal as well as spatial correlations is a viable technique for hybrid coding of digital image sequences.

Acknowledgments

Much of the work described herein was supported by the Advanced Research Projects Agency of the Department of Defense and monitored by the Wright-Patterson Air Force Base under Contract No. F-33615-76-C-1203 and by the Naval Ocean Systems Center, San Diego, California, under Contract No. N00123-75-1192.

The author wishes to acknowledge Dr. Ali Habibi of TRW systems for his contributions, particularly in the formative stages of research on hybrid coders. The author also acknowledges Dr. Edwin H. Wrench, Dr. Robert W. Means, Harper J. Whitehouse, Jeffrey M. Speiser, and James M Alsup of the Naval Ocean Systems Center; Dr. William K. Pratt of the University of Southern California Image Processing Institute; and Col. H. M. Federhen, US Army, of the Advanced Research Projects Agency for their contributions to the advancement of hybrid transform/predictive coder technology.

References

Ahmed, N., Natarajan, T., and Rao, K. R. (1974). *IEEE Trans. Comput.* **c-23**, 90–93.

Alsup, J. M., Means, R. W., and Whitehouse, H. J. (1973). "Real Time Discrete Fourier Transforms Using Surface Acoustic Wave Devices," ARPA AP4, Order No. 2303, Code No. 3G10. Naval Undersea Center, San Diego, California.

Habibi, A. (1971). *IEEE Trans. Commun. Technol.* **com-19**, 61–66.

Habibi, A. (1974). *IEEE Trans. Commun.* **com-22**, 614–624.

Habibi, A., and Hershel, R. S. (1974). *IEEE Trans. Commun.* **com-22**, 692–696.

Max, J. (1960). *IEEE Trans. Inf. Theory* **it-6**, 7–12.

Means, R. W., Whitehouse, H. J., and Speiser, J. M. (1974). *Proc. Natl. Telecommun. Conf.* pp. 61–66.

Noble, S. C., Knauer, S. C., and Giem, J. I. (1973). *Proc. Int. Telemeter. Conf.* Vol. 9, p. 496.

Pratt, W. K. (1978). "Digital Image Processing." Wiley, New York.

Rao, K. R., Narasimhan, M. A., and Gorzinski, W. J. (1977). *IEEE Trans. Syst., Man Cybernet.* **smc-7** 728–734.

Roese, J. A. (1976). "Interframe Coding of Digital Images Using Transform and Hybrid Transform/Predictive Coding Techniques," USCIPI Rep. 700. University of Southern California, Image Processing Institute, Los Angeles.

Roese, J. A., Habibi, A., Pratt, W. K., and Robinson, G. S. (1975). *Proc. Int. Conf. Commun.* Vol. 2, pp. 17–21.

Roese, J. A., Pratt, W. K., and Robinson, G. S. (1977). *IEEE Trans. Commun.* **com-25**, 1329–1339.

Rudnick, J. J., Claffie, G. M., and Richards, J. R. (1977). "Bandwidth Reduction System," Final Rep., Contract N00123-76-C-0746. Advanced Technology Laboratories, Radio Corporation of America, Camden, New Jersey.

Speiser, J. M. (1973). "High Speed Serial Access Implementation for Discrete Cosine Transforms," ARPA QR3, Order No. 2303, Code No. 3G10. Naval Undersea Center, San Diego, California.

Speiser, J. M. (1976). "The Prime Cosine Algorithm," ARPA QR6, Order No. 2303, Code No. 3G10. Naval Undersea Center, San Diego, California.

Tescher, A. G. (1974). "The Role of Phase in Adaptive Image Coding," USCIPI Rep. 510. University of Southern California, Image Processing Institute, Los Angeles, California.

Frame Replenishment Coding of Television

BARRY G. HASKELL

Radio Communications Research Department
Bell Laboratories
Holmdel, New Jersey

A frame replenishment coder–decoder (FRODEC) takes advantage of the considerable similarity between successive frames of television in two ways:

(1) The parts of the picture that do not change between frames are not transmitted; at the display they are reconstructed simply by repeating from the previous frame.

(2) The changing parts of the picture that are sent are coded with varying resolution depending on subjective requirements for acceptable picture quality and the bit rate available for transmission.

With videotelephone or conference television where typically cameras are stationary and scenes consist mainly of small areas moving in front of a relatively large stationary background, a considerable saving in transmission can be achieved compared with PCM, or, in many cases, with analog transmission. In this situation the required transmission bit rate is determined by the amount of movement that must be accommodated and by how fast the coder must recover from a sudden scene change, which may be caused by such things as camera switching, putting up a new chart or graph, or a sudden change in lighting.

With broadcast television where there is a great deal of camera movement and scene changing, the savings are relatively less than with video-telephone or conference television. Although the percentage of stationary background area is normally much lower, there still exists considerable frame-to-frame redundancy, which can be exploited by redundancy reduction coding. In addition, by varying the resolution of moving areas to display only what is required for subjective acceptance, further savings can be obtained.

At the present time, with low-resolution monochrome videotelephone used for interpersonal communication ($\approx$1-MHz bandwidth), frame replenishment coding degradations can be made negligible at bit rates of about 0.75 bit per picture element or 1.5 Mbits/sec (Limb *et al.*, 1974). At lower bit rates less movement can be accommodated without visible defects. At a bit rate of about 0.1 bit per picture element or 0.2 Mbit/sec, only low-key conversations with the subject sitting relatively still can be transmitted without annoying degradations (Haskell and Schmidt, 1975). Graphics are handled quite well (within the resolution limits of the original signal) at all bit rates in this range, the principal degradation being the delay time required to display full resolution after a sudden scene change.

For medium-resolution videotelephone or conference television ($\approx$4-MHz bandwidth), good results have been obtained in the range 0.2–0.75 bits per picture element or 1.5–6 Mbits/sec (Haskell *et al.*, 1977; Iinuma *et al.*, 1975). Coding distortion is detectable in this range, but most viewers find it not objectionable for interpersonal communication. Color pictures have also been coded at 6 Mbits/sec.

For broadcast color signals (NTSC, bandwidth = 4 MHz), the quality constraints are much more stringent. Good results have been obtained by sampling the composite signal at three times color carrier frequency and coding at 2 bits per picture element or 22 Mbits/sec (Ishiguro *et al.*, 1976). However, subjective tests remain to be carried out to determine broadcaster acceptability. Bit rates obtainable at the present time for various picture formats are summarized in Table 6-1.

6.1 HISTORY

It has long been recognized that it is wasteful to send more than 50 separate television frames per second in order to avoid flicker visibility. Good motion rendition, after all, requires at most 30 frames per second, and even at this rate successive frames are very much alike (Kell, 1929; Seyler, 1962). Early efforts at reducing this waste were aimed at more efficiently using the bandwidth available for analog transmission. For example, simply transmitting 15 frames per second and displaying each

TABLE 6-1

Analog signal	Bit rate (Mbits/sec)	Application	Reference
1 MHz, monochrome, 267 lines	1.5	Conferencing—low-to-moderate motion	Limb *et al.*, 1974
1 MHz, monochrome, 267 lines	0.2	Conferencing—low-motion only	Haskell and Schmidt 1975
4 MHz, monochrome, 525 lines	1.5	Conferencing—low-to-moderate motion	Haskell *et al.*, 1977
4 MHz, color, 525 lines	6	Conferencing—low-to-moderate motion	Iinuma *et al.*, 1975
4 MHz, color, 525 lines	22	Broadcast—all types of motion	Ishiguro *et al.*, 1976

Notes: Low-resolution, monochrome videotelephone signals of 1-MHz bandwidth typically require 14–16 Mbits/sec for simple PCM coding. DPCM coding uses about 6.3 Mbits/sec. Monochrome signals of 4-MHz bandwidth need 56–64 Mbits/sec for simple PCM coding. Color signals require about 88 Mbits/sec for PCM.

frame four times at the receiver to avoid flicker has been found to be useful for face-to-face video telephone (Brainard *et al.*, 1967). With this technique and appropriate time multiplexing, four television signals can be sent over one channel nominally reserved for 60 frames per second.

With $N:1$ line interlace, only one out of N lines are sent during each scan through the picture. The subset of lines thus produced during one scan through the picture is called a field. The remaining lines are sent similarly in the following $N - 1$ fields. All broadcast-rate television systems use $2:1$ line interlace. For N greater than 2, picture quality depends on the persistence of the display phosphor and the amount of motion in the scene (Cherry, 1974a). Dot interlace (Deutsch, 1973) at a factor of $N:1$ is similar to line interlace. Only one out of N samples are sent in each line, and N passes through the picture are required to send all of the samples. Again, picture quality depends on the persistence of the display phosphor and on the amount of motion in the scene (Cherry, 1974b; Stone, 1976).

In both interlacing techniques above, frame memory at the receiver enables line or sample repeating to avoid flicker visibility on normal persistence phosphors. However, degradations due to motion in the scene still occur in the form of visibility of the sampling pattern in moving areas (Mounts, 1967). An improvement can be obtained in this regard by interpolating in the moving areas of the picture instead of repeating (Pease and Limb, 1971; Fukinuki *et al.*, 1972). These techniques all produce a relatively constant bit rate with the result that, in terms of coding efficiency, the bit rate is still too high in stationary areas of the picture. Observations and ideas such as this inexorably led to the first experiments with frame replenishment of monochrome television (Seyler, 1963, 1965; Mounts, 1969).

Frame replenishment requires (1) a frame memory at the transmitter to enable comparison of two successive frames in order to select the moving-area picture elements for transmission (see Fig. 6-1), (2) a transmitter buffer to smooth the data rate prior to transmission over a constant-rate digital channel, (3) a receiver buffer, and (4) a frame memory at the receiver to repeat from the previous frame picture elements that have not been transmitted. Positional addressing information must also be sent so that the receiver knows where in the frame to place the received picture elements. Mounts (1967) describes conditional replenishment in which a PCM picture element value plus an address is sent for each pic-

FIG. 6-1.   Example of the location of moving-area picture elements, indicated by white dots, that are transmitted by a frame replenishment codec.

ture element that is changed by more than a certain threshold since the previous frame. With this algorithm operating at a channel rate of 1 bit per picture element, excessive movement causes the buffer to quickly fill, which in turn causes breakup of the moving areas of the picture.

Improvements on this rudimentary algorithm were rapidly forthcoming, so that by the time of the last review paper on interframe coding (Haskel *et al.*, 1972) much had been learned about coding low-resolution (1-MHz-bandwidth) monochrome videotelephone signals. For example:

• As in intraframe processing, predictive coding using variable word lengths of transmitted picture elements was found to be far more efficient than separate transmission via PCM.

• Methods of addressing changed picture elements more efficiently were discovered. Instead of addressing each changed picture element separately, it was found that they could be addressed in clusters (Candy *et al.*, 1971).

• Because of the blurring of moving areas due to camera integration (Pease and Limb, 1971), it was found to be unnecessary to transmit all moving-area picture elements during periods of rapid motion. Subsampling by 2:1 in the horizontal dimension approximately halves the data rate during such periods and helps prevent buffer overflow without degrading picture quality.

• It was learned that isolated frame differences can be ignored since they are probably due to noise. Therefore, under low-noise conditions the data rate can be measurably reduced.

• Buffer requirements for frame replenishment were better understood. A transmitter buffer of size B bits connected to a channel of rate R bits/sec introduces a source receiver delay of B/R sec (J. C. Candy and F. W. Mounts, informal communication, 1970). Since in a two-way videocommunication round-trip delay should be kept below 600 msec (R. C. Brainard, C. C. Cutler, and D. E. Rowlinson, informal communication, 1968), then if T is the total round-trip channel delay, a frame replenishment system must satisfy

$$2B/R + T \leq 600 \quad \text{msec} \tag{1}$$

to avoid annoying delay effects.

• Extremely large buffers do not result in much additional savings (Limb, 1972). Once a buffer is large enough to smooth the data over a field period, further savings in channel rate come about only by smoothing between human actions. These actions tend to be several seconds in duration, a period that is much too long a time over which to smooth data in a two-way communication.

• Since over the long term, videotelephone or conference pictures contain relatively little movement (movement usually only occurs in short bursts), combining data from several coders prior to buffering and transmission results in a large amount of data smoothing without adding very much delay or requiring large buffers (Haskell, 1972a). Combining data from a dozen or so sources results in a 2:1 reduction in required channel bit rate.

Since 1972, work on these and other aspects of frame replenishment coding has continued, and several operating prototype systems have been constructed. In the following sections the emphasis will be on basic techniques. However, since in a complete system the interaction among basic methods and the harmonious blending thereof is extremely important, examples of more or less complete algorithms will also be given. Also, the main interest will be in luminance coding, since color information typically is a relatively small percentage of the total.

6.2   EFFICIENT PREDICTIVE CODING

In a frame replenishment coder the moving-area picture elements need not be transmitted independently from one another. As with intraframe coders, a reduced number of bits per transmitted picture element can be achieved if advantage is taken of their correlation with nearby picture elements, both spatially and temporally. One method of accomplishing this is linear predictive coding (Connor *et al.*, 1972). As long as the picture elements used in the prediction are available to both coder and decoder, for example, picture elements A–V in Fig. 6-2, successful transmission is possible if the differential signal between an actual and predicted picture element value is sent. Table 6-2 gives some examples of linear prediction rules that are useful for frame replenishment coding of moving-area pic-

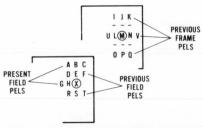

FIG. 6-2.   Two successive television frames with interlacing (two interlaced fields per frame). Picture elements (pels) *X* and *M* are exactly one frame period apart in time.

TABLE 6-2

SOME MOVING-AREA LINEAR PREDICTOR RULES

Transmitted signal $X - P_X$	P_X (see Fig. 6-2)
Frame difference	M
Element difference	H
Element difference of frame difference	$M + H - L$
Line difference of frame difference	$M + B - J$
Field difference	$(E + S)/2$
Element difference of field difference	$H + (E + S)2 - (D + R)/2$

ture elements. An implementation of frame replenishment coding with linear prediction is shown in Fig. 6-3. For each pel X, the predictor uses previously coded pels to compute a prediction P_X. The differential signal $X - P_X$ is quantized and coded. If X is a moving-area pel, as determined by the segmenter, the differential code plus addressing information are fed to the buffer to await transmission, and a new pel value $\tilde{X}$ is passed to the frame memory to be used later by the coder.

It was recognized quite some time ago (Pease and Limb, 1971) that as the speed of motion in a television picture increases, the spatial correlation between moving-area picture elements will also increase owing to the

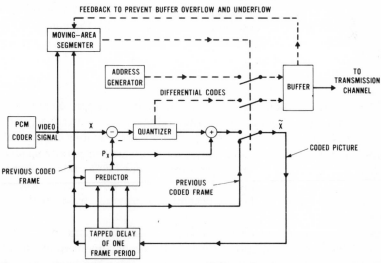

FIG. 6-3. Frame replenishment coder that transmits moving-area picture elements (pels) via predictive coding.

integrating effect of the television camera. Moreover, the temporal correlation among such picture elements will decrease. Thus, a spatial predictive coder, e.g., element-differential PCM (Pease and Limb, 1971; Haskell
et al., 1973; Limb *et al.*, 1974; Wendt, 1973), would seem to be a good
candidate for frame replenishment. For this type of coder the differential
signal entropy and, consequently, the number of bits per moving-area picture element (if variable-word-length coding is used) will decrease as motion increases. This is exactly the desired behavior if buffer overflow is to
be avoided.

To quantify this observation, a number of measurements were carried
out of the moving-area element-differential entropy as a function of the
speed of movement (Haskell, 1972b, 1975; Wendt, 1973; Bostelmann,
1976), and results were compared with the moving-area frame-differential
entropy (see Fig. 6-4). As expected, for slow speeds, frame-differential
coding was better, and for high speeds element-differential coding was
superior, the crossover point being at approximately a speed of one picture element interval per frame period. At this speed (for horizontal motion) the frame difference equals the element difference (Connor and
Limb, 1974).

When using element-differential coding in moving areas of the picture,
horizontal subsampling increases the entropy of the element-differential
signal, thus reducing the effectiveness of element-differential coding.
Also, when the element-differential signal is quantized, as it must be for
digital transmission, additional noise is introduced into the picture. This
increases the difficulty of segmenting the picture into moving areas and
stationary background areas. More will be said on this topic later. In spite
of these difficulties, element-differential prediction may have a place in
frame replenishing coding if the FRODEC must be able to handle a signal
that has been previously coded with intraframe EDPCM (Limb *et al.*,
1974).

Other linear predictors for coding moving-area picture elements have
also been studied. Previous field picture elements are particularly attractive, since they are spatially even closer than the previous element along
the line in most signal formats. However, they are temporally spaced by
one-half frame period from the picture element being coded, so that as
motion increases, the differential signal entropy will increase. The same
holds true for linear predictors that utilize previous frame picture elements.

Measurements of moving-area differential signal entropies are presented in Fig. 6-4 as a function of speed of a moving mannequin's head for
several higher-order linear predictors using 1-MHz-bandwidth videotelephone signals. It should be observed that entropies of intraframe differen-

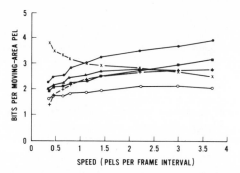

FIG. 6-4.   Entropies of various moving-area differential signals obtained from a scene containing a moving mannequin's head. ●, Frame difference; x, element difference; ■, field difference; ▲, element difference of frame difference; +, line difference of frame difference; ○, element difference of field difference.

tial signals (element differences) decrease with speed, while entropies of interframe differential signals increase with speed. In Fig. 6-4 all signals have been quantized to 35 levels. This number of levels is too large by a factor of approximately 2 for all except frame and field differences. But, since entropy is determined almost completely by the inner quantized levels, a meaningful comparison can nevertheless be made using these results. The best of the linear predictors transmits element differences of field differences. Relatively low entropies can also be obtained by transmitting the line-difference-of-frame-difference signal or element differences of frame differences.

For speeds above one picture element interval per frame period none of the predictors possesses a 2:1 advantage over the others. Thus, subsampling (not sending all picture elements) in the moving area is required for most efficient coding. If 2:1 horizontal sampling is to be used, then the linear predictor must not use the previous picture element along the line. If 2:1 vertical subsampling is to be used, the linear predictor must not use the previous field picture elements. Of the better predictors, the line-difference-of-frame-difference predictor fulfills both of these requirements. It has been used in a system for 0.1 bit per picture element coding of 1-MHz-bandwidth videotelephone signal (Haskell and Schmidt, 1975).

Use of the picture elements in the previous line by the linear predictor has serious consequences in the presence of transmission errors (Connor, 1973c). In such cases, the decoding error propagates downward. In addition, if variable-word-length coding causes loss of samples, the error propagates rightward, thus causing distortion in the entire lower right side of the picture. This error remains until it is corrected by other means. Thus, in the presence of digital transmission errors, the linear predictor should use only picture elements from the same line or the same line of the previous frame. A reasonable compromise is to use element-difference-of-frame-difference predictive coding. More will be said on this topic later.

6.3   SEGMENTING THE PICTURE INTO MOVING AND NONMOVING AREAS

Segmentation of the picture into moving areas that have changed significantly since the previous frame and into stationary background areas that have not changed significantly is basic to the operation of any frame replenishment coder. If the noise on the input signal is small, then simple thresholding (at approximately 1.5% of maximum) of the frame difference followed by rejection of isolated above-threshold differences is sufficient to define the minimal area that must be transmitted for adequate rendition of movement. Because of the large correlation between adjacent picture elements, there will be many insignificant frame differences, even within moving objects, with the result that the moving area, as defined above, will not be very contiguous. Sending positional information for highly noncontiguous areas can require a large number of bits if corrective measures are not taken. Suppose, for example, that horizontal clusters (runs) of moving-area picture elements are transmitted by sending addresses referenced to the beginning of the line, followed by amplitude information for each picture element, followed in turn with an end-of-run word distinguishable from all of the amplitude words. For this addressing strategy small gaps between runs are much more efficiently sent by redefining the picture elements therein as moving-area picture elements. This is called "bridging the gap." If A bits are used to address each cluster, E bits are used for the end-of-cluster word, and the average number of amplitude bits per picture element in the gap is P, then gaps smaller than $(A + E)/P$ picture elements should be bridged (Candy et al., 1971b).

More efficient addressing results if the beginning of each cluster of moving-area picture elements is addressed not with respect to the beginning of the line, but with respect to some other cluster that has already been transmitted. Cluster positions are highly correlated vertically and temporally. Sending the difference between the present cluster address and that of a cluster suitably chosen from the previous line, field, or frame, using a variable-word-length code for the differential addresses, can save 50% in addressing bits in videotelephone or conference television (Haskell, 1976a). However, during periods of moderate to rapid movement, when clusters are long, positional information is usually a relatively small percentage of the total (less than 20%). And since performance of a single frame replenishment coder is usually determined by its peak bit rate during such periods, the address bit saving is often not worth the additional coder complexity. If buffer and channel sharing by several frame replenishment coders is contemplated, however, the performance is determined by the average bit rate during slow movement, when the clusters are relatively short. During these periods the positional information is a much higher percentage of the total, and more efficient addressing may be much more worthwhile.

When the input video signal is corrupted by noise, segmenting the picture is not as straightforward as in the low-noise case. If the peak signal-to-rms-noise ratio falls much below 40 dB, simply raising the frame-difference significance threshold to eliminate the effects of noise causes too many subjectively important moving-area picture elements to be deleted and gives rise to the well-known "dirty window" effect (Mounts, 1969). It is in this situation that account must be taken of the differing properties of frame differences caused by noise and those caused by movement (Limb *et al.*, 1974; Connor *et al.*, 1973a, b). For example:

(1) Frame differences caused by white noise are spatially uncorrelated, whereas frame differences caused by movement are highly correlated spatially because of the high correlation between adjacent picture elements.

(2) High-detail moving areas—in particular, edges of moving objects—typically generate much larger frame differences than low-detail moving areas.

(3) Moving areas have high spatial contiguity.

(4) Moving areas have high temporal contiguity.

(5) Noise frame differences have negative temporal correlation in moving (replenished) areas and positive correlation in stationary background (unreplenished) areas (Connor and Limb, 1974).

These properties can be exploited to segment the picture more effectively in the presence of noise. For example, simple low-pass filtering of the frame difference in one dimension or two dimensions takes advantage of property 1 and can drastically reduce the effects of (relatively white) noise. Properties 2 and 3 can be utilized by hysteretic N out of M segmenting (Pease and Limb, 1971) as follows: An array of M picture elements surrounding (spatially or temporally) the one of interest is examined for significant frame differences. If more than N_1 are detected, "moving area" is assumed. This commonly occurs at the left edge of a moving object. The whole array is then moved to the right, and picture elements continue to be defined as "moving" until fewer than N_2 significant frame differences are detected. Typically, N_2 is less than N_1, thus, making the process hysteretic. Property 4 can be exploited by providing a 1-bit field or frame memory for the segmenter output signal. Then, segmenting in the present field can be influenced by whether or not the same area in the previous field or frame was deemed "moving area." Property 5 can be exploited by adaptive filtering of the frame-difference signal depending on whether moving areas or stationary areas are under consideration (Limb *et al.*, 1974).

Special problems arise when the input signal to be coded has previously been intraframe coded and reconstructed by element-differential PCM (DPCM) or transform coding, for example. This situation might occur in a network in which intraframe coding is used for short-haul transmission, and frame replenishment coding is employed for long-haul transmission. In this case the noise in the picture is no longer picture independent. In regions of high detail where the coarse outer levels of DPCM intraframe quantizer are used, the noise is larger and typically of lower frequency than in low-detail regions of the picture. In order to effectively segment such a signal, in addition to the above techniques, the dependence of the frame-to-frame noise on in-frame picture content must be taken into account. This is conveniently accomplished by examining element-to-element differences within the areas of interest and adjusting the frame-difference significance threshold to match the expected amount of frame-to-frame noise caused by the intraframe coding. In Connor *et al.* (1973a) and Limb *et al.* (1974) frame replenishment coders that accept a DPCM-coded signal as input are described. The latter achieves a transmission rate of 0.75 bit per picture element and, in addition, stores an element-differential PCM-coded signal in the frame memory, thus reducing the memory size by about 50% compared with storing PCM values.

In the implementation of any frame replenishment coding system, attention must be given to the problem of dc level shifts. Since many analog components are only ac coupled, dc restoration prior to measuring frame differences is a minimum necessity to enable proper segmenting during periods of movement. Otherwise, dc level changes cause frame differences over large parts of the stationary background area. Automatic gain control (AGC) can be another source of frame differences over large parts of the stationary background area. Many AGC circuits are controlled by the average picture value instead of the peak value (which is more suitable for analog-to-digital conversion). When objects move into or out of the picture and create a change in average value, the AGC action generates significant frame differences in all or in large parts of the stationary background area. Other low-frequency disturbances, such as heterodyning between camera field frequency and ac power frequency, can also cause significant frame differences in the stationary background area.

The effects of these types of low-frequency disturbances can be dealt with (assuming they cannot be removed) by compensation techniques at the coder or at both the coder and decoder. Such methods involve measurement of the low-frequency frame differences and alteration of the picture to compensate and thereby avoid sending stationary background picture elements (K. A. Walsh, private communication, 1971).

6.4   TEMPORAL FILTERING

Filtering along the time axis reduces the temporal resolution in a picture, i.e., the rapidity with which a given picture element can change in brightness. According to sampling theory, the lower the temporal resolution, the lower the required sampling rate (frame rate) for faithful reproduction. Thus, initially, the main interest in temporal filtering was for reducing the transmitted frame rate by introducing blurring into the moving areas instead of the jerkiness normally associated with frame repeating (Cunningham, 1963).

Television cameras typically integrate light over a frame period and dump the result as each picture element is scanned. This mechanism provides temporal filtering of a sort. Temporal resolution can be reduced by lowering the camera sweep rate and by providing memory at the receiver to satisfy flicker invisibility requirements. Camera lag, i.e., incomplete dumping, also results in temporal filtering. However, camera integration and lowering of the sweep rate is often insufficient and/or impractical (Haskell and Schmidt, 1975). In such case temporal filtering requires memory external to the camera for implementation.

Finite impulse response sample data filters typically require several stages of delay for implementation. This is impractical for temporal filtering of television signals, since each stage of delay requires a frame memory. Unless large savings accrue therefrom, frame replenishment coders can normally afford only one frame memory at the coder and one at the decoder, thus limiting the temporal filter to a one-stage recursive configuration, such as that shown in Fig. 6-5. Weighting values of $\alpha \leq 0.5$ introduce significant blurring, so that 2:1 frame repeating causes relatively little jerkiness with moderate amounts of movement.

Besides making frame repeating more palatable, temporal filtering can be used in frame replenishment coders to blur the moving area (Haskell

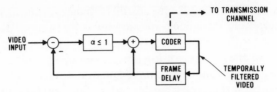

FIG. 6-5.   Interframe coder preceded by a single-pole temporal filter.

et al., 1975; Yasuda *et al.*, 1977) in order to reduce the entropy of moving-area predictive coders. It also makes subsampling effects less visible. For these applications the amount of temporal filtering, i.e., the value of α in Fig. 6-5, can be varied according to the amount of motion in the scene. For slower motion a value of α close to 1 could be used; whereas for more rapid motion that might cause buffer overflow, a smaller value of α would be employed. Replacing the multiplier in Fig. 6-5 by a nonlinearity in which $\alpha < 1$ for small frame differences and $\alpha = 1$ for large frame differences has been found to improve the quality of moving edges in the picture as compared to using a smaller constant value of α (Ishiguro *et al.*, 1976).

Temporal filtering also ameliorates the effects of noise that is uncorrelated from frame to frame. This might be due either to the camera or to quantization in moving-area predictive coding. Thus temporal filtering can make the segmenting task easier.

6.5   ADAPTIVE MOVING-AREA RESOLUTION

Most frame replenishment coder algorithms are designed so that as motion within the otherwise stationary scene causes the number of picture elements in the moving area to increase, the number of bits allocated per moving-area picture element decreases so that the overall bit rate is more constant than it would be otherwise. This can be accomplished in a variety of ways, all of which result in a reduction only of the moving-area resolution (either spatial, temporal, or amplitude) as motion increases.

Distinct from this situation is the abrupt scene change that occurs, for example, when switching from one camera to another. In this case, a change occurs in nearly all picture elements in the frame. The bit rate of most frame replenishment coders is not nearly high enough to send a new full-resolution picture in one frame period. However, it has been found (Seyler and Budrikis, 1965) that this is not necessary. Viewers cannot perceive full resolution for at least several frame periods after a scene change. Thus, a frame replenishment coder need only transmit a very low-resolution picture immediately following a scene change. If full resolution can be built up within a reasonable time (8–10 frame periods), picture degradation will not be noticed.

The objective of adaptive moving-area resolution is to keep the generated data rate more constant than it otherwise would be, and therefore avoid requiring extremely large buffer memories or overflowing buffers of more practical size. The most convenient measure of whether moving-area resolution should be altered is the likelihood of near-term buffer overflow or underflow. Typically, if the buffer is filling rapidly, resolution is decreased, and resolution is increased if the buffer is nearly empty. This measure is not an instantaneous indication of movement, but if the buffer is of moderate size, e.g., 5–10% of frame memory, the time lag is not a serious handicap. A sometimes serious drawback of using this measure is that it is not possible to distinguish between small areas moving fast and large areas moving slowly.

It is not known how to optimally control moving-area resolution for a given channel bit rate and buffer size. Most resolution control algorithms have been designed on an ad hoc basis by trial and error. Reducing resolution in the moving area as buffer fullness exceeds certain thresholds gives reasonably good results as long as some hysteresis is built in to avoid oscillations between different resolutions. Without hysteresis it is possible for the top and bottom of a picture to be displayed with different resolution, which may be objectionable if the difference is visible. A simple technique for avoiding oscillations is to reduce the moving-area resolution when the buffer queue length exceeds a certain threshold. But, only when the queue length falls below a much lower threshold is the moving-area resolution improved again.

Temporal and spatial resolution in the moving areas can be reduced by using temporal filtering. With this, bit rate per moving-area picture element is reduced somewhat if predictive coding with variable word length is used.

Bit rate is reduced much more, however, when subsampling is used. Vertical subsampling of 2:1 works quite well because picture elements are typically spaced closer vertically than horizontally. However, as a result of the 2:1 line interlace used in most systems, vertical picture elements are spaced temporally by approximately one-half frame period. Thus, 2:1 vertical subsampling results in no amplitude bits being transmitted in alternate fields. Ideally, in such fields stationary background picture elements would be obtained from the previous frame, and moving-area picture elements would be obtained by interpolation between adjacent picture elements. To avoid transmitting positional information for such fields, it has been found acceptable to estimate the location of the moving area from that of an adjacent field (Connor *et al.*, 1973a).

For moderate-speed movement 2:1 vertical subsampling gives good results. At high speeds, however, a slight jerkiness may often be detectable unless some temporal filtering is employed. This is due to a mispositioning of moving edges. If correctional information is transmitted only. for these edges, then only a small number of additional bits are required, and picture degradation is virtually removed. This technique is called conditional vertical subsampling (Pease, 1972).

Horizontal subsampling at a factor of 2:1, like vertical subsampling, gives approximately a 2:1 data-rate reduction and results in little degradation for moderate speeds of movement. Moving-area segmentation is somewhat complicated by this, however, by the fact that the interpolated picture elements will possess more frame-to-frame noise. This problem can be alleviated if, in each frame, the same subsampling pattern is employed, and if frame differences corresponding to picture elements that might be interpolated are removed from consideration by the segmenter. An additional problem for vertical and horizontal subsampling is that high data rates causing buffer overflow occur if either relatively small areas move rapidly or large areas move slowly. In the latter case, subsampling degradation is easily visible, since temporal filtering (either camera integration or external) does not reduce the spatial resolution sufficiently to mask the subsampling effects. In such cases conditional subsampling can be employed to send all picture elements only at moving edges in order to reduce subsampling degradation. However, the receiver must be able to discern which of the nominally untransmitted picture elements are to be sent. This can be accomplished by sending an indicator bit, but this strategy can defeat the bit-rate advantage of subsampling. A better way is to carry out the conditional transmission on the basis of some measure of picture detail already available at the receiver, e.g., element differences or frame differences (which are also large at moving edges).

Amplitude resolution can be changed by varying the quantization of the predictive coder. In particular, spreading the inner levels further apart reduces the entropy and, therefore, the bit rate if variable-word-length coding is used. However, this also leads to an increase in quantization noise, which generally lessens the entropy reduction somewhat and makes segmentation more difficult. Coarser quantization is less effective than subsampling in reducing bit rate, but (aside from conditional subsampling) it does have the virtue that moving-area resolution can be reduced gradually.

The adaptive moving-area resolution techniques previously described have been incorporated into a multimode frame replenishment codec (Haskell *et al.*, 1977) for coding a 525-line, monochrome, 4-MHz-bandwidth picture at 1.5 Mbits/sec (0.19 bit per picture element at 8-MHz sampling rate) for videotelephone or videoconferencing applications. In this work, a versatile simulation system was constructed, which was capable of carrying out in real time most of the picture-processing functions mentioned above, but whose parameters were set through an attached minicomputer and resident software. The minicomputer was synchronized with the video system via interrupts, and in real time was capable of adaptively controlling the processing and interrogating the buffer queue length. Almost as important, the minicomputer allowed for rapid testing of the entire system for malfunctions.

Segmentation in this system is fairly straightforward. The frame difference is low pass filtered and threshold detected with two alterable thresholds, $T2 > T1$. Differences larger than $T2$ are immediately classified as significant, whereas differences exceeding $T1$ must undergo isolated point rejection before being classified. Following this step, small gaps between clusters of changes are redefined as "changed" to increase addressing efficiency.

A variable amount of temporal filtering is included to reduce entropies of differential signals, noise on the input signal, and quantization noise. Also used is 2:1 horizontal, 2:1 vertical, and 4:1 vertical subsampling. Moving-area picture elements are sent by means of the element-difference-of-frame-difference signal, where instead of using the immediately previous picture element in the prediction, two picture elements back are used to allow for horizontal subsampling and to ease somewhat hardware implementation. Using this prediction and variable-word-length coding, average bit rates are in the range of 2 bits per transmitted picture element.

Twelve modes (0–11) are used in the algorithm described. In general, switching to the next higher (movement) mode takes place as soon as the buffer queue length exceeds an upper limit specified for that mode. However, switching to a lower (movement) mode only occurs at the end of a coded field if at that time the buffer queue length is below a lower limit specified for that mode. This avoids oscillations between modes, which otherwise could cause unnecessary impairment and needless filling of the buffer.

Addressing data include 9 bits for horizontal synchronization, 9 bits per start-of-cluster address, and 5 bits per end-of-cluster word. A 100-Kbit buffer is employed at both coder and decoder.

In the lower modes where relatively high resolution is maintained, 11-level quantization of the differential signal is employed. However, for the higher modes 6-level quantization is used. Variable-word-length coding is utilized for both quantizers, with one 5-bit word reserved for end-of-cluster signaling. Varying the quantization and temporal filtering requires that changes be made in the segmenting as well. Thus, different modes utilize different frame-difference low-pass filters and different thresholds. Subsampling is utilized straightforwardly under buffer control in the following order: vertical 2:1, horizontal 2:1, vertical 4:1, frame repeating. The last option is used only during camera movement or scene changes.

Rudimentary subjective tests were carried out using the following standard 5-point degradation scale:

> 5   Imperceptible
> 4   Perceptible but not annoying
> 3   Slightly annoying
> 2   Annoying
> 1   Very annoying

Subjects were told to regard a PCM-coded picture as having a perfect score of 5. With the frame replenishment coder operating at 1.5 Mbits/sec, mean opinion scores varied from above 4 for slow-to-moderate motion to approximately 3 for rapid movement (see Fig. 6-6). Camera motion was not included in these tests.

6.6   MOVEMENT COMPENSATION

It has not gone unnoticed that when a scene contains objects moving more or less in translation, more redundancy exists than is taken advantage of by frame replenishment, which sends only moving areas (Gabor and Hill, 1961; Haskell and Limb, 1972; Rocca, 1972). If the velocity of movement is known and is reasonably constant over the moving area, then a very good prediction of the present frame moving area should be obtainable from a translated version of the previous frame. Then the difference between the actual picture element values and the predicted values should have low entropy, thus enabling transmission at low bit rates. The prediction only fails adjacent to edges of moving objects where newly uncovered background area exists. However, this area tends to be relatively small compared to the total amount of moving area in the picture. If objects in the scene are rotating or moving toward or away from the camera, then the assumption of translational movement is violated. However, if the scene is partitioned into smaller regions, then within each region the translational movement assumption is approximately valid if the moving objects are not too small.

To take advantage of this property in a frame replenishment codec, the foremost requirement is some means for measuring velocity or, equivalently, the frame-to-frame translation. This has been accomplished by computing correlations between a moving area in the present frame and various translations of the corresponding area in the previous frame. The translation with the highest correlation is then assumed to be the correct one, and predictive coding can then take place. The traditional measure of correlation (average of point-by-point product) can be used, but it is rather expensive to implement computationally. The average magnitude of point-by-point differences is a simpler measure of correlation and gives reasonably reliable estimates of frame-to-frame translation. However, with either of these methods, frame-to-frame translations are usually measured only to the nearest picture element interval, whereas movement typically produces a frame-to-frame translation by a noninteger number of picture elements.

Two techniques have been studied for measuring translations by nonintegral picture element spacings. The first incorporates the theory of minimum-mean-square-error linear prediction (Haskell, 1975). Since nonintegral picture element translations imply interpolation between picture elements to obtain the prediction, the resulting prediction P_X is a linear combination of picture elements in the previous frame

$$P_X = \sum_i a_i Y_i \qquad (2)$$

where a_i's are weighting coefficients and Y_i's are picture element values from the previous frame. Using well-known mathematical techniques, it is possible to choose the weighting coefficients a_i to minimize the average value of $(X - P_X)^2$ in the moving area of a region to be transmitted. In its most straightforward implementation, two passes are required over each field to be coded—one pass to determine the weighting coefficients and a second pass to carry out the predictive coding. Also, the values of the weighting coefficients must somehow be conveyed to the receiver. Using this approach there is no reason why the Y_i's must be restricted to the previous frame. By also including previously transmitted picture elements in the same field and in the previous field, intraframe redundancy can be exploited. Differential signal entropies (per moving-area picture element) have been measured for 1-MHz-bandwidth videotelephone scenes containing a moving mannequin's head, as well as for scenes containing live subjects. Results were significantly lower than with other nonadaptive

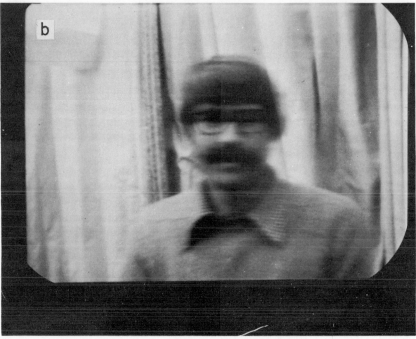

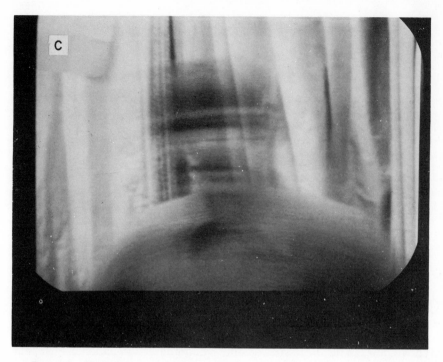

FIG. 6-6.   Single frames of 525-line monochrome television coded at 1.5 Mbits/sec in which moving-area resolution is reduced as motion increases. (a) No motion; (b) slow-to-moderate motion; (c) rapid motion. (From Haskell *et al.*, 1975).

linear predictive coders, indicating a possible 2:1 reduction in entropy per moving-area picture element (Haskell, 1975).

The other approach to measuring frame-to-frame translations by non-integral pel spacings utilizes the relation between spatial-differential and temporal-differential signals when translational movement exists (Limb and Murphy, 1975b; Cafforio and Rocca, 1976). Figure 6-7 illustrates the frame-to-frame displacement of a moving edge. From the figure, the sum of the element differences in either frame is h, whereas the sum of the

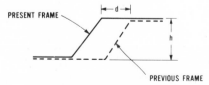

FIG. 6-7.   Frame-to-frame displacement of a moving edge.

frame differences is the area between the two curves. Dividing one by the other (magnitudes only) yields the desired displacement quantity

$$d = \frac{dh}{h} = \frac{\Sigma|\text{frame differences}|}{\Sigma|\text{element differences}|} \qquad (3)$$

Examination of the signs of the element and frame differences indicates the direction of motion; equal signs as shown in Fig. 6-7 implies leftward motion, whereas unequal signs implies rightward motion. Summing over the area of a moving object yields an average displacement value for the object. This technique works quite well if the spatial differentiation is in the direction of movement. In general, however, horizontal, vertical, and temporal differences must be combined to estimate vertical and horizontal components of velocity.

Measurements of differential signal entropy using this technique for estimating frame-to-frame translation and using cubic polynominals for interpolation between picture elements have been carried out on 64×64 picture element (no interlace, 50-Hz frame rate) pictures containing a moving mannequin's head (Brofferio and Rocca, 1977). Results indicate about a $2:1$ reduction in entropy per moving area of picture element compared with sending element differences in the moving area.

Interframe coding using movement-tracking techniques, as discussed above, has, so far, been studied only by computer simulation using a relatively small number of consecutive frames. In order to adequately determine television picture quality with frame-to-frame coding (and intraframe coding, as well), many frames must be displayed. Thus, a much more ambitious effort must be launched in this direction before a reasonably complete multimode FRODEC that uses these methods can be evaluated.

6.7 COLOR CODING

Two approaches have been investigated for implementing frame replenishment codecs for standard composite television signals. In the first approach, the composite signal is decomposed into luminance and two color-difference signals, while the second approach involves direct coding of the composite signal.

Since horizontal color bandwidth is already relatively small, vertical color bandwidth can be compromised somewhat, without sacrificing picture quality unduly, by alternately sending only one of the two color signals during each line period. At the receiver, line repeating is used to recover the untransmitted color information. If the color signals are band-limited to about one-fifth the luminance bandwidth (not much of a sacrifice considering that most color monitors are not capable of displaying even this color bandwidth), then each color signal can be time compressed by a factor of 5 and transmitted during the luminance signal blanking period. The coding task has, by this approach, been reduced from one of transmitting three separate signals to one of transmitting a single time-division multiplexed signal that can be treated in the same manner as in a monochrome frame replenishment coder.

This approach has been taken in coders that can send a 525-line signal with videotelephone or conference television quality at about 0.75 bit per picture element or 6 Mbits/sec. Ishiguro *et al.* (1975) code a time-division multiplexed signal using frame-differential coding for the moving-area picture element amplitudes, 2:1 horizontal subsampling, 2:1 vertical subsampling, and variable-frame-difference significance thresholds in much the same way as Candy *et al.* (1971) utilized for 1-MHz monochrome videotelephone signals. Degradations using these bit-rate reduction techniques appear subjectively to be about the same as with monochrome pictures. Oddly enough, however, the transmission of color information in this system accounts only for about 10% of the total bit rate, even though it comprises 20% of the input signal.

In another system which codes a time-division multiplexed signal at 6.3 Mbits/sec (Yasuda *et al.*, 1977), moving-area picture elements are sent via element-difference-of-frame-difference predictive coding using variable word lengths. Horizontal and vertical subsampling are incorporated as needed under control of the buffer fullness. In addition, the amount of temporal filtering (α in Fig. 6-5) is also controlled by the buffer queue length. However, only a very rudimentary frame-difference-threshold segmenter is used, with thresholding following temporal filtering. Addressing of moving-area picture elements is also somewhat different than has been used in the past. Instead of attempting to minimize the number of moving-area picture elements transmitted, this coder partitions the picture into 1×8 picture element blocks and sends all picture elements in blocks that contain one or more segmented picture elements. One bit per block must also be transmitted to indicate whether or not it contains any segmented picture elements. Picture quality has been judged to have a mean opinion score between 3 and 4 on the standard 5-point scale.

Coding an NTSC color signal at 6.3 Mbits/sec yields picture quality that is probably sufficient for videotelephone or conference television, but it is definitely not sufficient for broadcast color television. In fact, there is considerable doubt as to whether even time-division multiplexing by itself is sufficiently good for broadcast television. The alternatives remaining are

(1) code the color components separately (or in concert), but time-multiplex the three resulting bit streams just before transmission; or

(2) code the composite color signal itself.

The latter approach was used by Ishiguro *et al.* (1976) to code an NTSC composite signal with high quality at 22 Mbits/sec. Monochrome frame replenishment coding techniques cannot usually be applied unmodified to an NTSC composite color signal. If the sampling rate is a multiple of the line rate (as in monochrome systems), then large frame differences are caused by the reversal of color carrier phase from frame to frame. To alleviate this, pairs of lines are converted by this coder into a sum (mostly luminance) and a difference (mostly chrominance) prior to processing. The polarity of the difference signal is then inverted every frame period in order to minimize frame differences due to this component. The process is reversed at the receiver.

For slow-to-moderate motion, the sampling rate is approximately three times the color subcarrier frequency, and moving-area picture elements are sent by element-difference-of-frame-difference predictive coding using three picture elements back instead of the previous picture element so that samples used in the prediction will be more nearly in color subcarrier phase. A modest amount of temporal filtering is also used for the smaller frame differences in order to ameliorate the effects of quantization and camera noise.

With increased movement, more temporal filtering is employed, the sampling rate is reduced to approximately twice the color subcarrier frequency, and a more complex linear predictor is used. Since a sampling rate of twice the color subcarrier frequency is below the Nyquist rate for a 4-MHz bandwidth, aliasing components are present; these would be objectionable if not removed. In this coder they are removed for frequencies at or above the color subcarrier frequency by staggering the sampling pattern from line to line and employing a comb filter that takes advantage of vertical correlations in the picture.

Segmenting is relatively simple. Thresholding of the predictor-differential signal (not the frame difference) with a variable threshold depending on buffer occupancy is all that is used. Addressing is carried out in a manner similar to Yasuda *et al.* (1977), in that the picture is divided into blocks that are or are not transmitted depending on whether they contain significant changes. Variable quantization is also used under control of the buffer.

Subjective picture quality at 22 Mbits/sec is perfect for slow-to-moderate motion, and nearly so for most cases of rapid motion, including scene changes, zooming, and fast pans. Slow pans over detailed backgrounds where moving objects are tracked produce distortions perceptible to expert viewers. However, the overall applicability to broadcast transmission remains to be determined.

6.8 ERROR CONTROL

With intraframe coding where each frame is transmitted separately, the effect of a digital transmission error lasts only for a frame period. However, with interframe coding, such effects can last much longer. In general, the more one removes redundancy from a television signal through the use of sophisticated coding techniques, the more important each bit of transmitted information becomes, and the more noticeable are the effects of digital transmission errors. For example, with simple frame-differential transmission of every picture element, an error appears in only one picture element and lasts indefinitely unless some error correction strategy is employed, e.g., incorporating leak into the feedback loop (Connor et al., 1972). With frame replenishment, leak is not very effective since not all picture elements are sent in every frame. Furthermore, if higher-order DPCM and/or variable-word-length coding is used, defects due to transmission errors can spread beyond one picture element, possibly into adjacent lines.

Forward acting error control has been incorporated into frame replenishment coders in which effects due to an error are confined for the most part to one line. Channel error-correcting codes, such as BCH or convolutional codes can be utilized (Ishiguro et al., 1976). Special protection of sync and cluster demarcation words is also worthwhile in order to minimize the area affected by a transmission error (Yasuda et al., 1976). In spite of these precautions, however, errors are bound to appear in the pictures sooner or later, and further steps must be taken to deal with them.

Typically, several lines per frame are sent via PCM. This is called forced updating (Candy et al., 1971). In this way, in a few seconds, every picture element in the frame can be updated with correct values, thus eliminating any residual effects resulting from errors that survive the channel error-correcting codes. It has also been reported (Yasuda et al., 1976) that the receiver buffer must be made considerably larger than the transmitter buffer if overflow is to be avoided in the presence of transmission errors.

Several seconds is a long time for a highly visible error defect to remain at the display. Through the use of highly reliable error detection codes, it is possible for the receiver to tell which lines contain errors. If these lines are then replaced, for example, with an average of adjacent lines, then the effects of errors (if their rate is reasonably low) can be made much less visible (Connor, 1973c; Bowen and Limb, 1976). This technique usually requires that once an erroneous line is replaced by an average, replacement of that line must continue during succeeding frames until PCM values arrive for that line.

Error detection followed by a request for retransmission is usually not feasible. First, for the high data rates usually entailed in video transmission, very large buffers would be required. Second, for the long distances often involved, too much delay would be introduced for two-way video communication. However, if substitution of an erroneous line, as described above, were followed by a request for PCM transmission of that line during some later frame, then the duration of error effects could be markedly reduced in comparison with strictly forward-acting techniques.

If the effects of a digital transmission error propagate to adjacent lines, as they would for example with DPCM that uses picture elements from previous lines, then line substitution does not work. Substitution from the previous frame would not be very disturbing if movement were slow, but in rapidly moving areas, picture breakup would occur, and substitution of the entire field would probably be preferable. Subdivision of the picture into smaller blocks which are coded independently of one another might alleviate the situation somewhat. In any event, substitution could not be carried out for very long—one or two frames at most. A request for retransmission would have to be issued to minimize the visibility of effects due to transmission errors.

6.9 CONCLUSION

Interframe coding techniques employed heretofore exploit the statistical redundancies present in the input video signal due to frame-to-frame similarities as well as in-frame similarities. They also try to make use of subjective redundancies resulting from the inability of viewers to see spatial or temporal detail under certain conditions of movement and/or brightness transitions.

The use of local statistical redundancy has been, up to the present, fairly straightforward. Linear predictive coding removes much of the long-term average correlation—both intraframe and interframe—from the video signal. By making the prediction adaptive, it is possible to take advantage of short-term statistical variations within a frame, as well as the changing frame-to-frame correlations caused by translations of moving objects. Further gains in this direction involving transform coding, scene analysis, context-dependent processing, etc., show promise but remain to be studied in much detail.

The subjective implications of many of the interframe coding techniques currently in use have been studied for the most part on a cut-and-try basis. This is especially true in a multimode frame replenishment coder where simultaneous optimization of the parameters of each mode is extremely difficult given their interdependence under operational conditions. The combined subjective effects of, for example, temporal filtering, quantization, and subsampling have yet to be studied on a scientific basis. Temporal masking effects which could be exploited by adaptive quantization have also received very little attention. Thus, much remains to be done before a good understanding can be claimed of the phenomena involved in interframe coding.

The feasibility of implementing these relatively complex coding algorithms continues to improve. Costs of digital storage have declined dramatically in recent years and show every indication of maintaining this trend. In addition, the availability of random-access memories, read-only memories, and microprocessors at reasonable cost considerably simplifies the design of reliable and easily tested systems. As these devices become cheaper and digital transmission becomes widespread, more and more use will be found for sending television signals via frame replenishment coding.

REFERENCES

Achiha, M., and Fukinuki, T. (1971). *Image Eng. Conf., 2nd, 1971* No. 2–6.
Achiha, M., and Fukinuki, T. (1972). *Gen. Meet. Inst. Electr. Commun. Eng., 1972* No. 1691.
Bostelmann, G. (1976). *Nachrichtentech. Z.* **29**, 261–264.
Bowen, E. G., and Limb, J. O. (1976). *IEEE Trans. Commun.* **com-24**, 1208–1212.
Brainard, R. C., Mounts, F. W., and Prasada, B. (1967). *Bell Syst. Tech. J.* **46**, 261–271.
Brofferio, S., and Rocca, F. (1977). *IEEE Trans. Commun.* **com-25**, 448–455.
Brofferio, S., Cafforio, C., DelRe, P., Quaglia, G., Racciu, A., and Rocca, F. (1974). *Alta Freq.* **43**, 836–843.
Cafforio, C., and Rocca, F. (1976). *IEEE Trans. Inf. Theory* **it-22**, No. 5.
Candy, J. C., and Mounts, F. W. (1971). U. S. Patent 3,571,807.
Candy, J. C., Franke, M. A., Haskell, B. G., and Mounts, F. W. (1971). *Bell Syst. Tech. J.* **50**, 1889–1917.
Cherry, E. M. (1974a). *J. SMPTE* **83**, 708–710.
Cherry, E. M. (1974b). *J. SMPTE* **83**, 711–718.
Connor, D. J. (1973c). *IEEE Trans. Commun.* **com-21**, 695–706.
Connor, D. J., and Berrang, J. E. (1974). *Natl. Telecommun., Conf. Rec., 1974* pp. 54–60.

Connor, D. J., and Limb, J. O. (1974). *IEEE Trans. Commun.* **com-22,** 1564–1575.

Connor, D. J., Brainard, R. C., and Limb, J. O. (1972). *Proc. IEEE* **60,** 780–791.

Connor, D. J., Haskell, B. G., and Mounts, F. W. (1973a). *Bell Syst. Tech. J.* **52,** 35–51.

Connor, D. J., Limb, J. O., Pease, R. F. W., and Scholes, W. G. (1973b). U. S. Patent 3,716,667.

Cunningham, J. E. (1963). Sc. D. Dissertation, Department of Electrical Engineering, Massachusetts Institute of Technology, Cambridge.

Deutsch, S. (1973). *IEEE Trans. Commun.* **com-22,** 65–75.

Fukinuki, T., Achiha, M., Miyata, M., and Fukushima, K. (1972). *Transm. Study Comm. Television Soc. Jpn. Rep., 1972.*

Gabor, D., and Hill, P. C. J. (1961). *Proc. IEE* **108B,** 303–315.

Graham, R. E. (1953). U.S. Patent 2,652,449.

Haskell, B. G. (1972a). *Bell Syst. Tech. J.* **51,** 261–289.

Haskell, B. G. (1972b). *IEEE Int. Conf. Commun., Conf. Rec., 1972* Vol. 8, pp. 31–51.

Haskell, B. G. (1974). *IEEE Trans. Inf. Theory* **it-20,** 119–120.

Haskell, B. G. (1975). *Bell Syst. Tech. J.* **54,** 1155–1174.

Haskell, B. G. (1976a). *IEEE Trans. Commun.* **com-24,** 140–144.

Haskell, B. G. (1976b). U.S. Patent 3,952,535.

Haskell, B. G. (1976c). Proc. 20th Anniv. Tech. Symp. Soc. Photo-Opt. Eng., *1976* pp. 87-23.1 to 87-23.10.

Haskell, B. G., and Limb, J. O. (1972). U.S. Patent 3,632,865.

Haskell, B. G., and Schmidt, R. L. (1975). *Bell Syst. Tech. J.* **54,** 1475–1495.

Haskell, B. G., Mounts, F. W., and Candy, J. C. (1972). *Proc. IEEE* **60,** 792–800.

Haskell, B. G., Limb, J. O., and Pease, R. F. W. (1973). U.S. Patent 3,767,847.

Haskell, B. G., Gordon, P. L., Schmidt, R. L., and Scattaglia, J. V. (1975). *Natl. Telecommun., Conf. Rec., 1975* Vol. 1, pp. 22-23 to 22-24.

Haskell, B. G., Gordon, P. L., Schmidt, R. L., and Scattaglia, J. V. (1977). *IEEE Trans. Commun.* **com-25,** No. 11.

Iinuma, K., Iijima, Y., Ishiguro, T., Kaneko, H., and Shigaki, S. (1975). *IEEE Trans. Commun.* **com-23,** 1461–1466.

Ishiguro, T., Iinuma, K., Iijima, Y., Koga, T., and Kaneko, H. (1975). *Int. Conf. Digital Satellite Commun. Rec., 3rd, 1975.*

Ishiguro, T., Iinuma, K., Iijima, Y., Koga, T., Azami, S., and Mune, T. (1976). *Natl. Telecommun. Conf. Rec., 1976* Vol. 1, pp. 6.4-1 to 6.4-5.

Kell, R. D. (1929). British Patent 341,811.

Limb, J. O. (1972). *Bell Syst. Tech. J.* **51,** 239–259.

Limb, J. O. (1973). *Bell Syst. Tech. J.* **52,** 1271–1302.

Limb, J. O., and Murphy, J. A. (1975a). *IEEE Trans. Commun.* **com-23,** 474–478.

Limb, J. O., and Murphy, J. A. (1975b). *Comput. Graphics Image Process.* **4,** 311–327.

Limb, J. O., and Pease, R. F. W. (1971). *Bell Syst. Tech. J.* **50,** 1877–1888.

Limb, J. O., Pease, R. F. W., and Walsh, K. A. (1974). *Bell Syst. Tech. J.* **53,** 1137–1173.

Miyahara, M. (1973). *Electron. Commun. Jpn.* V **56-A,** 46–56.

Mounts, F. W. (1967). *Bell Syst. Tech. J.* **46,** 167–198.

Mounts, F. W. (1969). *Bell Syst. Tech. J.* **48,** 2545–2554.

Pease, R. F. W. (1972). *Bell Syst. Tech. J.* **51,** 787–802.

Pease, R. F. W., and Limb, J. O. (1971). *Bell Syst. Tech. J.* **50,** 191–200.

Rocca, F. (1972). *Symp. Picture Bandwidth Compression, 1969* p. 675.

Rocca, F., and Zanoletti, S. (1972). *IEEE Trans. Commun.* **com-20,** 960–965.

Seguin, H., and Petit, C. (1974). *Ann. Telecommun.* **29,** 271–280.

Seyler, A. J. (1962). *Proc. IEEE* **109,** 676–684.

Seyler, A. J. (1963). *Proc. IEEE* **51**, 478–480.

Seyler, A. J. (1965). *Proc. Inst. Radio Electron. Eng. (Aust.)* p. 355.

Seyler, A. J., and Budrikis, Z. L. (1965). *IEEE Trans. Inf. Theory* **it-11**, 31–43.

Stone, R. F. (1976). *IEEE Trans. Broadcast.* **bc-22**, 21–32.

Wendt, H. (1973). *Int. Elektron. Rundsch.* **27**, 2–7.

Yasuda, H., Kanaya, F., and Kawanishi, H. (1976). *IEEE Trans. Commun.* **com-24**, 1175–1180.

Yasuda, H., Kuroda, H., Kawanishi, H., Kanaya, F., and Hashimoto, H. (1977). *IEEE Trans. Commun.* **com-25**, 508–516.

Binary Image Compression

RONALD B. ARPS*

Department of Electrical Engineering
Linköping University
Linköping, Sweden

Binary image compression can be considered a special case of the more general problem of gray-scale picture coding. The images here are assumed to be digital, static, and monochromatic and are confined to two-level pels rather than multilevel picture elements (pixels).[1] Figure 7-1 diagrams the overall flow through a typical encoder for binary images, from the scanning of a source document to the generation of compressed bits. Each block represents a stage in the coding process. Listed below each stage are some of the major parameters affecting it.

Note that a kind of compression is accomplished by the thresholder in quantizing all amplitudes to 1 bit/pel rather than 6 or 8 bits/pel, as is the starting point for most gray-scale image compression. The spatial quantization performed by the dissector in digitizing the image also accomplishes a form of compression, when compared to the continuous infor-

---

* Present address: IBM Dept. F08/G26, 555 Bailey Avenue, San Jose, California 95150.

[1] For *binary* image coding the term "pel" is commonly used to specify a picture element with 1-bit/pixel amplitude resolution (see Arps, 1971, or White *et al.* 1972).

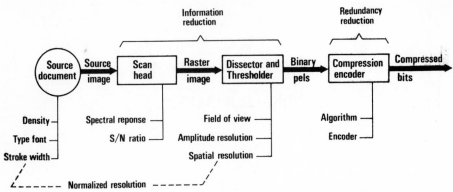

FIG. 7-1. Parameters in a binary image compression encoder.

mation in the original document. Furthermore, the scan head spectral response and field of view are often selected to eliminate "irrelevant" information. All of the above quantization steps are forms of "information reduction," in which an irreversible transformation takes place with some loss during the digitization process.

By comparison, the classical noiseless coding or "redundancy reduction," which is discussed in this chapter, deals only with the design of completely reversible one-to-one transforming algorithms. Figure 7-2 illustrates such a lossless transformation. Figure 7-2a is a binary digital image of a business document and Fig. 7-2b is a binary pseudoimage representing the transformed data. The left-justified black pels indicate the number of bits needed to describe each horizontal scan line, while the white pels represent the savings due to compression. Note the correlation between Fig. 7-2a and b, especially evident in the large number of bits required to encode scan lines containing text and the small number of bits needed to represent empty scan lines. The digital image in Fig. 7-2a can be reconstructed identically, given only the amount of coded bits indicated in Fig. 7-2b for each scan line.

As they are presented here, the steps of information and redundancy reduction are separate operations to be executed in cascade. This contrasts with gray-scale coding techniques like DPCM or delta modulation (see Chapter 3), in which both kinds of reduction occur simultaneously. For the images being considered, this separation occurs as a natural result of originally creating them with only two amplitudes. Once this has been done, the opportunity for amplitude information reduction is essentially exhausted. Typically, the spatial resolution has also been held to a bare minimum and further reduction of this type is inadvisable as well. As a re-

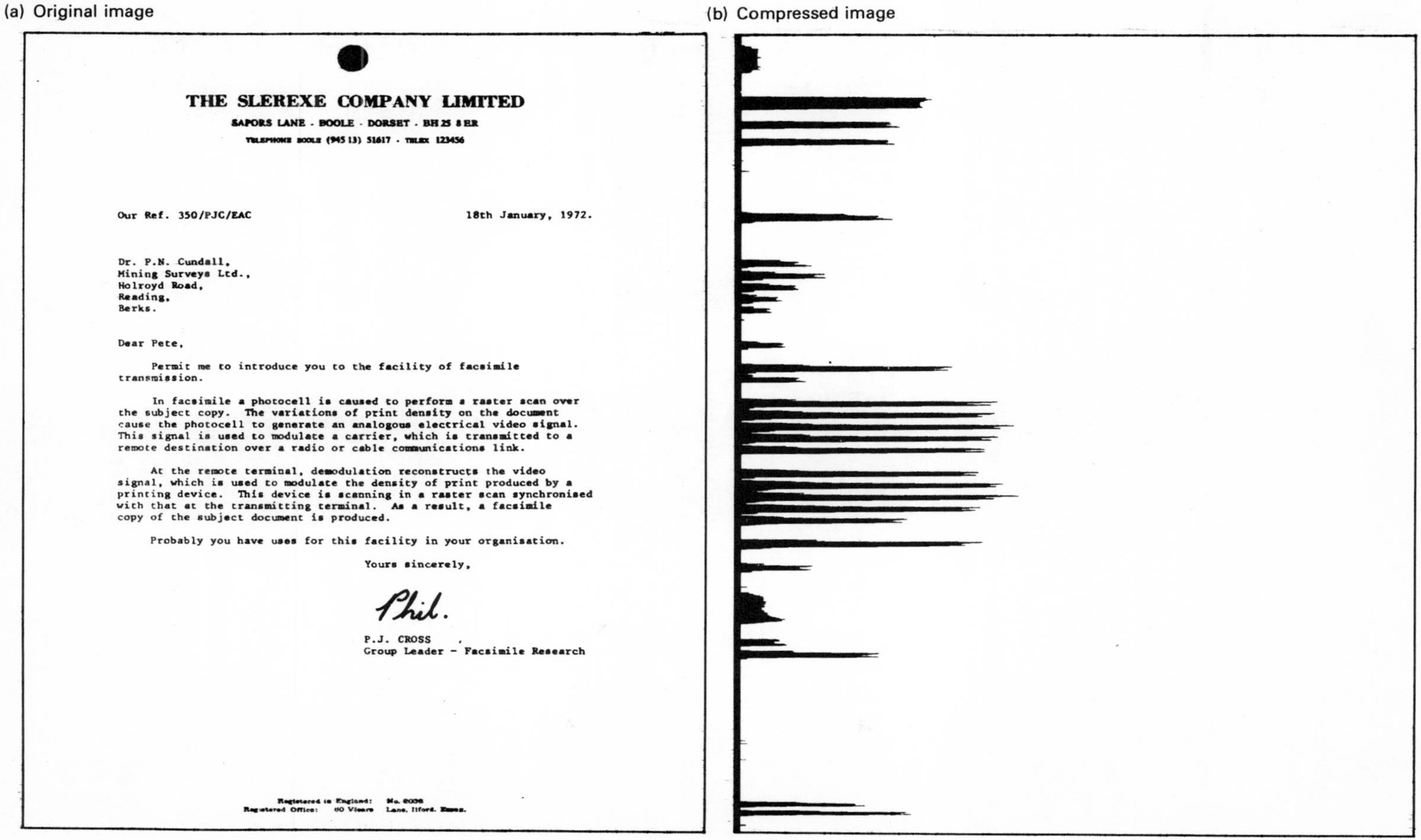

(a) Original image

(b) Compressed image

FIG. 7-2. Example of binary image compression.

sult, the remaining compression to be treated here consists entirely of redundancy reduction.

A further consideration is how to design for protection from noise and channel errors. For simplicity, this will also be treated as a separate operation to be performed in cascade using some form of "redundancy insertion." In practice, simultaneous design for noiseless coding and error protection is done if a fail-soft response to errors is required. Generally, this results in a requirement that the noiseless coding be line independent or at least independent for groups of lines. For some fail-soft algorithms, see Weber (1975), Koller (1975), Eto *et al.* (1977), Renelt (1977), Musmann and Pre'iss (1977), or Huang (1977).

This summary of noiseless coding for binary images will proceed in four parts. First some historical background will be presented, followed by the fundamental problem and a summary of relevant tools from information theory. The last two parts will cover the state of the art, broken down into "raster" and "area" algorithms. These algorithms will be evaluated in terms of their source models and related bounds. Their numerous possible implementations will not be described. However, specific codebooks and coding schemes can readily be characterized in terms of their efficiency in attaining the bounds for these algorithms.

The latter division of algorithms into two groups is based on the amount of image memory they require and on the structure of their image data. Raster algorithms are primarily one dimensional and operate on the data from a raster image scan (with only one or two scan lines of memory). In contrast, area algorithms are truly two dimensional and assume the existence of all (or a meaningful part) of the image in a random-access memory.

In these last two parts, no attempt will be made to be exhaustive in covering the current art. Rather, the major contributions will be emphasized, while large areas of similar work will be consolidated into a unified summary. Analytic relationships between algorithms and bounds on algorithm performance, however, will be emphasized and systematically included wherever possible. This approach will make possible the broad overview that is desired here. For a related overview, see Huang (1977).

7.1 Historical Trends and Comments

Activity in the field of binary image compression dates back at least to the formalizing of information theory by Shannon and Weaver (1949). Soon after, Laemmel (1951) published an extensive report on binary image compression including many of the basic concepts used today. Because Laemmel's work was not published in a major journal, many of his algorithms were reinvestigated much later by others. Another significant author of this period was Elias (1950), who laid the foundation for predictive coding.

The first publications about measurements on binary image data and on compression hardware occurred in the late 1950s. Deutsch (1957) made statistical measurements on a small sample of text. Michel (1958) extended this to measurements on full pages of text and line drawings. Frolushkin (1958) also made measurements during this period, covering handwriting as well as text and line drawings. Michel et al. (1957) described a complete system design with binary image compression as did Wyle et al. (1961). It is interesting that neither system design had been actually implemented.

The 1960s saw further development of compression algorithms. Making statistical measurements became commonplace, and the actual implementation of systems culminated in some commercial facsimile devices. Facsimile was always seen as the major application for binary image compression. However, analog facsimile for business documents was in existence long before the 1950s. How is it that digital facsimile only developed commercially in the last decade and is just now on the verge of widespread use?

The maturing of this field today can be attributed to several factors. Among them must be included the emergence of computing power, copy machines, and low-cost digital hardware. Significant computing power was needed to simply gather the statistics to design good codes. Low hardware costs were needed so that facsimile could be afforded by enough customers to create a meaningful network of units between which to communicate. Early products were marketed for time-sensitive, low-fanout applications like transmission of newspaper plates to secondary printing facilities.

The impact of copy machines was felt in the marketing of facsimile. There was rapid movement from unfamiliarity or even concern for committing valuable papers to machines to routine acceptance of the duplication and automatic handling of all kinds of documents. Selling facsimile machines as copiers that can communicate by telephone is now evolutionary rather than revolutionary. Copiers have even laid the groundwork of a business infrastructure in which to introduce facsimile equipment (copier rooms, servicing, etc.).

Another factor responsible for the field's maturing now is that improved compression algorithms are steadily reducing the time needed to transmit an image. Analog facsimile machines require from 3 to 6 minutes to transmit a standard business document over a switched telephone network. By contrast, digital machines with compression can reduce this time to less than 1 minute.

The impending introduction of large numbers of digital facsimile machines into national networks has generated international efforts in the CCITT (1977) to standardize them. This in turn has further stimulated manufacturers by the prospect of a large interconnected market. These discussions on standardization have also accelerated algorithm development. In addition to current competition for the low-performance standard, other standards are slated to be discussed in the future. High-performance algorithms offered in addition to the standard may become a basis for product competition.

Other application areas like computer image processing are also emerging with different requirements for binary image compression. They have spawned a second generation of algorithms (see Morrin, 1975) that require more than just compression capability. These algorithms must encode data in such way that they can be processed without decompression. This subject will be elaborated on near the end of this chapter.

7.2 SOURCE CHARACTERIZATION

The reader is assumed to have a basic understanding of noiseless source coding as it is summarized in any of the many texts on information theory (for example, Abramson, 1963). On the surface, the task of compressing binary images appears to be a straightforward application of such source coding. As will readily become apparent, however, a globally optimal solution is impractical; and since compromises must be made, an art emerges. (This section expands on a tutorial by Arps, 1975.)

Source Models

The data to be encoded comprise a sequence of binary image fields, where the term "fields" is used for generality and to emphasize the need to select the right field of view. This sequence will be modeled as the output from a discrete source which is assumed to be ergodic and stationary. The individual fields will be assumed to be independent. If these two-dimensional source outputs each contain a total of V pels, then the source alphabet can be represented as some set G with the image fields as symbols g_k selected from among all possible binary V-tuples

$$G \equiv \{g_k: k \in \{1, 2, \ldots, 2^V\}\} \tag{1}$$

This will be called the "global" source model and is illustrated in Fig. 7-3.

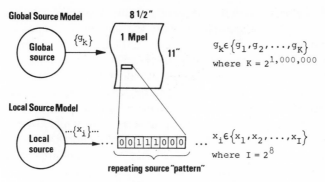

FIG. 7-3. Basic models for binary image compression.

Typically, the corresponding symbol probabilities $P(g_k)$ must be estimated in order to calculate the potential for compression before designing
an appropriate code.

Before proceeding further, the implications of this global model
should be fully appreciated. The major market today for binary image
coding lines in the application of digital facsimile. This can be generalized
to include any application that needs digital data compression for
common DIN A4 size[2] ($\approx 8.5 \times 11.0$ in.) pages. With a minimal sampling
resolution (see Arps *et al.*, 1969; Arps, 1970a) of roughly 4×4 pels/mm
($\approx 100 \times 100$ pels/in.), one quickly discovers that V is approximately 10^6.
When this value is applied to Eq. (1), it becomes apparent that the alphabet G must range over some $2^{1,000,000}$ symbols! Estimating probabilities
and encoding for such a global source is simply intractable. Physically,
such a code book would assign an individual code word to every page
(image field) that could possibly exist at the above resolution values.

The generally accepted strategy, therefore, is to model the image field
as the result of some repeating "local" source X, where each source
symbol x_i represents a piece of the field. These pieces are usually mutually exclusive image segments that "tile" together to build up the total
page. If these segments are regular in their two-dimensional form, then
they correspond to a well-defined image "pattern" for the local source
model. Figure 7-3 illustrates an example pattern consisting of 1×8
groupings of adjacent pels, resulting in a symbol alphabet consisting of
binary U-tuples

$$X \equiv \{x_i : i \in \{1, 2, \ldots, 2^U\}\} \tag{2}$$

---

[2] "DIN" is an abbreviation for Deutsche Industrie Norm (German Industry Standard).
Outside of the United States, the DIN paper size standards are commonly used.

where $U = 8$ pels/symbol, and there are only 2^8 symbols. This, at least, is a source model small enough to allow the design of a code and practical coding hardware.

With the myriad of local models that can be proposed, a systematic method is needed for comparing and evaluating them. Typically, appropriate coders are designed for each model, and their performance is simulated using identical data for a fair comparison (see Table 7-1). Generalization of the results from such simulations is difficult, however. Pulling together the analytic structure needed to make generalizations and comparisons is one of the goals of this chapter, along with presenting an overview of the field.

The concept of a coder designed for a given source model is a familiar one. However, for many algorithms, coders are reported in the literature without an explicit accompanying source description. It is assumed here that the alphabet(s) of symbols in a coder implicitly define a source model. Such a converse source should be developed, if a source model has not been explicitly specified.

When a group of algorithms are to be compared, their individual source models will be treated as approximations to the underlying global source G. Two basic approaches will be used for systematic analysis:

(1) Occasionally, these models can be directly compared using identities from information theory. All that is needed is the assumption that their distributions are properly estimated from identical data.

TABLE 7-1

COMPARISON OF COMPRESSION ALGORITHMS, GRAPHICS CODING CONTEST, 1976 PICTURE CODING SYMPOSIUM[a,b]

CCITT document[c]	White skipping (Huang)	Truncated Huffman (Segin)	ITC-II (Rothgordt)	PDQ (Huang)	Contour (Morrin)	2-D Markov (Preuss)
1	383,820	229,050	225,534	161,460	140,867	137,277
2	554,809	262,641	218,032	96,650	78,859	94,189
3	751,926	446,251	404,319	250,720	221,260	203,407
4	1,119,690	689,921	680,367	592,200	538,842	470,352
5	764,875	458,541	415,506	276,710	249,424	228,566
6	616,553	388,565	334,730	152,890	130,996	134,438
7	1,120,041	843,050	800,774	582,000	549,210	515,062
8	2,112,534	543,433	411,022	189,720	198,468	169,287
Total	7.4M	3.9M	3.5M	2.3M	2.1M	2.0M

[a] Reference: Arps (1976).

[b] Results expressed in compressed bit/field.

[c] CCITT test documents at 7.7×8.0 (pel/mm)^2 from the Technical University of Hannover. Each document is $2128 \times 1728 = 3,677,184$ pel/field.

(2) Where direct analytic comparison is difficult, various "underlying" global source models that are simple and mathematically well behaved are assumed. The algorithms are then analytically compared or bounded assuming that their source alphabet distributions are estimated from data generated by these underlying global models.

Table 7-2 gives a quick look ahead to the type of results that will be obtained using the latter approach. Four underlying models or page generating processes are being related to six algorithms and to each other. Their interrelationships, along with the conventional and pictorial notation used, will be explained as this section develops.

Source Bounds

Local source models are compared in terms of the number of bits they each use to encode a given image field. To avoid the details of actual coders, such comparisons are made using the entropy for the model. Many coders can be designed for a given model, and these are then evaluated in terms of their efficiency in attaining the entropy of that specific source. The basic equations used for analysis are illustrated below for the simple model of Fig. 7-3. To apply these concepts to more complicated

TABLE 7-2

Algorithms Classified by Entropy Upper Bounds

Upper Bound		Algorithm	
Underlying Process	Entropy	Entropy[a]	Model
0th-order (independent) pel process	▨ $\left(= \boxed{▨} \right)$	$\geq \begin{cases} H_p(R_{sr}) \\ \\ H_p(R_{rl}) \end{cases}$	Michel (1957), scheme 4 Michel (1957), scheme 3
1st-order pel process	VI VI ▢▨	$\geq \begin{cases} H_p(R_{sm}) \\ H_p(R_{pm}) \end{cases}$	Michel (1957), scheme 2 Capon (1959)
3rd-order adjoint error process	⊞	$\geq H_p(R_{ae})$	Wholey (1961)
3rd-order conditional error process	VI VI $\left(⊞ = \right) ⊞$	$\geq H_p(R_{ce})$	Preuss (1975a)

[a] Entropy symbols listed without their constraints (e.g., see Eqs. (50), (60), and (68)).

models will require generalization of these expressions using identities from information theory.

First, the local source entropy $H(X)$ in bits per symbol is defined in terms of the symbol probabilities $P(x_i)$ to be

$$H(X) \equiv - \sum_{i=1}^{I} P(x_i) \log_2 P(x_i) \tag{3}$$

Then, the number of local source symbols $N_f(X)$ that are combined to represent the total field must be determined. For this example, with a source pattern of fixed size U and with a field size V

$$N_f(X) = V/U \tag{4}$$

The product of Eqs. (3) and (4) gives the field-normalized entropy[3] in bits per field

$$H_f(X) \equiv N_f(X)H(X) \tag{5}$$

based on the local source, which is assumed stationary.

A common, but possibly misleading, measure of the potential from a source model is its compression bound $C_B(X)$. This ratio compares the field entropy with V, the total number of pels in the field

$$C_B(X) \equiv V/H_f(X) \tag{6}$$

and is expressed in units[4] of pel/bit. Compression is a deceptive measure of performance because it is a ratio. It is normalized by the input image size, which can be excessive if the field dimensions or spatial resolution is too generous. To keep the bit cost visible, field entropy is recommended as a figure of merit. For facsimile applications, field entropy translates directly to transmission time.

Rather than compare the performance of source models using field normalization, many researchers normalize their results to the average entropy or compression bound per pel. This may be visualized by combining Eqs. (4), (5), and (6) to compute

$$C_B(X) = U/H(X) \tag{7}$$

[3] Subscript notation: (a) Subscripts p, s, f are used to modify any function to indicate that its units are normalized per pel, per source alphabet symbol, or apply over the whole field, respectively. If no subscript is shown, normalization per source alphabet symbol is assumed. (b) Subscripts indicating the specific member in a set are not shown in many cases where the meaning will not suffer (i.e., writing x instead of x_i). (c) Subscripts indicating time dependence are only shown where necessary. Otherwise stationarity is assumed.

[4] It is helpful to distinguish between bits of *uncoded* data and bits of compression-*coded* data. This is commonly accomplished by using the term "pel" instead of "uncoded bit," since each binary pel corresponds to exactly one bit. Then the unqualified term "bit" is understood to refer to a "coded bit" (see Arps, 1971, or Huang, 1977).

Its inverse is the pel entropy for the source X given by

$$H_p(X) = H(X)/U \qquad (8)$$

These pel-normalized performance equations do not illustrate the actual coding process as well as the previous field-normalized expressions do. As such, they are harder to generalize for the analysis of complex models. For example, they obscure the assumption of stationarity in Eq. (5). For some source patterns (e.g., without a fixed size U) it may become difficult to write simple expressions such as Eqs. (7) and (8). Writing similar equations for multiple-source models may be awkward as well. Generally, expressions for complicated models are more naturally written at the global level. Therefore, performance analysis as outlined by Eqs. (3)–(6) is recommended, with pel normalization afterward if desired.

Source Codes

For the basic problem depicted by the global model in Fig. 7-3, there is only an alphabet with fixed symbol size that must be variable-length encoded. However, for the local source model there is freedom to select whether the input pattern sizes or output word lengths (or both) are to be variable.

Fixed-to-variable-length coding is illustrated in Fig. 7-4 for the simple case of a local source X with a fixed 1×2 pel source pattern. The variable-length code words $W(X)$ are shown as passing through a noiseless channel. The decoding is unique and instantaneous, as implied by the use of a decoding tree. Huffman (1952) coding can be used to optimally encode such a source if the required table lookup is feasible.

Variable-to-fixed-length coding is illustrated in Fig. 7-5 by a run-length coding example. In this kind of run-length coding, variable-size source

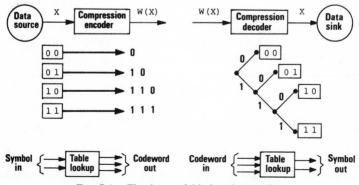

FIG. 7-4. Fixed-to-variable-length encoding.

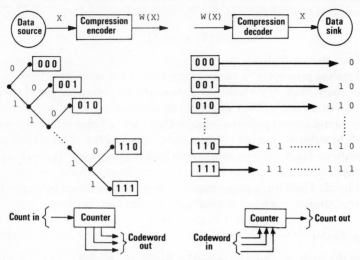

FIG. 7-5. Variable-to-fixed-length encoding.

patterns span "runs" of adjacent pels of the same state and are terminated by a pel of the opposite state. Such codes are easy to implement, requiring little more than counters for encoding and decoding. Papers describing other algorithms for variable-to-fixed-length coding have been written by White *et al.* (1972), Schalkwijk (1972), and Jelinek and Schneider (1972). Optimal variable-to-fixed-length coders may be difficult to design owing to the high order of joint pel statistics required to fully characterize their local source models.

For the case of fixed-to-variable- and/or variable-to-fixed-length coding, a general set of notation and relationships can be defined as follows. Assume that a set of binary code words has been derived for the local source X with an integer set of code word lengths

$$L(X) \equiv \{l(x_i): i \in \{1, 2, \ldots, I\}\} \qquad (9)$$

in bits per symbol. For variable-to-fixed-length coding, these lengths will be a constant L. The average length for these code words is

$$\bar{L}(X) \equiv \sum_{i=1}^{I} P(x_i) l(x_i) \qquad (10)$$

Correspondingly, a variable set of pattern sizes can be specified as

$$U(X) \equiv \{u(x_i): i \in \{1, 2, \ldots, I\}\} \qquad (11)$$

pels per symbol. For fixed-to-variable-length coding, these sizes will simply be a constant U. The average size for these patterns is

$$\bar{U}(X) \equiv \sum_{i=1}^{I} P(x_i)u(x_i) \tag{12}$$

Note that in contrast to Eq. (2), a more general definition for the alphabet X has been assumed. This is given by

$$X \equiv \{x_i: i \in \{1, 2, \ldots, I\}\} \tag{13}$$

Equations (11)–(13) have thus generalized the source model without affecting Eqs. (3), (5), and (6). However, for the general case, Eq. (4) must be replaced by simply counting the number of symbols into which the field is decomposed.

The evaluation of a prospective coder is analogous to the analysis of its corresponding source model in Eqs. (3)–(6). The average code word length in Eq. (10) corresponds to the entropy in Eq. (3). For cases where $U(X)$ is fixed at a constant value U, Eq. (4) can again be used to calculate the number of symbols per field $N_f(X)$. Similarly, for alphabets where U is not fixed, $N_f(X)$ must be determined by counting up the symbols in the total field.

The length of the coded bit string representing real data, however, does not have to be the multiple of an *average* value as in Eq. (5). Instead, the result from actually encoding a specific page is deterministic and can be expressed as

$$L_f(X) \equiv \sum_{n=1}^{N_f(X)} l(x_{in}) \tag{14}$$

bits per field, where $l(x_{in})$ is the actual length of the nth code word.

Analogous to Eq. (6), the performance for the actual code is specified as a compression ratio

$$C_R(X) \equiv V/L_f(X) \tag{15}$$

Source Optimization

The art of designing better algorithms is typically separated into a search for improved source models followed by the development of well-matched coders. This separation is helped by using entropy bounds like Eq. (5) to evaluate prospective models, without undue concern for details of the coders that will follow. Once a model has been selected, then competing coders can be evaluated for how close to the model bounds they perform. The performance measure used is a percentage comparison called coding efficiency, defined as

$$\eta \equiv (100)C_R(X)/C_B(X) \equiv (100)L_f(X)/H_f(X) \tag{16}$$

The following simple concepts are often used in the course of evaluating modifications to an existing source model. These basic tools characterize the changes in source entropy that occur when the model defining a source alphabet is perturbed.

1. Distribution "smoothing" ("peaking"): Given a source alphabet X, any change in any two probabilities that tends to further equalize (unequalize) their respective values causes an increase (decrease) in the source entropy $H(X)$.

2. Distribution "expanding" ("collapsing"): Given a source alphabet X, increasing (decreasing) the number of symbols in the alphabet by breaking up one symbol into two (combining two symbols into one) causes an increase (decrease) in the source entropy $H(X)$. It is assumed above that the corresponding symbol probability is also being broken apart (probabilities are also being combined).

3. Distribution "mixing": Consider two source alphabets X, Y with identical symbols but different distributions $P(X)$, $P(Y)$ and different entropies $H(X)$, $H(Y)$. Any new source Z with distribution $P(Z)$ generated as the weighted average of $P(X)$, $P(Y)$ will have an entropy $H(Z)$ that is greater than the corresponding weighted average of $H(X)$, $H(Y)$. A similar statement can be made if many alphabets are mixed. This concept is based on the "convexity" of the entropy function.

The development of better models can also be aided by visualizing several basic concepts and identities from information theory. A pictorial notation for joint, conditional, and marginal entropies (Arps, 1971) is introduced below, next to the defining equations for these functions. This notation for entropies is presented in terms of image patterns for some simple local source, where the patterns have been drawn according to a special set of rules[5], some of which will not be used until Sec. 7.3.2:

(a) Pels defining a "present" source symbol are crosshatched.
(b) Pels defining a "present" *error* source symbol are dotted.
(c) Pels defining any "previous" source state dependence are white.
(d) Dotted pel outlines are used for "positional" information only.
(e) Overbars above a pel pattern indicate an "adjoint" source.

Thus, the basic entropy definitions are
Joint entropy:

$$X\ Y$$

$$H(X, Y) \equiv - \sum_{i=1}^{I} \sum_{j=1}^{J} P(x_i, y_j) \log_2 P(x_i, y_j) \tag{17}$$

---

[5] The pel identifiers (e.g., X and Y) in the pictorial notation will be dropped if the sources are stationary and no confusion can arise. If all terms in a pictorial equation span the same pels, then each pattern will be assumed to be left justified. Where needed, dotted outlines will be used to indicate uninvolved pels [see Eq. (22)]. Alternatively, pictorial equations may use labeled axes to provide positional information (see Fig. 7-6).

Conditional entropy:

X Y

$$H(Y|X) \equiv - \sum_{i=1}^{I} P(x_i) \sum_{j=1}^{J} P(y_j|x_i) \log_2 P(y_j|x_i) \qquad (18)$$

Marginal entropy:

X Y

$$H(Y) \equiv - \sum_{j=1}^{J} P(y_j) \log_2 P(y_j) \qquad (19)$$

The pictorial entropies defined in Eqs. (17)–(19) can be related to joint, conditional, or marginal source models that are to be encoded accordingly. For example, the joint entropy pattern in Eq. (17) implies that pel pairs define the source alphabet, that the symbols are all possible 2-tuples, and that probabilities for all these symbols are to be estimated from the data. In contrast, a second "extension" (see Abramson, 1963) of the source implied by Eq. (19) would generate an alphabet of 2-tuples with probabilities derived by multiplying together estimates of the underlying single-pel probabilities for sources X and Y.

The pictorial notation for the nth extension of a source will be drawn as pattern with separation between the n independent repetitions of the basic pel model. Thus, the nth extension of the source implied by Eq. (19) is indicated as

$$H(Y^n) = nH(Y) \qquad (20)$$

The nth extension of a conditional source is also possible and will be drawn by simply adding the relevant "previous" state pels to the first part of the pattern.

Some useful identities from Ash (1965) are summarized next. The fundamental interrelationship among the above entropy functions is

$$H(X, Y) = H(X) + H(Y|X) \qquad (21)$$

Notice the similarity here to the basic interrelationship among joint, conditional, and marginal probabilities. The entropy interrelationship is only additive, instead of multiplicative. As shown, this equation is to be visualized in terms of pel patterns for successive local sources. It is also useful for analyzing compound source models, where $H(X)$ represents a choice among multiple models and $H(Y|X)$ represents the probability-weighted entropies of these models. In this sense, Eq. (21) can be thought of as the *generalized grouping axiom* described in detail by Ash (1965) in his Figure 1.3.1, Lemma 1.4.1, and Problem 1.10. Examples of published algorithms that require compound source models for proper analysis include those of Huang (1972) and Usubuchi *et al.* (1975).

The relationship between conditional and marginal entropies is given by the inequality

$$\square \!\!\!\!\square \leq \square \!\!\!\!\square \qquad H(Y|X) \leq H(Y) \tag{22}$$

with equality if and only if (iff) the underlying probability distributions for the source X and source Y are independent. Combining Eqs. (21) and (22) yields

$$\square \!\!\!\!\square \leq \square \!\!\!\!\square + \square \!\!\!\!\square \qquad H(X, Y) \leq H(X) + H(Y) \tag{23}$$

with equality iff X and Y are independent. Here again the conditions for equality in Eqs. (22) and (23) resemble the basic conditional and joint probability interrelationships given independent marginals, except that for entropies, Eq. (23) is additive rather than multiplicative.

To each of these relationships physical meaning can be given that will aid in the selection of better models and give insight into breaking down the global compression problem. Equation (22) means that a pel Y can be sent with fewer bits, on the average, if any dependence on the previous pel X can be utilized in a conditional source-coding scheme. With binary pels, extensions of the conditional and marginal sources must be taken to approach these pel-normalized entropies using actual coders [use Eq. (20)].

Equation (23) shows that where dependency exists in the image, the coding of groups of pels based on joint statistics has a lower bound than coding a sequence of individual pels. If the successive pels on the right-hand side of the equation have distributions that are identical, then these pels can also represent coding based on the nth extension of a single pel-repeating source. This equation then contrasts the coding of pel groups based on joint statistics with the coding of pel groups based on individual pel statistics. The result is still the same; encoding based on the joint statistics is superior when there is dependency between pels. For general comparison with other source pattern entropies [e.g., Eq. (22)], these pel group results must be subsequently pel normalized.

The lower entropies obtained with joint pel sources can also be attained using conditional sources. Figure 7-6 illustrates the simplest case,

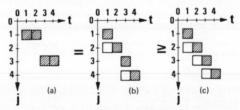

FIG. 7-6.   Advantage of overlapping conditional source patterns.

based on Eq. (21). The horizontal axis represents the pels in a scan line, while the downward vertical axis indicates successive messages as the processing proceeds from left to right. Figures 7-6a and b show two cases with equal entropy over the four pels. The entropy inherent in sending a pel pair such as X and Y can, alternatively, be achieved by first encoding X and then conditionally encoding Y given X. The following theorem shows how conditional source models may achieve even lower entropies.

THEOREM 1: OVERLAPPING CONDITIONAL SOURCES: *The total entropy used to represent a field when modeling with overlapping conditional sources*

$$H(X_0) + H(X_1|X_0) + H(X_2|X_1) + H(X_3|X_2) + \cdots$$

is less than or equal to the total entropy used to represent a field when modeling with adjacent joint sources

$$H(X_0,X_1) + H(X_2,X_3) + \cdots$$

This theorem is demonstrated in Fig. 7-6c. By comparison with Fig. 7-6b, the third time increment of Fig. 7-6c possesses a conditional rather than marginal source model. By applying Eq. (22) for this third time increment, it becomes apparent that the overall entropy has been decreased in Fig. 7-6c as compared to that in b. The equality of entropies in Figs. 7-6a and b using Eq. (21) then completes the proof.[6]

The important identity of Eq. (21) can be generalized for larger joint pel patterns as

$$H(X_1, X_2 \ldots, X_n) = H(X_1) + H(X_2|X_1) + H(X_3|X_1, X_2)$$
$$+ \cdots + H(X_n|X_1, X_2, \ldots, X_{n-1}) \quad (24)$$

When applied to the global source-coding problem of Eq. (1), this relationship breaks G down into a sequence of symbols from different conditional source models. The resulting string of sources is still too complicated to be practical. Their local image patterns should ideally be identical so that the same encoder can be used repeatedly throughout the image. For tractability, the dependency of these patterns should also be limited

---

[6] This result should not be confused with the ultimate equality of pel-normalized joint and conditional source entropies for *one* symbol (no overlapping) and with pattern sizes approaching infinity (see Huang, 1977, Eqs. 3 and 4).

to some fixed lower order. Note that even with identical patterns in the pictorial equation, the corresponding encoders may still be different until stationarity can be assumed. The resulting challenge is then: how can the global source be broken down into a sequence of simple, limited-dependency sources or, preferably, into a stationary source repeating with identical distribution and dependency?

If, in addition, complete independence can be assumed between successive source symbols, the local source model becomes even simpler. Eq. (23) can be generalized for larger joint pel patterns as

$$H(X_1, X_2, \ldots, X_n) \leq H(X_1) + H(X_2) + H(X_3) + \cdots + H(X_n) \qquad (25)$$

where equality holds iff successive symbols are independent. Again the identical patterns may still represent a nonstationary sequence and imply the use of different encoders or an adaptive encoder. However, with stationarity the distributions become identical. Of course, the simple 1-pel patterns shown here can represent larger, more complex patterns that are macroscopically independent.

Thus, the familiar independent, identically distributed (i.i.d.) constraint arises as a goal when selecting the ideal pattern for a repeating local source. If this constraint were satisfied, optimal algorithms could be designed without encoding on a global basis. The above is only an idealization, of course, but serves as a guide for investigations in this area. In practice, the challenge is to find repeating source patterns that enclose significant amounts of dependency (usually local dependency) while remaining practical.

7.3.   RASTER ALGORITHMS

Raster algorithms constitute the oldest and largest class of compression schemes for binary image data. As in television, they assume that input data are derived from a line-by-line scan of the image field (typically left to right, sequentially from top to bottom). Unlike TV, however, no interlacing of data is assumed and line-to-line correlations play a significant part in the more complex binary image coders. Models and bounds for the most significant algorithms are described here. A short overview of the major methods of coding in use can be found in Huang (1977).

7.3.1 Line-Independent Models and Bounds

The examples in Figs. 7-4 and 7-5 illustrated some simple source models for raster image data. Their respective source patterns were fixed-length 1×2 pel blocks and variable-length runs of 1 terminated by a 0. The latter pattern is but one of several used for "run-length" coding.

Run-length coding has been in use since the earliest days of information theory (Shannon and Weaver, 1949; Laemmel, 1951, p. 12). Enough variations exist that some detailed definitions are helpful. A set of increasingly complex methods for "parsing" streams of binary data forms the basis for the set of run-length coding definitions illustrated by Figs. 7-7, 7-8, and 7-14. For ease of comparison, these methods will be described with the same set of binary data, given in both Figs. 7-7a and 7-8a. For reference, the pels are assumed to be labeled from left to right as $X_1, X_2, \ldots, X_T$, for the T pels in a line of adjacent independent pel patterns X_t.

The simplest algorithms utilize a single run-length source to model the data. This implies the use of only one coder in the implementation, a significant cost requirement in the early days of hardware development. Figure 7-7 illustrates three such ways to parse binary data using only one source alphabet.

Figure 7-7b represents "simple" run parsing, in which a run is defined to be a contiguous set of pels of one state bounded by pels of the opposite state. From run to run, the state of these contiguous sets is seen to alternate. All the runs are delineated by enclosing them in rectangles, marked from above with their lengths.

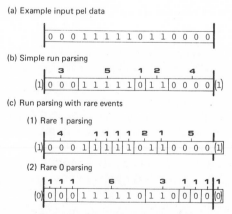

FIG. 7-7. Run parsing with binary data. Boundary conditions: (a) none; (b) $X_0 = \bar{X}_1$, $X_{T+1} = \bar{X}_T$; (c1) $X_0 = X_{T+1} = 1$; (c2) $X_0 = X_{T+1} = 0$.

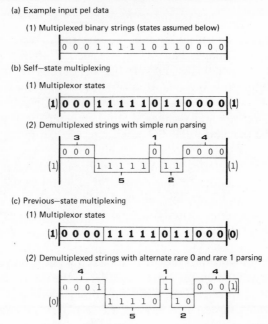

(a) Example input pel data

(1) Multiplexed binary strings (states assumed below)

0 0 0 1 1 1 1 1 0 1 1 0 0 0 0

(b) Self—state multiplexing

(1) Multiplexor states

(1) 0 0 0 1 1 1 1 1 0 1 1 0 0 0 0 (1)

(2) Demultiplexed strings with simple run parsing

(c) Previous—state multiplexing

(1) Multiplexor states

(1) 0 0 0 0 1 1 1 1 1 0 1 1 0 0 0 (0)

(2) Demultiplexed strings with alternate rare 0 and rare 1 parsing

FIG. 7-8. Run multiplexing with binary data. Boundary conditions: (a) none; (b) $S_0 = X_0 = \bar{X}_1$, $S_{T+1} = X_{T+1} = \bar{X}_T$; (c1) $S_0 = 1$, $S_{T+1} = X_T$; (c2) $X_0 = 0$, $X_{T+1} = \bar{X}_T$.

Figures 7-7c1 and c2 show parsing methods in which one state is considered "rare" and the other state predominates. Parsing occurs immediately after each occurrence of the rare state. For example, runs in rare 1 parsing are defined as strings of contiguous 0's *plus* the 1 that terminates the string. Any 1's immediately preceded by a 1 are considered to terminate a string of *zero* 0's. From this point of view, they are short runs by themselves with a run length of unity. Rare 0 parsing in Fig. 7-7c2 should be interpreted exactly like rare 1 parsing, except that the 0's and 1's are interchanged.

Boundary conditions (b.c.), have been added to all diagrams for completeness. They are shown in parentheses as the states assumed to exist beyond both ends of the example data. These b.c. are also defined in equation form in the figure captions. For example, $X_{T+1} = \bar{X}_T$ in Fig. 7-7b yields $X_{T+1} = 1$ and terminates the last run (contiguous 0's, since $X_T = 0$).

All of the b.c. are selected to ensure that the data start with the beginning of a run and finish with the end of a run. They are not necessarily the same from one method of parsing to another, as can be seen by comparing Fig. 7-7c1 and c2. Notice in Fig. 7-7c1 that the inclusion of terminating pels of rare event runs results in cases where the b.c. bit must be included in the last run. For uniformity, rare event parsing methods are assumed to always include this b.c. bit unless explicitly stated otherwise, even if it adds a dummy run to the line.

Simple Run Models

When these parsing methods are used to define a source, the possible run lengths form an alphabet that is also a random variable

$$R \equiv \{r_j : j \in \{1, 2, \ldots\}\} = \{r \in 1, 2, \ldots\} \tag{26}$$

with a set of unusual properties. The integer run lengths r_j are ordered to coincide with the index of alphabet symbols j [e.g., $r_j = j = r$]. Also, they can be ordered to coincide with the variable-source-pattern lengths $u(r)$ [e.g., $u(r) = r$ with $r = 1, 2, \ldots$]. This constrains the pattern lengths to be monotonically increasing, unique, consecutive integers.

Early writers in binary data compression, Shannon and Weaver (1949), Laemmel (1951), and Elias (1955), used variations of rare event parsing for their run-length sources. The run lengths they defined did not include the terminal rare pel, and run lengths of zero were needed [e.g., $u(r) = r + 1$ with $r = 0, 1, \ldots$]. Recent authors like Preuss (1975a) or Huang (1977) implicitly use the alphabet defined by Eq. (26) when defining a source. This definition will be assumed to hold, unless stated otherwise.

Having defined a source model, one must take care that the encoding/decoding process it implies is realizable. In particular, "look-ahead" methods that can be used for encoding may give rise to noncausal decoders that need unavailable future information. In simple run parsing, explicit information about the state X_t of pels in a run has been omitted. The states are assumed to alternate from run to run, but the first run must be initialized. The b.c. $X_0 = \bar{X}_1$ of Fig. 7-7b represents an unrealizable decoder requirement; it cannot start decoding X_1 without knowing X_0.

The typical solution to this problem uses the fact that margins are white at the left edge of most DIN A4 pages and $X_1 = 0$. This is a situation where one state predominates and transmission "by exception" can be used. No message is sent if the predominant starting state occurs (the "default" condition). A message is only sent when the "exception" condition (e.g., $X_1 = 1$) occurs. Making provision for an exception message "expands" the size of the source alphabet X and causes a slight increase in the entropy of $H(X)$. The number of messages $N_f(X)$ also increases. However, the combined effect of both increases on the field entropy in Eq. (5) is typically negligible.

Underlying Independent Pel Process, H(X) ≡ ▨

Two summation formulas are useful to introduce at this point:

$$\sum_{r=1}^{\infty} q^{r-1} = 1/(1 - q) = 1/p \tag{27}$$

$$\sum_{r=1}^{\infty} rq^{r-1} = 1/(1 - q)^2 = 1/p^2 \tag{28}$$

Various run-length models can be compared analytically if the image field is assumed to be generated by a simple underlying process. The first process to be assumed generates the field as a sequence of i.i.d. binary pels X with probability distribution $P\{X = x_i\} = \{p, q\}$. This is a sequence of Bernoulli trials based on the probability for black and white pels in the image being p and q respectively. If the pel states x_i are assigned binary values [e.g., $x_i = i - 1 = x$ for $i = 1, 2$] the alphabet becomes a random variable $X = \{x \in 0, 1\}$ with a *point binomial* distribution

$$P\{X = x\} = p^x q^{1-x} \tag{29}$$

Based on this, one can write the probability for a rare 1 run of length r (Laemmel, 1951, p. 14) as

$$P\{R_{r1}{}^0 = r\} = pq^{r-1} \tag{30}$$

where $r = 1, 2, \ldots$. The superscript 0 indicates the assumption that an underlying model with "zero memory" or independent pels is used.[7] By symmetry, the probability for a rare 0 run of length r can be written as above but with p and q interchanged. This expression is also known as the probability for the memoryless "waiting time" to the first 1, in a sequence of Bernoulli trials (Feller, 1968, Section XIII,9). Since the pels in the sequence of Bernoulli trials are independent, the runs they generate are also independent (memoryless). If one assumes the existence of run lengths out to infinity,[8] use of Eq. (27) verifies that it is a valid probability distribution. Equation (30) then becomes the *geometric* distribution.

Using Eq. (28), the expected value for the distribution (the average run length) is

$$\bar{r}_{r1}{}^0 = \sum_{r=1}^{\infty} rP(r) = \sum_{r=1}^{\infty} r(pq^{r-1}) = 1/p \tag{31}$$

[7] Superscript notation: Superscripts will only be used as a reminder that an underlying Markov pel process is assumed and then only for random variables B, R, and for runlength averages $\bar{r}$.

[8] Infinite-run-length models are used with finite-length scan lines in the following way. Assume the scan line to be a "window" on the infinite process. If the beginning or end of the line falls in the middle of a run, expressions like Eq. (32) are used to properly include incomplete runs in any analysis.

pels per symbol. The sum of terms in the tail of the distribution (beyond an arbitrary run length r) can be expressed as

$$P\{R_{r1}^0 > r\} = \sum_{i=r+1}^{\infty} pq^{i-1} = pq^r \sum_{j=1}^{\infty} q^{j-1} = q^r \tag{32}$$

by using Eq. (27) and a change of the dummy variable $j = i - r$. This value for the tail of the distribution can be helpful, when finite limitations on the maximum observable run length cause an infinite distribution to be inconvenient.

The basis for choosing this version of the geometric distribution, rather than the alternate form pq^r with $r = 0, 1, \ldots$, can be found in the discussion surrounding the properties in Eq. (26). A further basis lies in the simplicity of form in expressions like Eqs. (28), (31), and (32) when compared to expressions of the other version.

Given this geometric distribution for a rare 1 run source R_{r1}^0, its source entropy can now be calculated in closed form. This closed form appears in the proof of the next theorem for a general rare event run source R_{re}^0, in which the pel entropy for R_{re}^0 is also shown to have a simple expression.

THEOREM 2: RUNS BASED ON INDEPENDENT (ZEROTH-ORDER MARKOV) PELS. *Assume a binary source X generating an infinite stationary sequence of i.i.d. pels. Let this sequence be modeled by a geometrically distributed rare 1 or rare 0 source. Then the corresponding pel entropy $H_p(R_{re}^0)$ for the rare event run source R_{re}^0 equals the entropy $H(X) = H\{p, q\}$ for the underlying pel source.[9] The entropy per symbol $H_s(R_{re}^0)$ is $\bar{r}_{re}^0 H\{p, q\}$, where $\bar{r}_{re}^0$ is the average run length for the run source.*

The closed form for $H_s(R_{r1}^0)$ is found by combining Eqs. (3) and (30) to get

$$H_s(R_{r1}^0) = - \sum_{r=1}^{\infty} (pq^{r-1}) \log_2(pq^{r-1})$$

$$= -p \log_2 q \sum_{r=1}^{\infty} (r-1)q^{r-1} - p \log_2 p \sum_{r=1}^{\infty} q^{r-1} \tag{33}$$

$$= (1/p)(-q \log_2 q - p \log_2 p) = \bar{r}_{r1}^0 H\{p, q\}$$

where Eqs. (27), (28), (31), and again (3) have subsequently been used.

Equation (8) must now be generalized using Eq. (12) for variable-size source patterns $U(X)$ to define the pel-normalized entropy as

$$H_p(Y) = H_s(Y)/\bar{U}(Y) \tag{34}$$

---

[9] The notation $H\{\cdot, \cdot\}$ means the entropy for the set of probabilities in braces $\{\cdot, \cdot\}$.

Changing the dummy alphabet Y in Eq. (34) to R_{r1}^0 and combining with Eq. (33) yields

$$H_p(R_{r1}^0) = \frac{H_s(R_{r1}^0)}{\bar{U}(R_{r1}^0)} = \frac{\bar{r}_{r1}^0 H\{p, q\}}{\bar{r}_{r1}^0} = H\{p, q\} \tag{35}$$

where Eq. (12) has also been used. Interchanging p and q in Eqs. (30), (31), (33), and (35) produces the same result for a rare 0 run source R_{r0}^0, demonstrating that the theorem applies to either form of rare event source R_{re}^0, and completing the proof.

Capon (1959) showed this result in different form, as part of a theorem for runs based on pels from a first-order Markov source. Huang (1972) introduced the more concise derivation above in the course of summarizing Capon's theorem. Notice that the rare 1 run source R_{r1}^0 in Eq. (33) behaves like a variable-length extension of the underlying i.i.d. pel source X, with the term n in Eq. (20) replaced by an average extension $\bar{r}_{r1}^0$. Also, the two forms of rare-event sources are shown to have the same pel entropy, in spite of their different behaviors illustrated in Fig. 7-7c. The key difference lies in the number of runs and the average length of the runs they use while producing the same pel entropy. With different average run lengths, the variable-length extensions they represent will not be the same, causing differences in the attainable efficiency of their corresponding coders.

A separate but related theorem specifies the maximum symbol entropy over all possible run source distributions. The distribution producing the maximum entropy is determined as well. This entropy bound assumes that the mean value of the distribution $\bar{r}$ is given and constrained during the maximization process.

THEOREM 3: MAXIMAL-ENTROPY RUN DISTRIBUTION. *For an arbitrary run source* R, *with distribution* $P\{R = r\}$ *and mean value* $\bar{r}$, *the maximum symbol entropy is* $H_s(R_m) = \bar{r}H\{p_m, q_m\}$, *where* $p_m = 1 - q_m = 1/\bar{r}$. *This maximal entropy source* R_m, *has a geometric distribution* $P\{R_m = r\} = p_m q_m^{r-1}$ *with* $r = 1, 2, \ldots .$

The proof is detailed in a paper by Huang (1974), in which he uses the method of Lagrange multipliers with constraints

$$\sum_{r=1}^{\infty} P(r) = 1 \tag{36a}$$

$$\sum_{r=1}^{\infty} rP(r) = \bar{r} \tag{36b}$$

When converted to the notation used here $(i \rightarrow r, a \rightarrow \bar{r})$, the results in

Huang's Eqs. (15) and (16) become the first identities in Eqs. (37) and (38). The subsequent identities reformulate these expressions to complete the theorem. Thus

$$P\{R_m = r\} = \left(\frac{1}{\bar{r} - 1}\right) \left(\frac{\bar{r} - 1}{\bar{r}}\right)^r = \frac{1}{\bar{r}} \left(\frac{\bar{r} - 1}{\bar{r}}\right)^{r-1} = p_m q_m^{r-1} \quad (37)$$

and

$$H_s(R_m) = \bar{r} \log_2 \bar{r} - (\bar{r} - 1) \log_2 (\bar{r} - 1)$$
$$= \frac{1}{p_m} (-p_m \log_2 p_m - q_m \log_2 q_m)$$
$$= \bar{r} H\{p_m, q_m\} \geq H_s(R)|_{\bar{r} \equiv 1/p_m} \quad (38)$$

where the expressions in p_m result from recognizing the geometric distribution with parameter $p_m = 1/\bar{r}$ in Eq. (37). The inequality in Eq. (38) emphasizes that a source R with arbitrary distribution,[10] but with run length $\bar{r}$, has a symbol entropy $H_s(R)$ that is bounded by the maximum symbol entropy $H_s(R_m)$. Only the average run length need be specified for this bound to apply.

Theorems 2 and 3 can be combined by equating the parameters of their respective geometric distributions $(\bar{r}_{re}^0 = \bar{r})$. For example, if an image is generated by an i.i.d. pel source with $P\{X = x\} = \{p, q\}$ and if geometrically distributed rare 1 runs R_{r1}^0 are modeled, then $\bar{r} = \bar{r}_{r1}^0$, and $p_m = p$. Equations (33) and (38) can be combined to show that the rare 1 entropy $H_s(R_{r1}^0)$ bounds the entropy $H_s(R)$ for all other runs R having the same average run length $\bar{r} = \bar{r}_{r1}^0 = 1/p$. For rare 0 runs, the same statements are true but with p and q interchanged and $\bar{r} = \bar{r}_{r0}^0 = 1/q$. This important bound can be pel normalized by $\bar{r}$ using Eq. (34), and the result for both types of rare event source displayed in terms of two alternative run length constraints

$$\boxed{} \geq \underbrace{\boxed{}}_{} \; /\bar{r} \qquad H\{p, q\} \geq H_p(R)|_{\bar{r} \equiv 1/p \text{ or } 1/q} \quad (39)$$
$$\bar{r} \equiv 1/p \text{ or } 1/q \quad,$$

with equality iff the run source R is a rare event source R_{re}^0 generated by the pel source X. In retrospect, this is merely a pel normalized generalization of Eq. (25) for the case of a variable-length extension $n = \bar{r}$.

Interlaced Run Models

Some compound models using pairs of sources are introduced in Fig. 7-8. Patterns for the individual sources are again runs as defined in Fig.

---

[10] This includes *noninfinite* distributions as can be seen by combining all terms in the tail of the geometric distribution with other terms so that the value of $\bar{r}$ is preserved. By "collapsing" the distribution size, the corresponding source entropy $H_s(R)$ decreases.

7-7. However, runs generated by the two sources are interlaced to produce what will be called a "run-multiplexed" source model.

The simple runs of Fig. 7-7b have merely been separated in Fig. 7-8b, resulting in one source with simple runs of 1 alternating with another source generating simple runs of 0. As in simple run parsing, an initial condition must also be transmitted in order to start the receiver decoding with the correct pel state X_1 and thereby the correct run source. In Fig. 7-8b1 this amounts to initializing a "multiplexor state," which represents the source being used for a pel at any given time. The multiplexor state S_t alternates in step with the pel state ($S_t = X_t$); so the run model is called "self-state" multiplexing (R_{sm}).

In Fig. 7-8c2 the input data of Fig. 7-8a have been separated with alternate versions of rare event parsing, first with rare 1 parsing and then with rare 0 parsing. Note that the starting source is clearly specified for the receiver, since rare event coding can start with either pel state. It is only not allowed to finish on any pel state; so a terminating b.c. bit must again be added (as in Fig. 7-7c) to ensure that the data finish with the end of a run. The multiplexor (or source) state in Fig. 7-8c1 alternates by run as in Fig. 7-8b1 but with the characteristic $S_t = X_{t-1}$. In this case, the source selection is determined by the previous pel, so that this run model is named "previous-state" multiplexing (R_{pm}).

Underlying Dependent Pel Process, $H_p(X_t|X_{t-1}) \equiv$ ☐▨

Entropy bounds exist for these compound run source models similar to the bound in Eq. (38). The bounds are again developed using the assumption that some underlying pel source model completely characterizes the image. Capon (1959) introduced the use of a binary first-order Markov source to define the underlying pel model needed here.

The general case for Capon's model is shown in Fig. 7-9a along with two restricted cases in Figs. 7-9 b and c. The four possible pel state transitions, given knowledge of the current state, are labeled with their corresponding transition probabilities. The abbreviated notations for the conditional probabilities in Fig. 7-9a are implicitly defined by their positions in the transition probability matrix

$$P\{X_{t+1} = x_{t+1}|X_t = x_t\} = \begin{bmatrix} q_0 & p_0 \\ p_1 & q_1 \end{bmatrix} \equiv \mathbf{P} \tag{40}$$

Similarly, the abbreviated notations for the state probabilities are implicitly defined by their positions in the state probability vector

$$P\{X_t = x\} = [\pi_0(t)\pi_1(t)] \equiv \mathbf{\Pi} \tag{41}$$

The initial values for the state probabilities are $\pi_0(0)$ and $\pi_1(0)$, as is also

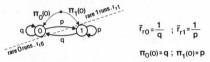

(a) General Case (Unequal Distributions, Dependent Pels)

$$\bar{r}_{r0} = \frac{1}{p_1} \; ; \; \bar{r}_{r1} = \frac{1}{p_0}$$

(b) Matched Case (Equal Distributions, Dependent Pels)

$$\bar{r}_{r0} = \bar{r}_{r1} = \frac{1}{p}$$

(c) 0th Order Case (Unequal Distributions, Independent Pels)

$$\bar{r}_{r0} = \frac{1}{q} \; ; \; \bar{r}_{r1} = \frac{1}{p}$$

$$\pi_0(0) = q \; ; \; \pi_1(0) = p$$

FIG. 7-9. Binary first-order Markov models (Capon's model).

shown in Fig. 7-9. For Fig. 7-9b and c the model is the same, but the general values for the transition probabilities have been constrained to $q_0 = q_1 = q$, $p_0 = p_1 = p$ and to $q_0 = p_1 = q$, $q_1 = p_0 = p$, respectively.

All of the various run models defined by Figs. 7-7 and 7-8 can be visualized in terms of transition sequences in Capon's model. For example, a rare 1 run in Fig. 7-9 is a sequence of 0-to-0 transitions (starting after a 1-to-0 transition) terminated by a 0-to-1 transition. A rare 0 run has the same definition, but with all 1's and 0's interchanged. The transitions used to generate rare 1 and rare 0 runs are mutually exclusive and have been separated in Fig. 7-9 by a dashed line, labeled to indicate for each side of the line the kind of run that is generated. If this dashed line is used to parse arbitrary sequences from the Markov chain into runs, a series of alternate rate 0 and 1 run symbols are naturally produced. These interlaced runs, as seen in Fig. 7-9, constitute the previous-state multiplexing model R_{pm} of Figs. 7-8c.

The above example will be helpful in visualizing the following proof for run pairs based on Capon's model.

THEOREM 4: RUN PAIRS BASED ON DEPENDENT (FIRST-ORDER MARKOV) PELS. *Assume a first-order Markov binary source* $(X_{t+1}|X_t)$ *generating an infinite stationary sequence of dependent pels. Let this sequence be modeled by paired symbols from alternate, geometrically distributed rare 1 and rare 0 run sources. Then the corresponding pel entropy* $H_p(R_{pm}^1)$ *for this compound run-pair source* R_{pm}^1 *equals the conditional entropy* $H(X_{t+1}|X_t)$ *for the underlying first-order Markov pel source.*

Assume that the Markov source has transition probabilities as defined by Eq. (40). The previous discussion about Fig. 7-9 illustrates how the four possible transitions in the Markov chain can be separated into mutually exclusive transition pairs that generate either rare 1 or rare 0 runs. Notice that their corresponding transition probability pairs p_0, q_0 and p_1, q_1 alternately replace each other and are separate point binomial distributions in the stochastic matrix of Eq. (40). As such, they generate alternate Bernoulli trial sequences that define mutually independent[11] but interlaced rare 1 and rare 0 runs according to Eqs. (29) and (30). Using Eq. (31), the average run lengths for these run sources are

$$\bar{r}_{r1}{}^1 = 1/p_0 \qquad \qquad (42a)$$
$$\bar{r}_{r0}{}^1 = 1/p_1 \qquad \qquad (42b)$$

These interlaced rare event sources combine to make the compound run-pair source $R_{pm}{}^1$. Based on Eq. (23), the symbol entropy $H_s(R_{pm}{}^1)$ for this compound source is simply the sum of the entropies for independent individual symbols in the run pair. The latter, in turn, can be rewritten using Theorem 2 with probabilities from Eq. (40) giving the result

$$H_s(R_{pm}{}^1) = H_s(R_{r1}{}^1) + H_s(R_{r0}{}^1) = \bar{r}_{r1}{}^1 H\{p_0, q_0\} + \bar{r}_{r0}{}^1 H\{p_1, q_1\} \quad (43)$$

bits per symbol. On the average, a run pair represents $\bar{r}_{r1}{}^1 + \bar{r}_{r0}{}^1$ pels. This fact can be used with Eqs. (34) and (43) to write the pel-normalized compound source entropy

$$H_p(R_{pm}{}^1) = \frac{\bar{r}_{r1}{}^1 H\{p_0, q_0\} + \bar{r}_{r0}{}^1 H\{p_1, q_1\}}{\bar{r}_{r1}{}^1 + \bar{r}_{r0}{}^1} \qquad (44)$$

To write the conditional entropy for the Markov pel source, the stationary state probabilities are needed. These can be computed from the transition probabilities using the observation that in the steady state, the number of 0-to-1 and 1-to-0 transitions are the same. This is equivalent to observing that the corresponding joint probabilities are equal. Thus

$$P\{X_{t+1} = 1, X_t = 0\} = P\{X_{t+1} = 0, X_t = 1\} \qquad (45a)$$
$$P\{X_t = 0\}P\{X_{t+1} = 1 | X_t = 0\} = P\{X_t = 1\}P\{X_{t+1} = 0 | X_t = 1\} \qquad (45b)$$
$$\pi_0(t)p_0 = \pi_1(t)p_1 \qquad (45c)$$

---

[11] To visualize this, write the probabilities for the individual pel transitions that generate the scan line in Figs. 7-8c1 and c2. Then factor them into subsequences corresponding to rare event runs:

$$[\pi_0(0)](q_0q_0q_0p_0)(q_1q_1q_1q_1p_1)(p_0)(q_1p_1)(q_0q_0q_0p_0)$$

Since the probability of the scan line can be expressed as a product of the individual run probabilities, the run probabilities are mutually independent.

where the last line uses the abbreviated notation of Eqs. (40) and (41). Solving for the state probabilities using $\pi_0(t) + \pi_1(t) = 1$, gives

$$\pi_0(t) = p_1/(p_0 + p_1) \tag{46a}$$
$$\pi_1(t) = p_0/(p_0 + p_1) \tag{46b}$$

The above shortcut is equivalent to solving the matrix equation $\mathbf{\Pi} = \mathbf{\Pi P}$ for the steady state values of $\mathbf{\Pi}$.

The conditional entropy for the pel source is written using Eq. (18). The right-hand summations are but the individual entropies $H\{p_0, q_0\}$ and $H\{p_1, q_1\}$ for the rows in Eq. (40), and their probabilities of occurrence are expressed by Eq. (46). The combined result is

$$H(X_{t+1}|X_t) = \frac{p_1 H\{p_0, q_0\} + p_0 H\{p_1, q_1\}}{p_0 + p_1} \tag{47}$$

Substituting Eqs. (42) into (47) produces the same expression as Eq. (44), completing the proof that

$$H_p(R_{pm}^1) = H(X_{t+1}|X_t) \tag{48}$$

This result is independent of the order of occurrence of the rare event sources used to form run pairs. Capon (1959) observed that if the last run length is dependent on the scan line length T, as $T \to \infty$ this dependency vanishes. In the absence of this restrictive assumption (see footnote 8), the run lengths are always mutually independent[11] of each other.

In his proof of Theorem 3, Huang (1974) made the observation that the identity of Eq. (48) for Capon's model is actually a bound on the entropy of run-pair sources. This result is similar to the bound in Eq. (39) for runs based on independent pels, except that a pair of simultaneous run-length constraints must be used. Consider a compound run model R_{pm} made up of arbitrary run sources R_{r1} and R_{r0} interlaced to produce run pairs. If Eq. (42) for the sources of Theorem 4 is used to constrain their average run lengths ($\bar{r}_{r1} = \bar{r}_{r1}^1 = 1/p_0$ and $\bar{r}_{r0} = \bar{r}_{r0}^1 = 1/p_1$), then separate application of Eq. (38) to the individual run sources in Eq. (43) yields a bound

$$H_s(R_{pm}^1) = \bar{r}_{r1}^1 H\{p_0, q_0\} + \bar{r}_{r0}^1 H\{p_1, q_1\}$$
$$\geq H_s(R_{r1})|_{\bar{r}_{r1}\equiv 1/p_0} + H_s(R_{r0})|_{\bar{r}_{r0}\equiv 1/p_1} = H_s(R_{pm})|_{\substack{\bar{r}_{r1}\equiv 1/p_0 \\ \bar{r}_{r0}\equiv 1/p_1}} \tag{49}$$

on the symbol entropy of R_{pm}. This inequality is expressed in terms of the compound run source R_{pm} based on the underlying Markov pel source $(X_{t+1}|X_t)$. When Eq. (49) is pel normalized (using $\bar{U} = \bar{r}_{r0}^1 + \bar{r}_{r1}^1$), it can be combined with Eq. (48) to write the upper bound in terms of the underlying process

$$\Box \mathbin{\!/\mkern-5mu/\!} \;\cong\; \underbrace{\mathbin{\!/\mkern-5mu/\!}\mathbin{\!/\mkern-5mu/\!}\cdots\mathbin{\!/\mkern-5mu/\!}\mathbin{\!/\mkern-5mu/\!}}_{}\,\underbrace{\mathbin{\!/\mkern-5mu/\!}\mathbin{\!/\mkern-5mu/\!}\cdots\mathbin{\!/\mkern-5mu/\!}}_{}\ /(\bar{r}_{r1} + \bar{r}_{r0})$$

$$\bar{r}_{r1} \equiv 1/p_0,\ \bar{r}_{r0} \equiv 1/p_1$$

$$H(X_{t+1}|X_t) \geq H_p(R_{pm})\big|_{\substack{\bar{r}_{r1}\equiv 1/p_0 \\ \bar{r}_{r0}\equiv 1/p_1}} \quad (50)$$

with equality iff the compound run source R_{pm} is a pair of interlaced rare event sources R_{pm}^1 generated by the dependent pel source $(X_{t+1}|X_t)$.

Analytic Model Comparison

The entropy upper bonds of Eqs. (39) and (50) can be compared using the inequality of Eq. (22). These interrelationships form the basis for analytical comparison of some basic run source models as summarized in Table 7-2. For examples, consider the run source models defined in Figs. 7-7 and 7-8. The source models for Figs. 7-7b, c1, and c2 are labeled R_{sr}, R_{r1}, and R_{r0}, respectively. The models for Figs. 7-8b and c and are labeled R_{sm} and R_{pm}, respectively.

Assume that the image is generated by a dependent pel source $(X_{t+1}|X_t)$. By Eq. (50), Capon's (1959) interlaced run source R_{pm}^1 has the maximum entropy $H(X_{t+1}|X_t)$. The code words produced by Michel's (1957) interlaced run source R_{sm}^1 are almost identical to those from source R_{pm}^1, as can be seen by comparing their output code words in Fig. 7-8. They differ only in that R_{pm}^1 adds an extra pel to the first run and R_{sm}^1 adds the run-length zero symbol to its run alphabets. As a result, their entropies are essentially the same. The run lengths for the simple run source R_{sr}^1 and the source R_{sm}^1 are exactly the same. They differ in that R_{sm}^1 has two alphabets, whose probabilities can be thought of as being combined to obtain the distribution for the single alphabet of R_{sr}^1. Such a "mixing" of alphabets increases the uncertainty unless the mixed alphabets are identical, so that $H_p(R_{sr}^1)$ is greater than or equal to $H_p(R_{sm}^1)$. These results can be summarized for assumed underlying *dependent pels* as

$$H(X_{t+1}|X_t) = H_p(R_{pm}^1) \approx H_p(R_{sm}^1) \leq H_p(R_{sr}^1) \quad (51)$$

Figure 7-9b illustrates a matched case with equal distributions, which is the quantized Poisson square wave discussed by Franks (1964) and Huang (1974). For this case, the two R_{sm}^1 alphabets are identical, and mixing them to form the R_{sr}^1 distribution produces the same result. Applying $p_0 = p_1$ to Eq. (46) shows that $\pi_1(t) = \pi_2(t) = \frac{1}{2}$. This is the case of equality in Eq. (51) where $H_p(R_{sm}^1) = H_p(R_{sr}^1)$.

Assume that the image is generated by an independent pel source X. By Eq. (39), the rare 1 and rare 0 run sources R_{r1}^0 and R_{r0}^0 generated by X

both have the maximum entropy $H(X)$. When these are combined into the alternating rare event source R_{pm}^0, they still produce the same pel entropy, as can be seen by combining Eqs. (48) and (22) for the case of equality (no pel dependence). This situation can be visualized in Fig. 7-9c, where the transition probabilities have been constrained to only have values p or q. The similarity between R_{pm}^0 and R_{sm}^0 has been discussed. In short, for assumed underlying *independent pels*

$$H(X) = H_p(R_{r1}^0) = H_p(R_{r0}^0) = H_p(R_{pm}^0) \approx H_p(R_{sm}^0) \tag{52}$$

Experimental Results

When these run models are cut free from the underlying pel model, their actual, unconstrained probability distributions can be estimated directly from the image data. Much more dependency exists in real images, resulting in nongeometric distributions and lower pel entropies. If a set of consistent[12] estimates are then made for the underlying pel model, its entropy can be used with Eqs. (39) or (50) to bound the entropy for the unconstrained run model.

Table 7-3 gives an important example based on the proposed CCITT standard digital facsimile algorithm, applied to the CCITT test documents. The modified Huffman code (see Musmann and Preuss, 1977) is compared to the estimated independent pel entropy, dependent pel (first-order Markov) entropy, and the pel-normalized entropy for its R_{sm} run model. Notice that the results match the relationship

$$H_p(X) \geq H_p(X_{t+1}|X_t) \geq H_p(R_{pm})\big|_{\substack{\bar{r}_{r1}\equiv 1/p_0 \\ \bar{r}_{r0}\equiv 1/p_1}} \tag{53}$$

which is obtained by combining Eqs. (22) and (50). One may question the validity of these results by asking if the test documents are really a "representative sample." Fortunately, this is an orthogonal problem in the area of sampling and inference. The relationships in this chapter hold true for any consistent sample data. Only the magnitude of the terms in inequalities like Eq. (53) will vary as the sample data are changed.

Figure 7-10 shows example distributions (Arps, 1969, 1971) for the interlaced run sources R_b and R_w of the compound source R_{sm}. The subscripts b and w refer to the black and white data pels, and the probabilities are marked as estimates to emphasize that the distributions are inferred

---

[12] Care must be taken in applying the entropy bounds in real situations. The entropies on both sides of any bound are calculated from probability estimates. For a bound to hold, a set of "consistent" estimators are needed (e.g., in Capon's model one needs to ensure that the estimates $\bar{r}_{r0}$ and $1/p_0$ have the identical value). Problems can arise at the scan line boundaries owing to incomplete runs (see footnote 8).

TABLE 7-3

MODIFIED HUFFMAN CODE (MHC) ANALYSIS

CCITT document[a]	Independent pel entropy	Dependent pel entropy	MHC pel entropy	MHC pel length	MHC efficiency	MHC field length
1	0.171	0.072	0.050	0.059	86.0	215,801
2	0.245	0.052	0.045	0.059	75.2	218,431
3	0.307	0.123	0.091	0.108	84.6	397,272
4	0.424	0.219	0.165	0.181	91.5	664,311
5	0.291	0.129	0.099	0.111	88.8	409,491
6	0.233	0.086	0.068	0.091	74.5	335,508
7	0.397	0.206	0.179	0.200	89.5	736,180
8	0.984	0.107	0.089	0.120	74.2	439,895
Notation[b] (units)	$H_p(R_{pm}^0)$ (bit/pel)	$H_p(R_{pm}^1)$ (bit/pel)	$H_p(R_{mh})$ (bit/pel)	$L_p(R_{mh})$ (bit/pel)	$\eta(R_{mh})$ (%)	$L_f(R_{mh})$ (bit/field)

[a] CCITT test documents at 7.7×8.0 (pel/mm)^2 from the Technical University at Hannover. Each document is $2128 \times 1728 = 3,677,184$ pel/field.
[b] For consistent[12] bounds, $H_p(R_{pm}^0)$, $H_p(R_{pm}^1)$ and $H_p(R_{mh})$ have been estimated from the document *plus* the column of right-hand b.c. bits specified by $X_{T+1} = \hat{X}_T$.

(a) Black pel runs

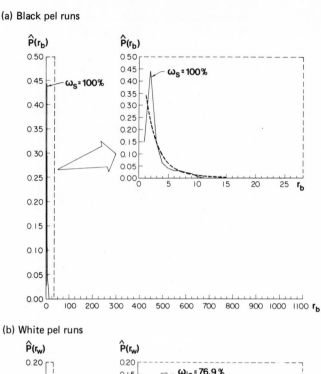

(b) White pel runs

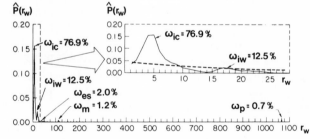

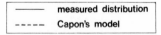

FIG. 7-10. Independent run-length distributions.

from real data. Also shown are the geometric distributions that are derived using Capon's model. Relative to the geometric distributions, the distributions of R_b and R_w have noticeable "peaking," accounting for their lower individual entropies. This peaking has been related to physical properties of the image data and in the R_b distribution represents the widths in pels of the black strokes. In the R_w distribution they represent the width of spaces between characters ω_{ic}, between words ω_{iw}, at the ends of sentences ω_{es}, at the left margin ω_m, and across the entire width of the page ω_p (for all-white lines). The physical insight obtained from Fig. 7-10 gave rise to investigations into the dependency between adjacent runs. The spaces within characters (or between strokes) ω_{is} were identified in the conditional run distributions that were obtained. Entropy bound improvements of 10% over the unconditional run source entropy $H_s(R_{sm})$ were reported (Arps, 1971).

Related investigations into the physical structure of binary images have been reported by Franks (1964) and Kunt (1975). Both authors compared measured correlation functions and power spectral densities with analytic models, on the basis of estimates of two image parameters, basically the two degrees of freedom needed to specify Capon's model. Franks's analog signal analysis reported extra concentrations of power at horizontal frequencies corresponding to the letter spacing in his single print line of typewritten copy. Kunt's digital signal analysis reported extra concentrations of power at vertical frequencies corresponding to the spacing between lines of print in his page of typewritten image data. Otherwise, their measured data matched the analytic models (included Kunt's data on a weather map).

The dependency between *alternate* runs (the same color) forms the basis for the algorithm reported by Weber (1975), which is used commercially. It is named "adaptive," but here it is classified as a conditional run coding algorithm. Stern and Heinlein (1974) extended this approach to also include the dependency of runs of the same color in the preceding scan line, reporting an improvement of 20 to 40% over the algorithm by Weber. They obtained this improvement almost entirely by use of the additional correlation between runs in the preceding and present line.

7.3.2   Line-Dependent Models and Bounds

The coding method explored by Stern and Heinlein resembles other algorithms that use dependence between the data in adjacent scan lines. These "line-dependent" algorithms generally produce higher compression ratios, but suffer more visible degradation when subjected to channel errors. They are the subject of a high-performance facsimile algorithm standard being considered next within the CCITT.

Line-Difference Models

The earliest line-dependent algorithm was a line-difference code proposed by Laemmel (1951). He used two preceding lines of image data to predict the locations of both ends of a run on the basis of preceding runs of the same color. Deviations from these predictions were expressed in terms of the number of pels . . . , 2, 1, 0, 1, 2, . . . needed to locate the run ends correctly. Additional provisions needed to be made for runs with no predecessor in the preceding line (a "new start") and runs with no successor in the following line (a "merge").

Other line-difference algorithms (PDQ by Huang, 1972; RAC by Yamazaki *et al.,* 1976; EDIC by Yamada, 1976) have been explored using only a single previous line to (vertically) predict the ends of a run. This class of algorithms has high performance, as can be seen for the PDQ algorithm in Table 7-1. Their main differences lie in the decision rules used to decide when to encode with a merge or a new-start symbol, rather than a prediction deviation symbol. Laemmel's code was different because of the order in which his prediction deviation and merge or new-start symbols were sent. Huang explored coding of the second edge in a black run, using a prediction of its location based on the first edge plus the length of the run in the preceding line. The NTT algorithm included the possibility for a merge of white as well as black (space as well as stroke) edge pairs.

Predictive Coding

In the same period that Laemmel (1951) wrote about line-difference coding as predicting the ends of runs, Elias (1950, 1955) was working on generalized predictive coding for information sources. Elias described the use of prior data samples to predict upcoming data samples, followed by encoding of only the errors from his predictions. His purpose was to encode using nearby dependence without having to use the multiple code books implicit in conditional source encoding. Thereafter, Wholey (1961) explored the application of predictive coding to binary image data. Some sample results from predictive coding of binary image data are shown in Fig. 7-11. Figure 7-11a is a closeup of part of an image. Figure 7-11b contains a corresponding pseudoimage, in which white pels indicate correct predictions and black pels indicate the location of prediction errors. (Note that for binary data the polarity and magnitude of a prediction error is completely specified, given knowledge of the corresponding predicted value.) This "error" image has been obtained from the image in Fig. 7-11a using an example two-dimensional predictor described below to produce the error random variable $E \equiv \{e \in 0, 1\}$. The predictor is shown in detail in Fig. 7-12.

At any time t, the state of the pel X_t can be predicted using some function of the prior states $F(X_0, X_1, \ldots , X_{t-1})$. Figures 7-12a and b illustrate how a shift register line memory is organized to continually make available the states of prior picture elements that are neighbors to the pel being processed.

(a) Original image

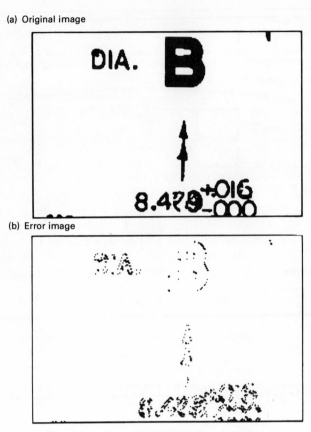

(b) Error image

FIG. 7-11.   Example of third-order prediction.

The predictors of interest define one-to-one transformations that can change a digital image into a corresponding set of prediction errors and back, with the final result being identical to the starting image. The comparison of X with its predicted value F is defined by an exclusive-OR "$\oplus$" operation, resulting in an error value E. Similarly, the inverse transformation consists of an exclusive-OR operation between the received error value E' and a reconstructed value of the prediction F', resulting in a reconstructed pel value X'. These transformations are written as

$$E = X \oplus F \tag{54a}$$
$$X' = E' \oplus F' \tag{54b}$$

The predictor should be confined to use only previous-state information so that in a decompressor this transformation will be "causal" and physically realizable.

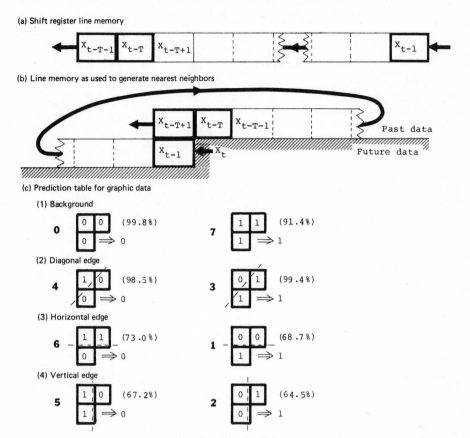

FIG. 7-12.   Example two-dimensional predictor.

Figure 7-12c defines an example third-order predictor function $F(\cdot, \cdot, \cdot)$ based on the prior pels X_{t-1}, X_{t-T}, and X_{t-T-1}, where T is the length of the scan line in pels. The three pels are from among the causal nearest neighbors to X and form a pattern that assumes the eight possible predictor states indicated. These states $S = \{s_j : j \in \{0, 1, \ldots, J\}\}$ with $J = 2^3 - 1$, are labeled by using a weighted sum of the individual pel values $j = (1)X_{t-1} + (2)X_{t-T} + (4)\ X_{t-T-1}$. For each predictor state $\{S = s\}$, the conditional probabilities $\hat{P}\{X = x | S = s\}$ for the values of X have been estimated from CCITT document 1 and listed in Table 7-4b. In Fig. 7-12c, the more likely pel value has been made the predicted value and is indicated to the lower right of the predictor state pattern (below the value in parenthesis for the estimated conditional probability of a correct prediction). For example, the combination $X_{t-1} = X_{t-T} = X_{t-T-1} = 0$ has

TABLE 7.4

THIRD-ORDER CONDITIONAL PROBABILITY ESTIMATES

(a) State probability

s	$\hat{P}\{S = S\}$
0	0.9647
1	0.0050
2	0.0042
3	0.0013
4	0.0014
5	0.0041
6	0.0049
7	0.0144

(b) Conditional pel probability

s	$\hat{P}\{X = 0|S = s\}$	$\hat{P}\{X = 1|S = s\}$
0	0.998	0.002
1	0.313	0.687
2	0.355	0.645
3	0.006	0.994
4	0.985	0.015
5	0.672	0.328
6	0.730	0.270
7	0.086	0.914

(c) Conditional error probability

s	$\hat{P}\{E = 0|S = s\}$	$\hat{P}\{E = 1|S = s\}$
0	0.998	0.002
1	0.687	0.313
2	0.645	0.355
3	0.994	0.006
4	0.985	0.015
5	0.672	0.328
6	0.730	0.270
7	0.914	0.086

(d) Marginal pel probability

$\hat{P}\{X = 0\}$	$\hat{P}\{X = 1\}$
0.975	0.025

(e) Marginal error probability

$\hat{P}\{E = 0\}$	$\hat{P}\{E = 1\}$
0.991	0.009

a corresponding prediction $F(0, 0, 0) \rightarrow 0$ because the value $X = 0$ followed this combination in 99.8% of all of its occurences in the sample data.

The transformation of an image into a pseudoimage of prediction errors does not accomplish any compression of itself. The predictor is but the preprocessing step in a model that now consists of a rare event run source, where the rare events are errors from the predictor. The compression performance of such a run source can be bounded assuming an underlying error-generating process as is described below.

The conditional probabilities $\hat{P}\{X = x | S = s\}$ used to derive the predictor can also be the transition probabilities for a kth-order Markov chain.[13] Over this chain, a kth-order *conditional pel* source (X/S) with pel entropy $H_p(X|S)$ can then be defined.

A kth-order *adjoint pel* source $(\overline{X|S})$ can also be defined over the chain (Abramson, 1963, p. 27). It has the same binary source alphabet as the conditional source, but with only unconditional probabilities $\hat{P}\{X = x\}$ that constitute a marginal distribution or state-weighted average of the rows in Table 7-4b. It is identical to the source obtained by *assuming* only an independent pel process X and deriving its distribution using consistent (see footnote 12) estimators on the same sample data. This marginal distribution is shown in Table 7-4d and determines what can be called either the kth-order adjoint pel entropy $H_p(\overline{X|S})$ or the independent pel entropy $H_p(X)$. That is,

$$H_p(X) = H_p(\overline{X|S}) \tag{55}$$

The estimated conditional probabilities for the predictor errors $\hat{P}\{E = e | S = s\}$ are listed in Table 7-4c. These are derived directly from Table 7-4b using Eq. (54) and Fig. 7-12. They can be used to define a kth-order *conditional error* source $(E|S)$.

Underlying Adjoint Error Process, $H_p(\overline{E|S}) \equiv$ ⊞

An underlying *adjoint error* source $(\overline{E|S})$ can be defined as well, on the basis of the marginal distribution of errors or the weighted average of the

---

[13] The Markov chain actually consists of the 2^{T+1} states that exist for the $T + 1$ bit positions in the line store shift register of Fig. 7-12. Although only three bit positions are used to form the predictor, the rest must be included for the chain to be *unifilar* (for the chain to go to a known state, given the present state and the output symbol X_t). The eight predictor states are then really combined values from groups of these 2^{T+1} "substates." However, they can be used to compute the right values for the conditional or adjoint entropies. The chain is ergodic, irreducible, and periodic with a periodicity of T. Because it is ergodic, steady state probabilities $P\{S = s\}$ are known to exist (see Ash, 1965, Chapter 6; Feller, 1968, Chapter XV).

rows of Table 7-4c. Its probability values $\hat{P}\{E = e\}$ take on the values p_e, q_e and are tabulated in Table 7-4e. If a kth order adjoint error process is assumed to generate the pseudoimage of Fig. 7-11, then its error probability can be used to define a geometric distribution for rare adjoint error runs $R_{ae}{}^k$ so that

$$P\{R_{ae}{}^k = r\} = p_e q_e{}^{r-1} \tag{56}$$

with $r = 1, 2, \ldots$. These runs constitute a variable-length extension of the adjoint error source.

Abramson (1963) showed that a conditional source bounds the entropy of its adjoint source. This result can be written for both the conditional pel source and its corresponding conditional error source as the inequalities

$$H_p(\overline{X|S}) \geq H_p(X|S) \tag{57a}$$
$$H_p(\overline{E|S}) \geq H_p(E|S) \tag{57b}$$

with equality iff $(X|S)$ or $(E|S)$ are zero memory sources (independent symbols).

Note that Tables 7-4b and c are identical except that some row values have been interchanged. This has no effect on the entropy of each row, and Eq. (18) can be used to show that

$$H_p(X|S) = H_p(E|S) \tag{58}$$

An inequality relating the adjoint pel source and adjoint error source can be derived by visualizing both of them as summations over the columns of their corresponding *joint* probability matrices. The row terms in both of these matrices are identical but sometimes interchanged. The interchanging of terms according to Eq. (54) can be viewed as a systematic method for "peaking" of the adjoint error distribution as compared to the adjoint pel distribution. Therefore, the adjoint error entropy is less than or equal to the adjoint pel entropy.

$$H_p(\overline{X|S}) \geq H_p(\overline{E|S}) \tag{59}$$

When an adjoint error source defines the underlying process, the resulting errors are assumed to be independent. Equations (55), (59), and (39) can then be used as a sequence of bounds for the rare error runs R_{ae} that are generated by a typical predictive coding algorithm (e.g., Wholey, 1961).

$$H_p(X) = H_p(\overline{X|S}) \geq H_p(\overline{E|S}) \geq H_p(R_{ae})|_{\bar{r} \equiv 1/p_e \ or \ 1/q_e} \tag{60}$$

These run entropies are therefore bounded from above by the independent pel process as is indicated in Table 7-2.

The corresponding adjoint error source $(\overline{E|S})$ can also be bounded from *below* by using Eqs. (57) and (58) so that

$$H_p(\overline{E|S}) \geq H_p(E|S) = H_p(X|S) \tag{61}$$

As a result, $(\overline{E|S})$ occupies a position in Table 7-2 somewhat analogous to the first-order pel process, lying between the zeroth-order pel and the third-order conditional error processes.

When compared to more conventional interlaced run codes, prediction followed by rare error coding offers a decrease in hardware cost by eliminating one run-length coder in exchange for a small amount of prediction circuitry. A scan line memory is usually already needed. More important, it increases the "robustness' of the algorithm or its ability to compensate for changes in the image data. With interlaced run codes optimized for one type of data, changes in spatial resolution or in the stroke width of lines and characters can cause drops in compression performance. The compression results for "negative," or white-on-black images can be even worse. For example, the truncated Huffman code is matched to a peak in the black run distribution at 2 or 3 pels/run. This code is described in the paper by Musmann and Preuss (1977), which also gives examples of the CCITT documents. The code's relative performance in Table 7-1 is at its worst for CCITT document 8, which has a large area of white-on-black text (compare relative to the best algorithm, the predictor-based 2-D Markov code). Predictive coding is completely indifferent to negative images and less affected by resolution and stroke-width changes. The rare error run distribution is less peaked, allowing for more variation.

The empirically derived predictions in Fig. 7-12 can be interpreted and given physical meaning, somewhat analogous to interpretation of the data in Fig. 7-10 (Arps, 1970b). If the combinations "0" or "7" in Fig. 7-12c1 are considered, they strongly suggest that the neighboring pels are part of a solid "background" of the same color. The diagram has accordingly been labeled "background," and predictions that the next pel will have the same color have a very high probability of success. The predictors in Fig. 7-12c2, 3, and 4 can be interpreted as detecting two-dimensional boundaries. If one assumes that the most likely boundaries in text and line drawings are locally straight edges, particularly vertical, horizontal, or diagonal edges, then all of the empirically determined prediction value can also be arrived at intuitively. The assumed edge types have been made the label for each subdiagram. The location of these edges in the predictor state patterns have been shown with a dashed line.

Such physical understanding of algorithm behavior has significant practical value. Given a finite ability to test large numbers of sample images, engineering judgment may be needed to project the performance of an algorithm from a limited sample. In Fig. 7-11 this example predictor can be seen eliminating large portions of the interior and edges of objects, for example, in the large letter B. Many runs of white (now nonerrors) continue through objects, decreasing the number of runs N_f. It is possible to extrapolate that this predictor does well in reducing the number of runs for most edge-based image data. Since the predictor is symmetric, it also works the same way for negative images. If the overall algorithm behavior can be related to physical image properties (edges, strokes, average run length, density, etc.), it becomes possible to characterize its performance for a class of images (text, line drawings, etc.) in terms of these properties. The number of samples in large performance tests may be significantly reduced by eliminating test images with overall properties that duplicate those of images that have already been measured.

Kobayashi and Bahl (1974) investigated adaptive predictors followed by rare event coding. When compared to a fixed predictor with values determined by a prescan of the image, the adaptive predictors made only small decreases in the percentage of prediction error p_e. For fourth- and seventh-order predictors, this reduction was only 12 and 7% respectively. With text, line drawing, or handwriting, prescan-matched third- or fourth-order predictors are usually very similar. This is probably due to consistency in the physical properties described above for the predictor of Fig. 7-12. The small improvement obtained with the above fourth-order adaptive prediction supports the observation that predictors are similar for such data.

White *et al.* (1972) recognized that line-difference coding is related to the coding of prediction errors, in that the run ends being coded are simply errors from a horizontal first-order predictor. They tried to extend their line-difference coding by applying it to higher-order prediction errors. However, they found insufficient correlation between errors in successive lines to obtain good results.

A more general approach called cross-array correlation coding (Arps *et al.*, 1977) solves this problem by line-difference coding between the error pseudoimage and the previous lines in a separate pseudoimage of "location events." The location events can consist of prediction errors or predictor states, or may not directly correspond to any prediction at all. All that is needed is that they be causal and reconstructable in the decompressor. For example, the first pel in all runs of black can define an array of location events.

The significance of this separation between errors and location events is that it permits individual optimization of the two terms in Eq. (5) that determine the overall field-normalized entropy. Increasing the order of prediction decreases the density of prediction errors, which are directly related to the number of symbols per field N_f. Decreasing the entropy per symbol H_s can best be done when one is free to choose between run-length coding, line-difference coding, and any other coding scheme in combination with a choice of location events. For example, successful line-difference coding of high-order prediction errors can be accomplished by referencing them to first-order prediction errors as location events.

The preceding algorithms limit themselves to basically one coder while trying to use the local dependence in an image. The following algorithms fully exploit this local dependence with less regard to hardware complexity.

Underlying Conditional Error Process, $H_p(E/S) \equiv$ ⊞

As Eq. (57) indicates, a conditional error source should have greater potential for compression than its adjoint source. This potential was measured for binary data (Arps, 1971) and is shown in Fig. 7-13 for increasing orders of dependency. Realization of this potential is complicated by the need to take an nth extension of the conditional binary source. Straightforward extensions of a conditional source (Abramson, 1963, p. 29) are quite cumbersome and are not clearly defined for two-dimensional patterns.

Preuss (1975a,b, 1976) developed an interlacing scheme for taking separate nth extensions for each of the subsidiary sources in a conditional binary source. It works with two-dimensional patterns and allows the extensions for each subsidiary source to vary independently as variable-length extensions made with rare event runs. Preuss' scheme is illustrated in Fig. 7-14 for the conditional binary error source produced by the example predictor of Fig. 7-12.

Figure 7-14a shows a scan line of error/nonerror E/N bits that have been generated from input pel data. A case with the predictor in state 2 is

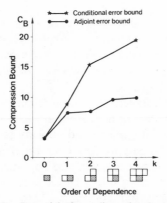

FIG. 7-13.   Potential of two-dimensional prediction.

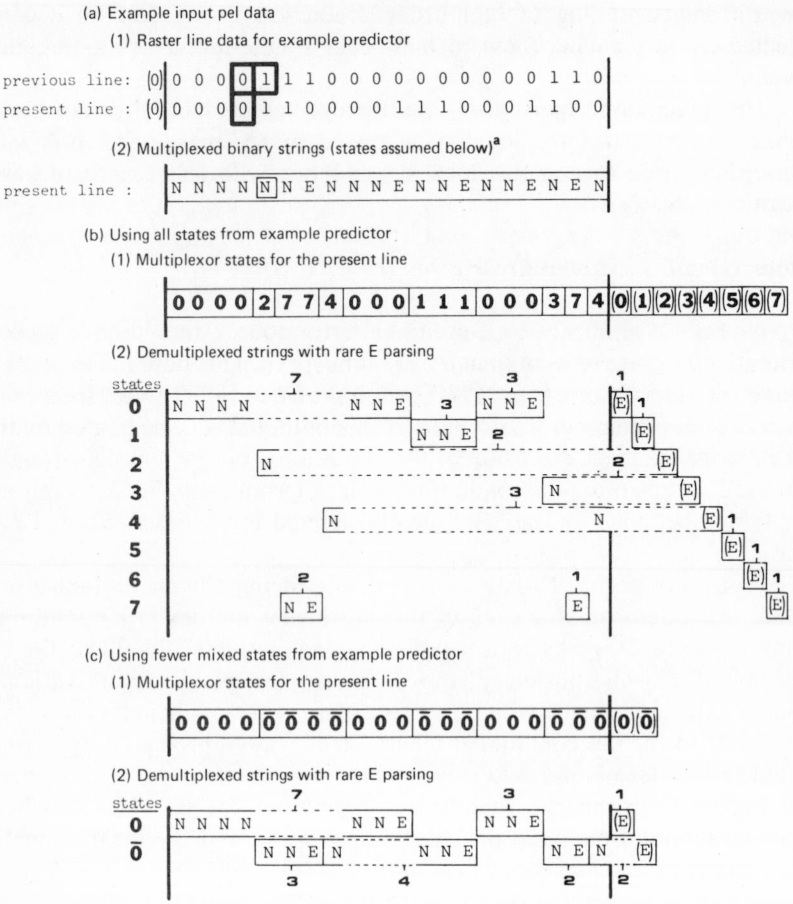

(a) Example input pel data

(1) Raster line data for example predictor

previous line: |(0)|0 0 0|0|1|1 1 0 0 0 0 0 0 0 0 0 0 1 1 0|

present line : |(0)|0 0 0|0|1 1 0 0 0 0 1 1 1 0 0 0 1 1 0 0|

(2) Multiplexed binary strings (states assumed below)[a]

present line : | N N N N |N| N E N N N E N N N E N N E N E N |

(b) Using all states from example predictor

(1) Multiplexor states for the present line

| 0 0 0 0 | 2 7 7 4 | 0 0 0 | 1 1 1 | 0 0 0 | 3 7 4 |(0)(1)(2)(3)(4)(5)(6)(7)|

(2) Demultiplexed strings with rare E parsing

(c) Using fewer mixed states from example predictor

(1) Multiplexor states for the present line

| 0 0 0 0 | 0̄ 0̄ 0̄ 0̄ | 0 0 0 | 0̄ 0̄ 0̄ | 0 0 0 | 0̄ 0̄ 0̄ |(0)(0̄)|

(2) Demultiplexed strings with rare E parsing

FIG. 7-14. Bit multiplexing with error data using predictor states. Boundary conditions: (a1) $X_0 = 0$; (a2) none; (b1) $S_{-k} = S_{T+k+1} = k$, for $k = 0, 1, \ldots, 7$; (b2) $X_{-k} = X_{T+k+1} = E$, for $k = 0, 1, \ldots, 7$; (c1) $S_{-1} = S_{T+2} = \overline{0}$, $S_0 = S_{T+1} = 0$; (c2) $X_{-1} = X_0 = X_{T+1} = X_{T+2} = E$. For (a2), error states shown as {N, E} rather than {0, 1} this figure only.

illustrated, so that the prediction $F(0, 1, 0) \rightarrow 1$ agrees with $X = 1$, yielding $F \oplus X = 0$ and thereby producing a nonerror N.

Figure 7-14b illustrates bit multiplexing, in contrast to the run multiplexing of Fig. 7-8. The multiplexor states S are the states[14] of the conditional error source. The data in Fig. 7-14b2 is demultiplexed into many parallel strings, but the process is governed by the states in Fig. 7-14b1 as

[14] Note that (unlike in the diagrams by Preuss) the values for the states S are shown in Fig. 7-14 at time position t, rather than $t-1$.

before. However, this form of demultiplexing is unrelated to the subsequent connecting of string symbols into runs. Since it is more general and bit oriented, it is called bit multiplexing.

Boundary conditions have again been shown for the ends of scan lines. General b.c. for the start of the line have been omitted to save space, but are summarized in the figure legend as before. All strings are starting a new run at the beginning of a line. Other variations are possible, but this set of b.c. has been found to yield consistent estimators (see footnote 12) and valid bounds.

Preuss (1975a,b, 1976) proved[15] that the rare error runs in the compound source of Fig. 14 have the same pel entropy as the underlying conditional pel process, when generated solely by that process. That will be demonstrated here using the following theorem for a conditional *error* process. The theorem is extended afterward to cover the corresponding conditional pel process.

THEOREM 5: BIT MULTIPLEXED RUNS BASED ON KTH-ORDER MARKOV ERRORS. *Assume a kth-order Markov prediction error source $(E|S)$ generating an infinite, stationary sequence of dependent error pels. Let this sequence be modeled by multiplexed runs from 2^k parallel, geometrically distributed rare error run sources, corresponding to the 2^k conditional source states. Then the pel entropy $H_p(R_{ce}{}^k)$ for this compound source $R_{ce}{}^k$ equals the conditional entropy $H_p(E|S)$ for the underlying kth-order Markov prediction error source.*

The results from earlier theorems, and examples can be applied once it is recognized that for an underlying conditional error process the above rare error runs are independent and geometrically distributed. The prediction errors themselves are dependent only on the Markov state and are assumed to be mutually independent from any other errors. As before, the errors for each state s_j can then be combined to generate independent (see footnote 11) geometrically distributed runs r_j from a rare 1 run source $R_{r1j}{}^k$, where errors are 1's and nonerrors are 0's. Defining the error probability for each state as $p_{ej} = 1 - q_{ej}$, the distribution is written as

$$P\{R_{r1j}{}^k = r_j\} = p_{ej}q_{ej}{}^{r_j-1} \qquad (62)$$

with $r_j = 1, 2, \ldots$.

The pel entropy for each separate run source $H_p(R_{r1j}{}^k)$ can immediately be obtained using Theorem 2. Thus

$$H_p(R_{r1j}{}^k) = H_p(E|S = s_j) = H\{p_{ej}, q_{ej}\} \qquad (63)$$

[15] Preuss does not clearly distinguish between $P\{X = x|S = s\}$ and $P\{E = e|S = s\}$ and omits pointing out that $H_p(X|S) = H_p(E|S)$, as shown in Eq. (58).

The pel entropy for the entire compound source is the pel-weighted averaged of these multiplexed sources,

$$H_p(R_{ce}{}^k) = \sum_{j=0}^{J} P\{S = s_j\} H_p(R_{r1j}{}^k) \tag{64}$$

where $P\{S = s_j\}$ is the steady state probability for a pel from state s_j. Combining Eqs. (63) and (64) produces an abbreviated form of Eq. (18) so that

$$H_p(R_{ce}{}^k) = \sum_{j=0}^{J} P\{S = s_j\} H_p(E|S = s_j) = H_p(E|S) \tag{65}$$

which completes the proof[16] of Theorem 5. Application of the identity in Eq. (58) extends the above theorem to the original image pels and proves Preuss's result that

$$H_p(R_{ce}{}^k) = H_p(X|S) \tag{66}$$

The bound in Theorem 3 by Huang (1974) can now be combined with Theorem 5 and Eq. (58) as above, to extend Preuss's result. Since the multiplexed runs are mutually independent, the bound can be applied to each of the runs separately.

Take an arbitrary compound error source R_{ce} made up of multiplexed run sources R_{r1j} with distributions that are more general than the geometrically distributed sources $R_{r1j}{}^k$ generated by the underlying process. If these more general sources are only constrained to have the same average run length $\bar{r}_j = \bar{r}_j{}^k = 1/p_{ej}$, then their pel entropies will be individually bounded as in Eq. (39) by the bound

$$H_p(E|S = s_j) \geq H_p(R_{r1j})\big|_{\bar{r}_j = 1/p_{ej}} \tag{67}$$

Combining these results, by taking the pel-weighted average over all the states s_j, produces the overall bound for the compound source

$$H_p(X|S) = H_p(E|S) = \sum_{j=0}^{J} P\{S = s_j\} H_p(E|S = s_j)$$
$$\geq H_p(R_{ce})\Big|_{\substack{\bar{r}_0 = 1/p_{e0} \\ \vdots \\ \bar{r}_j = 1/p_{ej}}} \tag{68}$$

[16] Unlike Eq. (46), in the earlier proof of Theorem 4 for Capon's model, no attempt was made here to explicitly obtain the steady state probabilities $P\{S = s\}$. Because of the complexity of the true underlying Markov chain (see footnote 13) it is difficult to explicitly solve for them. It is sufficient to know that steady state values exist before eliminating them in the proof.

where the leftmost identity was added using Eq. (58). The above entropy bound is written pictorially in Table 7-2. The number of bits actually used to encode some images using Preuss's scheme, are reported in Table 7-1.

Various algorithms attempt to use the dependency implicit in a conditional error process without the use of 2^k parallel coders as in Preuss's algorithm above. The encoding of the adjoint error source using a single error run coder is but one example. The superiority of conditional coding of error runs over adjoint coding comes from variations from state to state in the chance of a prediction error p_{ej}. The error run distributions that are generated for the individual states differ and should be coded individually for optimal results. The single-run alphabet used to encode the adjoint error source can be thought of as a mixture of the multiple alphabets from the conditional source. By convexity, this mixture will have greater entropy and a lower compression performance. From the point of view of an underlying conditional error source, dependency still exists between the error pels, but it is not being fully utilized. Some intermediate schemes that use pairs of run coders to encode the errors follow.

In the same articles as above, Preuss (1975a,b, 1976) described the algorithm of Fig. 7-14c where errors from the 2^k states are combined into groups for subsequent run-length coding. The two groupings he recommended are 0 and $\bar{0}$, corresponding to the state for white "background" and the remaining states that characterize "information" in a black-on-white document.

"Reordering" algorithms also divide prediction errors into groups before separately run-length coding them. Typically, they use only two groups of errors that are accumulated for a line and encoded contiguously, rather than multiplexed. Wah (1975) encoded the errors from a vertical first-order predictor. He also used this two-state predictor to *separate* the errors, directly producing only a pair of error groups.

Yasuda *et al.* (1975) used high-order predictors producing many states, but still separated the errors into two groups using a vertical first-order predictor. They also explored "macroscopic" reordering of the data in addition to the above "microscopic" reordering to encode some of the global dependency. All white vertical lines in Japanese text were separated out before applying the above microscopic ordering, resulting in a 10% further decrease in entropy.

Netravali *et al.* (1976) used high-order prediction to reduce the errors, but also used these prediction states to reorder the errors into two groups, as is done in Preuss's version of this algorithm. In addition, they reported a method for optimal separation of the errors into two groups by clustering the states based on their prediction error probabilities.

For a kth-order underlying conditional error process, the above algorithms with two state groups cannot exceed the performance[17] of Preuss's complete 2^k group algorithm owing to "convexity." However, they achieve much of its potential with only two run coders.

7.4 AREA ALGORITHMS

In spite of the fact that images are two dimensional in nature, economic constraints generally force them to be processed as one-dimensional raster data. Only recently, have falling memory costs made it possible to consider partial image buffers in commercial hardware. Even so, the cost of buffering full DIN A4 size images is still prohibitive for low-cost facsimile products.

The first algorithms to really take advantage of two dimensions operate within "strip buffers" that hold large groups of adjacent scan lines. Even by working within a strip, they can capitalize on some of the structure in images, without incurring too much of a hardware penalty. Such "area" algorithms, when compared to raster algorithms, should have a better chance of capturing the dependence in an image, thereby obtaining higher compression performance.

7.4.1 Block Coding

Laemmel (1951, pp. 7–10) quite naturally began his report on image compression with the analysis of an area algorithm. The local source patterns he investigated consisted of repeated rectangular blocks containing U pels. In a scheme that he called "block coding," Laemmel utilized the predominance of the "all-white" state, among the 2^U possible states that a block source, B, can assume.

His code started with a flag bit to transmit an all-white/non-all-white block condition. For the non-all-white case only, the flag was followed by U additional bits to describe the block in detail. He analyzed this simple "dual-mode" code in terms of an underlying independent pel process $P\{X = x\} = \{p, q\}$, with the result that the pel-normalized average length of a code word is

$$L_p(B_{dm}{}^0) = 1 - (1 - p)^U + 1/U \qquad (69)$$

---

[17] For real data, free from the assumption of a kth order underlying conditional error process, Netravali *et al.* (1976) reported empirical results that exceed those of Preuss (1975a). These results apply only to Preuss's simpler two-state-group algorithm and at this writing are being contested.

By viewing the blocks simply as nth extensions of the underlying pel source, one can combine Eq. (69) with the pel entropy $H_p(X) = H\{p, q\}$ to write a closed expression for the efficiency of this coder. The implicit alternative to this simple code is to Huffman code the block, as was illustrated for a simple case with $U = 2$ in Fig. 7-4.

Huang and Hussian (1975) explored the optimal block size for one-dimensional block coding. They extended Eq. (69) to another closed form on the basis of an underlying *first-order* Markov pel process. Their expression for the pel-normalized average code word length can be written in terms of the notation used here, as

$$L_p(B_{dm}^{1}) = 1 - \pi_0(t)q_0^{U-1} + 1/U \tag{70}$$

where $\pi_0(t)$ and q_0 are defined as in Fig. 7-9a. When they solved for the optimum block size, they found a very shallow minimum. Huang and Hussain also proposed a recursive form of block coding using a flag bit and dual-mode code for all-white scan lines, followed by a flag bit and dual-mode code for small blocks within the line when the line was not all-white.

De Coulon and Kunt (1974) systematically extended this recursive idea to related hierarchies of dual-mode-coded one- and two-dimensional blocks. The first flag bit indicated whether the largest block size was all white. If not, the flag indicated that the block was to be subdivided into blocks from the next size in the hierarchy. These smaller blocks, in turn, were dual mode coded with another flag bit and again subdivided if a non-all-white block occurred. At the lowest level in the hierarchy, subdivision was replaced with explicit representation of a non-all-white block.

A related algorithm, proposed by Usubuchi *et al.* (1975), was especially suited for implementation with 4-bit microprocessors. The blocks chosen were various powers of 4 bits in size. Furthermore, blocks were divided into four subblocks when they were not all-white. In such a case, flag bits from the four subblocks were grouped together into a code word, preserving a code structure that produced only 4-bit words. Variations that they investigated included Huffman coding of the smallest 4-bit (2×2) blocks and applying their algorithm to the errors from third-order predictive coding.

Experimental results for recursive block coding have been summarized by Huang (1977). His best performance was obtained using a hierarchy of square blocks, as compared to a rectangular hierarchy, or to no hierarchy at all. Kunt (1977) reported experimental results for two-dimensional block coding that he then compared to entropy bounds for structured pictures on the basis of an underlying first-order Markov pel model.

7.4.2 Contour Coding

A truly two-dimensional approach to binary image compression should exploit the structure inherent in most practical images. Schreiber *et al.* (1972) pointed out that for binary images, all of the information is contained in the outlines of objects. Given these outlines or "contours," filling in the spaces that they enclose regenerates the original image. The implementation of this idea is somewhat involved, especially if a complete one-to-one transformation is desired between any possible image and its contours. Morrin (1975, 1976) developed such an algorithm, based on coding the outer edges of all objects and holes in an image. He also extended this concept by extracting information during the encoding process about any "nesting" interrelationships among objects or holes.

Isolating the contours in an image can be viewed as a preprocessing step, analogous to converting a raster image into runs. This analogy is especially good if runs are thought of as describing the locations of transitions between areas of black and white pels. The contours are encoded using the property that their pels are contiguous and form closed "chains." The pel positions are described in terms of a sequence of "moves" around the contour, forming closed "chains." The chains are encoded in terms of the sequence of "moves" needed to circumnavigate a contour back to its starting point. The individual moves or sequences of moves are then variable-length coded to achieve further compression.

The result is an algorithm that not only yields high compression (see Table 7-1) but has many interesting properties as well. This encoding process isolates all the objects in the image and preserves them as contours in the compressed data. The image becomes an "order list" of these contours that can be manipulated in *compressed* form to edit an image. Addition or deletion of objects are corresponding additions or deletions to the order list. Many other operations can be easily performed on the compressed objects, including translation, 90° rotation, smoothing, and scaling. The isolation of all objects can also be useful for "segmentation" in an optical character recognition (OCR) algorithm.

7.4.3 Pattern Recognition

Pattern recognition, and in particular OCR, is sometimes viewed as a powerful form of data compression. For noiseless coding, however, this viewpoint is somewhat misleading in that recognition and its inverse are not one-to-one transforms. OCR, for example, only recognizes members of specific fonts and does not have the generality and completeness of a compression algorithm. In contrast, a "complete" noiseless coding scheme is a one-to-one transform that encodes all possible images. These ideas can be better explained in the context of some definitions concerning digital data and digital coding as shown in Fig. 7-15.

Figure 7-15a represents digital data in two broad classes—"diffuse" and "symbolic." Symbolic data are the familiar, byte-oriented ASCII or EBCDIC data processed in most computers today. In contrast to this, images are a form of diffuse data from which meaning and structural properties have not yet been extracted or "recognized." Diffuse data processing consists only of replication, editing, enhancement, etc., without any deep "understanding" of the data.

Recognition of characters from their digital images (OCR) is representative of what will here be called "cognition"—the conversion of diffuse data into symbols to facilitate processing of the meaning in the image. This is an expensive process requiring human intelligence or sophisticated hardware, illustrated as the cognition "barrier" in Fig. 7-15a. Its converse is called "generation," as in the computer generation of character images from their symbolic representation.

Figure 7-15b represents all forms of one-to-one digital data-coding algorithms. These include not only data compression/decompression algorithms but, for example, data encryption/decryption algorithms as well. Their operations can be viewed as orthogonal to the plane of digital data types. Compression algorithms for speech, image character, and vector data are all different, depending on the *a priori* characteristics of their respective data.

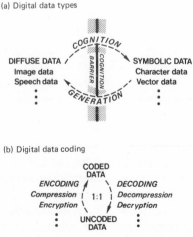

(a) Digital data types

DIFFUSE DATA / COGNITION \ SYMBOLIC DATA
Image data   BARRIER   Character data
Speech data \ GENERATION / Vector data

(b) Digital data coding

CODED DATA
ENCODING / \ DECODING
Compression | 1:1 | Decompression
Encryption \ / Decryption
UNCODED DATA

FIG. 7-15.   Orthogonality between cognition and coding.

In restricted cases, compression and cognition algorithms can also be compared in terms of their hardware cost and the compression that they achieve. For images containing printed matter in a font that is matched to the recognition algorithm, compression ratios roughly two orders of magnitude greater than those from data compression can be achieved by OCR. However, this is attained using roughly two orders of magnitude more hardware as well.

Contour coding, as defined above by Morrin, has an interesting interpretation in terms of these diagrams. It definitely performs data compression as in Fig. 7-15b, but it also does cognition, as in Fig. 7-15a, to extract the contours and nesting of objects in the image. However, it only recognizes microscopic properties in comparison to the relatively macroscopic recognition performed on characters with OCR. As such, it only penetrates part of the way through the cognition barrier. Conversely, as a decompressor it can plot successive points in an image and can thereby be used as a rudimentary generator of unit vectors. As an area algorithm, it requires more hardware than conventional facsimile compression schemes in return for its additional cognitive capability. However, this trade-off can be compatible with the requirements for compression in binary image-processing systems.

Ascher and Nagy (1974) proposed an hybrid compression and cognition scheme, designed for the encoding of printed matter. They assumed the use of an OCR system, backed up by a compression algorithm for objects that could not be recognized. Unrecognized objects that were identical or similar could all be encoded using a pseudocharacter, standing for a single compressed representation that needed only to be stored once.

Pratt *et al.* (1976) made some measurements for applying such a system to typewritten data. They used a segmentation algorithm for their OCR scheme that enclosed all objects within minimum-size rectangular "blocks." When objects were assumed unrecognizable, their corresponding blocks were compression coded instead. The recognized characters and coded blocks were then preceded with addresses to locate their position. Compression ratios of 37 to 1 or message lengths of 59 kbits/field were estimated for a typewritten test document similar to CCITT document 1. This indicates the potential for achieving compression ratios perhaps a factor of 2 or 3 greater than those obtained using nonhybrid schemes (see Table 7-1).

The above hybrid compression/cognition schemes use the power of pattern recognition without sacrificing the generality of lossless compression coding. What they do sacrifice is hardware simplicity and algorithm robustness. These algorithms may be subject to poor performance with data not containing the font for which the OCR is designed. However, the potential performance advantages are significant. It is in this area, and more generally in "area" algorithms, that significant compression performance improvements will probably be made in the future.

7.5 CONCLUDING COMMENTS

Being limited to a chapter, this work has only focused in depth on noiseless coding schemes for binary image compression. It addresses the redundancy reduction stage shown in Fig. 7-1 for the front end of a system with digital compression.

Furthermore, the emphasis here has only been on maximizing compression performance, expressed in terms of compression ratios or compressed image field sizes. It should be emphasized that this is but one measure for evaluating an algorithm to be used in a practical system. Further figures of merit to consider include compression performance, robustness, digitized image quality, noise immunity, complexity (cost, speed, etc.), and processibility of compressed data.

The compression performance of a given coder is highly data dependent. This is readily apparent in Table 7-1 where compressed image fields vary by a factor of 5 or 6 depending on the test document. Results for even the same document will also vary depending on the resolution used to digitize it. The robustness of an algorithm is its ability to perform well over a variety of input documents.

Digitized image quality is determined mainly by the information reduction steps in Fig. 7-1. This factor is generally traded off against compression performance as a function of the amplitude and spatial resolution of systems (Arps, 1969). As resolution increases, image quality improves, but at the cost of having large compressed image fields.

The noise immunity of a redundancy reduction algorithm becomes important if the system design does not provide enough error protection. When fail-soft algorithms are used, channel errors result in lower image quality. This degradation is in addition to the information reduction that occurs while digitizing the source document.

Complexity is an obvious factor to consider when comparing algorithms. It has a direct effect on the amount of hardware/firmware/software required for implementation and on the speed with which an algorithm can perform. Some less obvious effects of complexity are reflected in development, testing, and servicing costs.

The processibility of data in compressed form has been discussed as a significant property of contour coding algorithms (see Section 7.4.2). This figure of merit also applies to raster algorithms designed to "fail soft" in the face of channel errors. In order to recover from an error, portions of the compressed data must be deletable without impacting the rest of the field. Typically, this gives rise to constraints like independence between compressed scan lines (or groups of lines). Other applications constraining compressed data to be processible will probably arise as systems using binary image compression become more sophisticated.

The above list has purposely been left open ended. With the current activity in binary image compression for facsimile and its future application in binary image processing, new factors to consider will continually be added. Readers interested in further details may refer to the bibliography by Arps (1974).

List of Symbols

B block source symbol set
b block source symbol
E error source symbol set; error source random variable
e error source symbol; error source random variable value
F predictor source symbol set; predictor source random variable
f predictor source symbol; predictor source random variable value
G global source symbol set
g global source symbol
R runlength source symbol set; runlength source random variable
r runlength source symbol; runlength source random variable value
S multiplexor state symbol set; multiplexor state random variable
s multiplexor state symbol; multiplexor state random variable value
X local source symbol set; local source random variable
x local source symbol; local source random variable value
Y local source symbol set; local source random variable
y local source symbol; local source random variable value
Z local source symbol set; local source random variable
z local source symbol; local source random variable value

L code word length random variable; code word length (if constant)
l code word length random value
U local pattern length random variable; local pattern length (if constant)
u local pattern length random variable value
V global pattern length random variable; global pattern length (if constant)
v global pattern length random variable value
W code word set
w code word

E error source random variable value—"error" (Fig. 7-14 only)
N error source random variable value—"nonerror" (Fig. 7-14 only)
ω width (Fig. 7-10 only)

C compression
H entropy
P probability
η efficiency
π state probability

$\mathbf{P}$ probability matrix
$\mathbf{\Pi}$ state probability matrix

I maximum value of i index
i general index
J maximum value of j index
j general index
K maximum value of k index
k general index
N maximum value of "number of" index
n "number of" index
T maximum value of time index
t time index

k order of Markov source dependence
n order of source extension

p binary source probability value (first)
q binary source probability value (second)

Subscripts

0 general index value—"zero"; binary Markov source state value—"zero"
1 general index value—"one"; binary Markov source state value—"one"

R ratio
B bound

f field normalized
p pel normalized
s source normalized

I maximum value of i index
i general index
J maximum value of j index
j general index
K maximum value of k index
k general index
N maximum value of "number of" index (function)
n "number of" index
T maximum value of t index
t time index

m	maximal
n	order of source extension
r	runlength source random variable value

b	black (Fig. 7-10 only)
w	white (Fig. 7-10 only)
m	margin (Fig. 7-10 only)
p	page (Fig. 7-10 only)
s	stroke (Fig. 7-10 only)
es	end of sentence (Fig. 7-10 only)
ic	intercharacter (Fig. 7-10 only)
is	interstroke (Fig. 7-10 only)
iw	interword (Fig. 7-10 only)

e	error source
ej	error source for *j*th state
r0	rare "zero" source
rl	rare "one" source
re	rare event source
sr	simple run source
sm	self-state multiplexing source
pm	previous-state multiplexing source
ae	adjoint error source
ce	conditional error source
dm	dual mode source

Superscripts

0	*0* th order Markov underlying pel source
1	*1* st order Markov underlying pel source
k	*k*th order Markov underlying pel source
´	received value
^	estimated value
-	average value; logical complement (NOT function)
—	adjoint of a source

ACKNOWLEDGEMENTS

The author is indebted to Professor Ingemar Ingemarsson and Thomas Ericson of Linköping University and to the Swedish Board for Technical Development for supporting the preparation of this overview.

The graduate students in my class at Linköping also deserve special thanks for all their stimulating questions and help in reading this manuscript.

This material was prepared as internal publication LiTH-ISY-I-0210 of Linköping University, Linköping, Sweden and has been released in its entirety for publication by Academic Press.

REFERENCES

Abramson, N. (1963). "Information Theory and Coding." McGraw-Hill, New York.

Ascher, R. N., and Nagy, G. (1974). *IEEE Trans. Comput.* **c-23**, 1174–1179.

Arps, R. B. (1969). Ph.D. Thesis, Rep. No. 31, Radioscience Lab., Stanford University, Stanford, California.

Arps, R. B. (1970a). *SID Idea Symp., 1970* pp. 80–81.

Arps, R. B. (1970b). "Compression for Facsimile Using Two-Dimensional Dependence." NTG-Fachtagung Codierung, Braunscheweig, West Germany (unpublished presentation).

Arps, R. B. (1971). *Nachrichtentech. Fachber.* **40**, 218–226.

Arps, R. B. (1974). *IEEE Trans. Inf. Theory* **it-20**, 120–122.

Arps, R. B. (1975). *IEEE Int. Conf. Commun., Conf. Rec., 1975* pp. 7.1–7.3.

Arps, R. B. (1976). "Graphics Coding Contest." *Pict. Coding Symp., 1976* Session 5.

Arps, R. B., Erdmann, R. L., Neal, A. S., and Schlaepfer, C. E. (1969). *IEEE Trans. Man-Mach. Syst.* **mms-10**, 66–71.

Arps. R. B., Bahl, L. R., and Weinberger, A. (1977). U.S. Patent 4,028,731.

Ash, R. (1965). "Information Theory." Wiley, New York.

Capon, J. (1959). *IRE Trans. Inf. Theory* **it-5**, 157–163.

CCITT (1977). *CCITT Study Group XIV.* Temp. Doc. No. 13-E Nov. 14–18, 1977, pp. 1–8.

de Coulon, F., and Kunt, M. (1974). *Proc. Int. Zurich Semin. Dig. Commun., 1974* pp. C4(1)–C4(4).

Deutsch, S. (1957). *IRE Trans. Inf. Theory* **it-3**, 147–148.

Elias, P. (1950). Ph.D. Thesis, Harvard University, Cambridge, Massachusetts.

Elias, P. (1955). *IRE Trans. Inf. Theory* **it-1**, 16–33.

Eto, Y., Hirano, Y., and Fukinuki, T. (1977). *IEEE Trans. Commun.* **com-25**, 1170–1173.

Feller, W. (1968). "An Introduction to Probability Theory and its Applications," 3rd ed., Vol. I. Wiley, New York.

Franks, L. E. (1964). *Proc. IEEE* **52**, 431–432.

Frolushkin, V. G. (1958). *Telecommunications (USSR) (London)* **12**, 1278–1286; *Elektrosvyaz* **12**, 43–48 (1958).

Huang, T. S. (1972). *In* "Picture Bandwidth Compression" (T. Huang and O. J. Tretiak, eds.), pp. 231–266. Gordon & Breach, New York.

Huang, T. S. (1974). *IEEE Trans. Inf. Theory* **it-20**, 675–676.

Huang, T. S. (1977). *IEEE Trans. Commun.* **com-25**, 1406–1424.

Huang, T. S., and Hussian, A. B. S. (1975). *IEEE Trans. Commun.* **com-23**, 1452–1466.

Huffman, D. A. (1952). *Proc. IRE* **40**, 1098–1101.

Jelinek, F., and Schneider, K. S. (1972). *IEEE Trans. Inf. Theory* **it-18**, 765–774.

Kobayashi, H., and Bahl, R. (1974). *IBM J. Res. Dev.* **18**, 164–171.

Koller, J. U. (1975). Ph.D. Thesis, Swiss Federal Institute of Technology, Zürich, Switzerland.

Kunt, M. (1975). *Proc. IEEE* **63**, 327–329.

Kunt, M. (1977). *Inf. Cont.* **33**, 333–351.

Laemmel, A. E. (1951). "Coding Processes for Bandwidth Reduction in Picture Transmission," Rep. R-246-51, PIB-187. Microwave Res. Inst., Polytechnic Institute of Brooklyn, New York.

Michel, W. S., Fleckenstein, W. O., and Kretzmer, E. R. (1957). *IRE WESCON Conv. Rec.* pp. 84–93.

Michel, W. S. (1958). *Commun. Electron.* **35**, 33–36.

Morrin, T. H. (1975). *IEEE Int. Conf. Commun., Conf. Rec., 1975* pp. 7.17–7.21.

Morrin, T. H. (1976). *Comput. Graphics Image Proc.* **5,** 172–189.

Musmann, H. G., and Preuss, D. (1977). *IEEE Trans. Commun.* **com-25,** 1425–1433.

Netravali, A. N., Mounts, F. W., and Bowen, E. G. (1976). *Bell Syst. Tech. J.* **55,** 1539–1552.

Pratt, W. K., Chen, W., and Reader, C. (1976). *Proc. SPIE* **87,** 222–228.

Preuss, D. (1975a). *IEEE Int. Conf. Commun., Conf. Rec., 1975* pp. 7.12–7.16.

Preuss, D. (1975b). *Nachrichtentech. Z.* **28,** 358–363.

Preuss, D. (1976). Dr.-Ing. Dissertation, Technischen Universität Hannover, Hannover.

Renelt, G. (1977). *Electron. Lett.* **13,** 573–575.

Schalkwijk, J. P. M. (1972). *IEEE Trans. Inf. Theory* **it-18,** 395–399.

Schreiber, W. F., Huang, T. S., and Tretiak, O. J. (1972). *In* "Picture Bandwidth Compression" (T. S. Huang and O. J. Tretiak, eds.), Part 5.7, pp. 443–448. Gordon & Breach, New York.

Shannon, C. E., and Weaver, W. (1949). "The Mathematical Theory of Communication." Univ. of Illinois Press, Urbana.

Stern, P. A., and Heinlein, W. E. (1974). *Siemens Forsch. Entwickl. Ber.* **3,** 170–176; in abridged form: *Proc. Zurich Semin. on Dig. Commun., 1974* pp. C5(1)–C5(5) (1974).

Usubuchi, T., Iinuma, K., and Ishiguro, T. (1975). *IEEE Int. Conf. Commun., Conf. Rec., 1975* pp. 7.17–7.20.

Wah, P. K. S. (1975). *Electron. Lett.* **11,** 504–505.

Weber, D. R. (1975). *IEEE Int. Conf. Commun., Conf. Rec., 1975* pp. 7.4–7.7.

White, H. E., Lippman, M. D., and Powers, K. H. (1972). *In* "Picture Bandwidth Compression" (T Huang and O. Tretiak, eds.), pp. 267–281. Gordon & Breach, New York.

Wholey, J. S. (1961). *IRE Trans. Inf. Theory* **it-7,** 99–104.

Wyle, H., Erb, T., and Banow, R. (1961). *IRE Trans. Commun. Syst.* **cs-9,** 215–222.

Yamada, T. (1976). *IECE Jpn. TG IE* **ie76,** No. 69, 38–40; for Engl. transl., see *CCITT Study Group XIV, Proposal on coding scheme standardization for group 3 machines, Nov. 1976* pp. 8–10.

Yamazaki, Y., Wakahara, Y., and Teramura, H. (1976). *Natl. Telemeter. Conf., Conf. Rec., 1976* pp. 6.2.1–6.2.5.

Yasuda, Y., Arai, K., and Tsuno, K. (1975). *IECE Jpn. TG Commun. Syst.* **cs75,** pp. 41–48; in abridged form: *Abstr. Presentation, Pict. Coding Symp., 1977* pp. 45–46 (1977).

SUBJECT INDEX

A

Automatic gain control (AGC), 200

B

Bandwidth, 38, 141
  broadcast color, 190, 210–212
  compression of, 120, 122, 126, 153, 158
  frame replenishment coding, and 190, 196
  redistribution, 126, 129, 136
  requirements, 120, 143, 153, 169
  videotelephone signals, 79, 109, 190, 196–197, 205, 207, 211
BCH codes, 213
Bernoulli trials, 240, 246
Binary image compression, 219–272
  area algorithms, 222, 266–271
  historical trends, 222–224
  raster algorithms, 222, 236–266, 271
  source characteristics, bounds and codes, 224–236
Bit rate, 1, 148–149
  in binary image compression, 219
  bit error rate and, 107
  component/composite coding and, 100–102, 104
  distortion/noise and, 107–108, 110, 182–183, 186, 211
  frame replenishment coding and, 190, 192–193, 198–205, 211, 213
  hybrid coding and, 186
  "low," 122, 158
  in NASA model, 140
  PCM reduction of, 74–76, 80, 110
Block coding, 266–267
Buffers, 76
  buffer control algorithm and, 153
  feedback procedures, 129, 132–133, 147, 152, 154
  in frame replenishment coding, 192–194, 196, 199, 203–206, 211, 213–214

"strip" (binary image compression), 266
  in transform image coding, 128–139, 143, 147–149, 152–154

C

CCD, see Charge-coupled device
CCIR recommendations, 79, 80, 96, 107
CCITT standards, 224, 249, 252, 255, 259, 270
Charge-coupled device, 3, 118, 125
Color imagery, see also Visual phenomena
  color standards in, 3, 190, 211
  component/composite coding of, 100–104, 109–110
  DPCM signals, 84
  extension to encoding of, 65–67
  frame replenishment coding and, 210–213
  PCM coding for, 6, 14, 15
  predictive coding for, 79, 100–104, 109
  sensitivity to/perception of color and, 8, 35, 40–44, 65
  transform coding for, 17
Contour coding (binary image compression), 268, 270, 271
Contouring effect (image coding), 14, 88, 92
  contour predictor and, 91
Convolutional codes, 213
Cosine transform, see Transform image coding
Cost, 123, 215
Cross-array correlation coding, 260

D

Delta modulation, 16, 74, 76, 220
Differential pulse-code modulation, 6, 16, 50, 57, 59, 73, 141, 200, 220
  adaptive prediction and quantization, 78, 90–97, 100–101

277